More Than an Ally

More Than an Ally

A Caring Solidarity Framework for White Teachers of African American Students

SECOND EDITION

Michael L. Boucher, Jr.

BLOOMSBURY ACADEMIC
NEW YORK · LONDON · OXFORD · NEW DELHI · SYDNEY

BLOOMSBURY ACADEMIC
Bloomsbury Publishing Inc, 1359 Broadway, New York, NY 10018, USA
Bloomsbury Publishing Plc, 50 Bedford Square, London, WC1B 3DP, UK
Bloomsbury Publishing Ireland, 29 Earlsfort Terrace, Dublin 2, D02 AY28, Ireland

BLOOMSBURY, BLOOMSBURY ACADEMIC and the Diana logo are trademarks of
Bloomsbury Publishing Plc

First published in the United States of America 2020
This edition published 2026

Bloomsbury Publishing Inc does not have any control over, or responsibility for, any
third-party websites referred to or in this book. All internet addresses given in this
book were correct at the time of going to press. The author and publisher regret any
inconvenience caused if addresses have changed or sites have ceased to exist, but can
accept no responsibility for any such changes.

A catalog record for this book is available from the Library of Congress

ISBN: HB: 978-1-4758-7531-7
PB: 978-1-4758-7532-4
ePDF: 979-8-8818-6827-7
eBook: 978-1-4758-7533-1

Typeset by Newgen KnowledgeWorks Pvt. Ltd., Chennai, India
Printed and bound in the United States of America

For product safety related questions contact productsafety@bloomsbury.com.

To find out more about our authors and books visit www.bloomsbury.com
and sign up for our newsletters.

For Karen, who makes everything possible.

Contents

Preface to the Second Edition

Using *More Than an Ally: A Caring Solidarity Framework* in Teacher Education Classes and Professional Development

The past decade has been transformative, challenging, and deeply instructive for educators committed to equity and justice. The second edition of *More Than an Ally: A Caring Solidarity Framework for White Teachers of African American Students* emerges from a critical need to respond to the shifting landscape of education in the United States. This landscape has grown increasingly racially hostile, politically divisive, and professionally precarious for teachers. This updated edition seeks to bridge the gap between theory and practice more boldly and strategically, offering educators the tools and frameworks to navigate these challenging times.

The importance of this work is both profound and pressing. The history of communities of color is being systematically erased from curricula, leaving students deprived of the truthful story of our nation. States are passing laws that ban discussions of race, equity, and systemic injustice under the guise of protecting students while perpetuating ignorance and exclusion. Meanwhile, the erosion of support for public education at the federal level—and in many states—has left educators and students to fend for themselves in an increasingly hostile environment.

Teachers face not only the absence of advocates in Washington but also a growing wave of policies designed to undermine their work and devalue their profession from statehouses and even local school boards. This hostility has tangible consequences: experienced teachers are leaving the field in record numbers, burned out by excessive demands, systemic inequities, and a lack of support. At the same time, the pipeline of new teachers is drying up, leaving classrooms understaffed and students underserved. These realities demand boldness, clarity, and a renewed commitment to anti-racist, transformative education.

A Call for Bolder Action

The first edition of this book introduced the concept of Caring Solidarity—a framework that moves beyond allyship to advocate for transformative relationships between educators and the students and communities they serve. It called on white educators to interrogate their own privilege, dismantle their complicity in systemic inequities, and commit to standing in solidarity with their students.

This second edition builds on that foundation but recognizes that we must now move with greater urgency and intention. The stakes are higher, and the challenges are steeper. Caring Solidarity cannot remain a theoretical ideal; it must be a lived practice embedded in the daily decisions of educators and the systemic changes they fight for.

To Do This, We Must

- **Acknowledge the Hostility:** The racial hostility in America today is not an aberration—it is the natural result of decades of systemic inequities and unresolved historical injustices. Educators must name this hostility, confront it, and prepare to teach within it.

- **Center Truth and Resistance:** As curricula are stripped of the histories and voices of marginalized communities, educators must take up the mantle of resistance. This includes teaching the truths that students are being denied and equipping them with the tools to critically analyze the systems around them.

- **Equip and Empower Educators:** In the face of teacher shortages and increasing pressures, we must better prepare educators to do the work of Caring Solidarity. This means bridging theory and practice in actionable ways that are realistic, sustainable, and impactful.

Bridging Theory and Practice

The second edition of *More Than an Ally* seeks to be more practical without losing the depth of its theoretical underpinnings. Each chapter has been revamped and expanded. They are designed to guide educators in understanding what solidarity is and how to enact it in classrooms, schools, and communities. Practical tools—such as reflective questions, actionable lists, and real-world examples are woven throughout the book to make the framework accessible and applicable. These elements are designed to move educators from intellectual understanding to practical change, bringing the principles of Caring Solidarity into their teaching practice.

Grounded in Critical Theory

At its core, Caring Solidarity is rooted in theoretical foundations at the intersections of solidarity, whiteness, and systemic injustices like the school-to-prison pipeline. Each chapter unpacks these concepts, encouraging educators to move beyond surface-level understandings of diversity or inclusion and into a deeper engagement with how race, privilege, and power operate in educational systems.

A Framework for Personal and Professional Growth

Caring solidarity is a practice that should be lived, reflected upon, and continually refined. This book provides a roadmap for that process, making it a resource for teacher education programs, professional development workshops, and schoolwide book studies.

> In *Teacher Education Classes*, the book can be a foundational text that scaffolds learning over time. Professors can use reflective questions to spark critical discussions, practical lists to guide lesson-planning exercises to illustrate real-world applications of caring solidarity.
> In *Professional Development Settings*, the book's tools can be used to design reflective and practice-oriented workshops. Facilitators might use the chapters and actionable items to build specific discussions of classroom practice, pedagogy, and curriculum design.
> In *Schoolwide Book Studies*, the book provides a shared language and framework for collective growth. Its combination of theory and practice ensures that discussions lead to plans for systemic change.

A Hopeful Vision

Despite the challenges we face, this is a work of hope. I believe in the transformative power of education and the educators' ability to create classrooms and schools that reflect the values of justice, equity, and humanity. Caring Solidarity is not easy, but it is necessary. It requires courage, vulnerability, and an unwavering commitment to stand with students and communities, even when the stakes are high.

This second edition of *More Than an Ally* is an invitation to take up this work with renewed vigor, bridge the gap between theory and practice, embrace the complexities of teaching, and see education as a radical act of love and resistance. We can prepare educators to do more than pass on knowledge—we can prepare them to transform the world.

Acknowledgments

Many people have guided me over the years and have made it possible for me to produce this second edition of the book. First, I want to thank my brilliant, amazing wife, Karen Burgard, for her unwavering support. This book would not have been possible without you, Dollface. Secondly, I want to thank my hero and mentor, Robert Helfenbein. Rob, you are my model for how professors in the academy should approach research with communities and someone who truly understands the impact of centering those communities in that research.

There are so many people in Minneapolis who have made this work become a reality. My life in Minneapolis classrooms shaped me as an urban educator and I want to thank my students from Folwell and Sheridan, who taught me so much as a young teacher. I now have the privilege of seeing them as grown-ups with kids of their own, accomplishing so much, and I am proud to call them friends. To our cadre of once-young teachers, Jeff Sommers, Amy Strickland-Johnson, and Laura Yost-Manthey, we set out to change the world and succeeded. This book is a continued testament to all I learned from you as we grew together.

My students from South High School in Minneapolis continue to inspire and teach me as professionals, doctors, activists, artists, writers, parents, and academics. You taught me the meaning of solidarity and created it with me. Each student I taught at South still holds a special place in my heart, but I would like to take a moment to identify a few. Isiah, who helped me see solidarity when I wasn't looking, and Sha'Dasha Whitner taught me so much about myself as a white teacher, and that solidarity is always needed. We lost Dasha in 2024 to cancer at the young age of 34. She was a shining light. Very few people in this world lived their lives *out loud* the way she did, and she is missed by so many. I also want to acknowledge my student and friend, Vince Moniz, for his poetry, friendship, jokes, and encouragement. Vince, your friendship is so important to me, and your words bring me home in many ways.

I deeply appreciate my colleagues at South High School in Minneapolis. The teachers of South who laughed with me, encouraged me, and challenged me over the years, especially Doug Berglund, Diane Manley-Bagley, Tiffany Moore, Phyllis Hayes, Melinda Bennett, and Brian Fitzgerald; thank you all for your belief in me and your commitment to students. I still tell stories about you in my classes and hold you all as examples of what great teaching can be.

I want to thank the editors I have worked with at Rowman and Littlefield and Bloomsbury. Suzanne Canavan first encouraged me to do a book based on my research, and Carrie Brandon talked with me at the American Educational Research Association (AERA) and agreed to help me get a second edition out. Mil gracias to Sara Eiranova for her excellent design work on the diagram for Caring Solidarity, to South Alum Greta McClain for her work in Minneapolis and for allowing me to use images of her South High mural on the cover, and to Courtney Perry for allowing the use of her amazing photographs of Greta's work.

I am deeply grateful to my family—Vicki and Mike Boucher, my sister Beth Edgar, and her family—for your unwavering support and encouragement throughout my teaching and academic journey. You remind me that this work is not just academic but personal, rooted in the love and solidarity that families embody. Finally, I want to acknowledge and thank my child, Joshua Boucher. Joshua, our long talks about improving communities and being an activist for equity and justice have meant everything to me. Those conversations deeply influenced and shaped this work, and echoes of them resonate throughout these pages. I am so proud of you, Buddy, for the way you stand in solidarity with your community as a journalist. You understand what this work is about—you always have.

1 Great Teachers Need a Framework to Talk About Race

Propelled by people of color and their advocacy on behalf of themselves and their children, race has shifted from being a taboo topic to a central point in American political and social discourse. This move into public consciousness accelerated after the acquittal of George Zimmerman for the killing of Trayvon Martin in 2013 (Love, 2014). The use of social media and the Twitter hashtag #BlackLivesMatter by Alicia Garza, Patrisse Cullors, and Opal Tometi stirred a new generation of activists after the killing of Michael Brown in Ferguson, Missouri. Corresponding events and movements, such as the Movement for Black Lives, pushed white Americans to reexamine the country's history, structures, and essential nature.

This examination has resulted in race being discussed more openly and regularly, yet these conversations have not produced the increased awareness and empathy necessary to drive substantial change. Why is that? When race is discussed, the focus often remains superficial, avoiding solutions that dismantle the structures keeping powerful people in power and marginalized groups on the periphery. In schools, when race is addressed, it is too often done *to* people and not *with* them. This dynamic isolates those affected by systemic racism from participating in conversations about their own liberation. It frames the problem as one that must be solved by the marginalized while leaving the systems of privilege and power untouched.

The reluctance to engage deeply with structural change is not due to a lack of solutions—plenty of transformative ideas exist. The real barrier is the perceived cost of these changes. Redistribution of money, power, and privilege is seen as too great a sacrifice for those who benefit from the status quo. As a result, conversations about race often devolve into blaming the victims of racism, perpetuating stereotypes, and justifying inequities. This deflection shifts the focus away from systemic issues and reinforces the narrative that marginalized communities are responsible for their own oppression rather than acknowledging the societal forces and historical actors who made decisions specifically to oppress and exclude (Kendi, 2016).

In the current US climate, this hesitance is exacerbated by the backlash against racial equity initiatives and the deliberate erasure of race as a topic. Political leaders and media figures have labeled anything they dislike as "woke" or dismissed it as part of diversity, equity, and inclusion (DEI) agendas. This calculated strategy silences crucial conversations about the roots of racism and makes genuine progress very difficult. Legislation banning discussions of race, inequities, and critical perspectives in education aims to suppress truth-telling and maintain a false narrative of American exceptionalism.

These dynamics are especially troubling in schools, where the erasure of race from the curriculum undermines efforts to create informed, critical thinkers capable of addressing the realities of their world. By framing conversations about equity as dangerous or divisive, the systems of power ensure that these issues remain unresolved. As a result, schools, which should be spaces of liberation and critical engagement, often become sites where inequities are perpetuated and racism is reinforced.

To move forward, conversations about race must shift. They must include not only the naming of inequities but also a commitment to the radical reimagining of systems that uphold them. They must be *with* communities, not *to* them, and must focus on actionable steps rather than platitudes. Without these shifts, we risk continuing the cycle of talk without transformative results, leaving the structures of racism intact and the promises of equity unrealized.

After a successful career teaching in urban schools, I began this research in 2009 when it felt like America was poised for some reconciliation around race. The election of the nation's first Black president, Barack Obama, brought messages of hope and unity, signaling a moment when honest dialogues about inequities might finally take root. More people of color were entering leadership roles in public and private sectors, and racial justice themes were gaining visibility in popular culture and social media. For many, it seemed like the United States was ready to confront the legacies of racism that shape its institutions and culture.

However, a storm of resentment was brewing beneath this veneer of progress. The 2016 election shattered the illusion that the nation was moving steadily forward in race relations. Instead, it laid bare the deep undercurrents of white grievance, fear, and resistance to change. Millions of white Americans, disoriented by the shifting cultural and demographic landscape, clung defensively to privilege while becoming increasingly disconnected from the difference between fact and fiction (DiAngelo, 2011; Coates, 2017). This unraveling left even well-intentioned individuals struggling to comprehend how they might contribute to meaningful change—or what that change might require of them.

For white teachers, this confusion was compounded by their lead role in a society reckoning with race. Teachers have witnessed the rise of the #BlackLivesMatter movement, a response to the devaluation of Black lives in policing, law, government, and schooling. The movement laid bare the anguish experienced by African Americans whose bodies, children, histories, and very existence are treated as expendable whenever they challenge the priorities of the white majority (Anderson, 2017; Painter, 2010). Many teachers have observed or even participated in the backlash: the denial of systemic racism, the weaponization of "#AllLivesMatter" as a deliberate misinterpretation of justice, or the silencing of student protests that demanded accountability and change.

Trump's first presidency amplified white nationalist rhetoric, emboldened hate groups, and institutionalized new forms of discrimination through policies such as family separations at the border, bans on diversity training in federal agencies, and rollbacks of civil rights protections. Teachers in states like Texas now face the added challenge of navigating laws that ban books and discussions of DEI and restrict conversations about systemic racism in schools. The recent attacks on curriculum content, framed as a crusade against *wokeness*, seek to erase the histories of marginalized communities and further isolate students of color.

The second Trump presidency and its authoritarianism have created an even more hostile climate for teachers committed to justice. Policies like the expansion of US Immigration and Customs Enforcement (ICE) raids and continued bans on DEI make it increasingly difficult to foster inclusive learning environments. The message to teachers is clear: stay silent or face repercussions. Yet, despite these challenges, educators must resist the impulse to give in to despair. The stakes for students and communities are too high, and the cost of complicity is measured in lives harmed and opportunities denied.

The absurdity of today's discourse on race is that it centers the fragility of whiteness rather than the needs of those most affected by racism. For white educators seeking to create more just and inclusive classrooms, the noise of political debates and fearmongering can feel overwhelming. But this moment demands clarity and courage. Teachers must move beyond being passive observers of racism or self-identified *non-racists* and embrace the transformative work of solidarity with their students and communities of color (Applebaum, 2011; Gaztambide-Fernández, 2012).

This work is neither easy nor comfortable, especially in a climate where honest discussions about race are labeled as radical. Yet, it is essential. To teach in solidarity is to confront the systems of oppression that shape our schools and society. It is to acknowledge the power dynamics, dismantle them where possible, and advocate for equity at every turn. This is the charge for educators today—not just to resist the horrors of our current moment but to build the foundation for a more just and inclusive future.

Considering the tenor of the conversation around race, picking up this book and considering its contents is either an act of defiance or one of devotion. If it is defiance in the face of the increasing polarization of the political and social landscape in all its forms, or if the motivation comes from a devotion to the art, craft, and calling of being an impactful educator, this book should be helpful in either endeavor. It attempts to empower white teachers and teacher candidates to do the hard work of interrogating their racial privilege and joining in Caring Solidarity with their students (Keating, 1995). My research over the last decade has shown that white teachers seeking success in their work that serves predominantly African American students should look within and interrogate their own whiteness. They should look for ways to dismantle structures of racial oppression and privilege in their schools and communities. However, the road to that self-awareness is fraught with pitfalls.

Sullivan (2014) argued that the tendency of *racially aware* white people to enter spaces where they feel they can have an impact, like a racially segregated neighborhood, does more harm than good. She argued that when people move into these new spaces, these white people express their privilege and assume a missionary or savior standpoint (Warren & Talley, 2017). She urged, "Rather than setting aside one's whiteness in an attempt to learn about other races, white people can begin to do effective racial justice work by cleaning up their own house" (p. 20). While Sullivan makes a compelling argument for self-knowledge before doing the work of dismantling privilege, white teachers working in schools with African American students have already crossed color lines and are living in the racial dynamic, meaning that inaction or delayed action is not a viable choice. White teachers in multicultural and multiracial schools do not have the luxury of deciding where and when to make a difference by waiting and assessing the situation from the sidelines. These teachers currently work across the color barrier; thus, it is not a question of whether they will influence their students and communities because they do it every day, for better or worse.

Dismantling structures of oppression is currently being done in many fields and from many angles, including law, politics, policy, faith, and education. While all white people should participate in these multi-sided efforts, teachers have a special responsibility to *care for* and *care about* our students and communities of color. This means that teachers must take control of the one place we have control: our schools.

No One Can Just Close the Door and Teach

In frustration, teachers often say they close their doors and do their work, effectively shutting out the cacophony outside. However, schools in a healthy republic are the gardens of democratic thinking, reasoning, and skills, not marketplaces, engaged in a crass exchange of services. If anything is exchanged, it should be the narrow, flattened ideas of childhood for the complex, rich ideas of adulthood. Instead, too many view education as a value-laden transaction where those who shout the loudest are privileged in the market of ideas while those without volume are further marginalized.

Classrooms are the place to build a more equitable and sustainable society, and they should not be some neutral or neutered conduit for received knowledge. It is a foolish fantasy to believe that any neutrality is possible, but actively arguing that schools should be mere conveyors of received knowledge is to reject our democratic ideals. The mask of cultural neutrality in schools must be lifted to create a space where pluralistic ethics can flourish.

Teachers in multicultural and multiracial schools are in the best position to do the work of dismantling structures of oppression and white supremacy. Still, it will take more than reading the *I Have a Dream Speech* every January and a bulletin board of heroes every February.

Even in teacher education programs, because of segregated patterns of living in America, most teacher candidates have never had a meaningful exchange about race with a person racially different from themselves (Cochran-Smith, 2000). It can be scary, treacherous, and unsafe to talk about race, and given the opportunity, most people avoid talking about it outside of their own racial or social groups. However, as educators devoted to students and equity and justice in education, these uncomfortable conversations are necessary and should lead to action.

Solidarity is built with students and communities by replacing fear with understanding, discomfort with empathy, and avoidance with courage. Through education, care, and solidarity, educators committed to dismantling these structures first move themselves and others to a deeper understanding and connection to empower and inspire students. Thus, closing the door will not meet the needs of our students, communities or ourselves. To build a democracy, especially in this time of threat, we must engage, rather than retreat.

Who Am I?

To discuss teachers' positionality and gain the historical and personal context of how they can work in solidarity with students, it is important to have at least an outline of my personal history and positionality so that I can also be placed in context. Individual and family histories matter in that they have shaped and continue to influence us. Thus, one of the first steps to interrogating my standpoint is understanding how I came to that position. In short, I am a mostly white male who grew up in the suburbs of Minnesota and taught in an inner-city high school in Minneapolis. Today, I am a teacher educator and associate professor in San Antonio, Texas, USA.

As for my family history, on my mother's side, my ancestors came from Poland and England, along with many other immigrants in the 1800s. On my father's side, beginning in 1830, some of my ancestors were removed during the *Trail of Tears* from their homes and farms in what is now Mississippi and Alabama by the United States. They were placed in Southern Oklahoma's *Indian Territory*. By blood quantum, my grandmother was a quarter Choctaw and Irish, and my grandfather was mostly English and came from a poor family of farm laborers. I am a registered and voting member of the Choctaw Nation of Oklahoma.

Early in my life, my father obtained a position in Minnesota, where I grew up and spent most of the first forty-five years. Growing up in Minnesota, all my friends' parents were white, middle-class, and college-educated. It was the stable, uncomplicated life my parents wanted for me. Yet even though we seldom traveled, I felt there was a piece of me that belonged somewhere else. In my suburban upbringing, I was dissatisfied and uncomfortable identifying with the cultural norms of the Minnesota mix of Norwegians, Germans, and Swedes. Even though we seldom went to Oklahoma, I was always proud to be *something else* that others did not share.

Until the last few years, I had little contact with Choctaws in Oklahoma beyond my extended family, but the Choctaw Nation is integral to who I am. In college, I began carrying my Choctaw identification card in my wallet. That ID card is a good metaphor for my connection to the tribe for most of my life. I kept it with me, but it was not outwardly visible. These days, I have been more involved with being a tribal member from a distance, attending events, and keeping up with the news. I wear my Choctaw medallion at graduation every semester. Sitting with the other faculty in my puffy hat, robe, medals, and medallion, I am part of a larger community. My ancestors would be proud of their progeny as the first PhD in our family. It is my bantam of difference from the society around me, and growing up, I felt that being a Choctaw allowed me to be an outsider whenever I felt like it. However, in my young adulthood as an urban teacher, I came to realize that for all my imaginings of being an outsider, I was deeply rooted in the privilege afforded me by whiteness and middle-class economic status.

After graduating from college with a degree in social studies education, I gained a position in Minneapolis Public Schools, where I began becoming a professional educator. There, I found the diversity I had been desiring. I experienced cultures, ideas, and people who taught me how to be a more complete teacher and person. I taught middle and high school social studies for eighteen years until I left to pursue my PhD in Curriculum Studies and become a teacher educator.

In reflecting on my personal and family history, my positionality has been shaped by a complex interplay of privilege and cultural identity. Growing up in predominantly white, middle-class suburbia, my experiences were framed by the stability and advantages that came with that. At the same time, my Choctaw heritage offered me a subtle but persistent sense of otherness and a connection to a history and identity beyond the dominant culture in which I was raised. This duality has been a source of pride and a reminder of my privilege, especially as I navigated my career as an educator. Teaching in Minneapolis allowed me to confront these complexities head-on as I learned from the students and communities I served, deepening my understanding of solidarity and equity. Today, as a teacher educator, I continue to draw on this personal history to inform my work, striving to critically examine my standpoint while empowering future educators to do the same.

Strategic Essentialism and Diversity

The focus of this work is the teaching of African American students by white teachers. Those categories are imposed to begin a dialogue, but there is no assumption that those categories are static or isolated from the history of colonization, slavery, segregation, and white supremacy. However, unless artificial categories are overlaid to some degree, the discussion becomes so watered down that it becomes meaningless. This type of *strategic essentialism* allows for a conversation about race. According to Azoulay (1997), strategic essentialism is a "prerequisite for dialogue" about race (p. 102). This targeted framing opens up the intellectual space by grouping people, even in ways that do not always reflect the people's lived reality, to build an understanding of race as socially constructed. However, that should not get in the way of seeing that it is also a historical reality. To deny this leads people to the kind of color-blind ideology that only reifies the current social and political structure of white privilege and "color-blind racism" (Bonilla-Silva, 2010, p. 40).

Strategic essentialism should not be confused with essentialized frameworks like white supremacy, which assumes that white people are fundamentally better and more equipped to run things than people of color. White supremacy essentializes others who are not assumed to be white and places them into the category of diverse or non-white. At the same time, white people are considered normal and outside of race (Irving, 2014). All over the world, white people have created spaces for themselves and pushed others to the margins. However, in each context, Blackness and its response are different. It is also important to note that the binary of Black and white does not work in all global contexts and does not even scratch the surface of the range of human diversity.

A caveat is important here. Strategic essentialism is a device used temporarily to give space for discussion of real historical issues. Thus, when talking about Black and white people, the tool of essentialized racial categories allows for the discussion of race in the United States and the study of diverse classrooms. If strategic essentialism is never abandoned, the danger is that it will become real essentialism and move away from its original intent. With that danger in mind, teachers and researchers need to acknowledge that while some group identifications are real, that historical inequity is real, and that racism is real, the racialized concepts that ground these notions are socially constructed and not based on any biologically determinable differences (Helfenbein, 2003).

Capitalizing and Contextualizing White

In the first edition of this book, I chose to capitalize "White" when referring to white people. This decision was rooted in an effort to emphasize that whiteness is not a mere description, like hair or eye color, but a socially constructed category of racialization within the US context. At the time, capitalizing "White" was a deliberate move to draw attention to whiteness as a racialized identity and to help readers recognize its role in systems of privilege and power.

For this second edition, I have chosen to move away from capitalizing "white," aligning with the evolving practices within the field of Critical White (or Whiteness) Studies (CWS). Most CWS scholars now use the lowercase "white" as an intentional choice to decenter whiteness in academic discourse. This shift highlights its constructed and contextual nature while refusing to accord it undue prominence. Like "Black" and "Brown," "white" is an essentialized, racialized descriptor of group membership, not a neutral or scientific reflection of skin color. Quotations from other scholars in this book retain their original formatting, meaning you may encounter capitalized and lowercase usage depending on the source. This choice also acknowledges the need to evolve our language and frameworks in response to ongoing discussions in the field, ensuring the work remains relevant for educators and newer scholars engaging with these critical ideas.

I have also used the term "racialization" or "racialized" when referring to how people are perceived. It is a shift in thinking for many white people from the assumption that race is old and descriptive to seeing it for what it is, a relatively new way to categorize people. People are not naturally dropped into races. They have race imposed upon them as others categorize them. Thus, people are racialized to place them in the racial categories used to decide who is in power and who is excluded. The concept of mixed race is part of this discussion. As a matter of history, all people in the United States are mixed from different parts of the world. The concept of mixed race, however, means that some people are not easily put into racial categories and are difficult to racialize. Sometimes, this causes identity conflicts, as people do not know where they fit in racialized America. This volume will not address the specific issue of the important work on how mixed race relates to the concept of race.

If a mature conversation is to be had about teachers working across the color barrier, whiteness, both as a concept and a fact, must be addressed. The waters ahead are not easily navigated, but unless the gaps between teachers and students in terms of race, culture, income, political power, and privilege are embedded in the structure of reforms, they will not address the issues facing today's schools. As a matter of definition, I refer to white people as those of European descent who hold both social and economic power that comes with being perceived as a member of the white race. Whiteness and Blackness have historically been fluid and contextual. A related concept, anti-Blackness, refers to the pervasive bias and discrimination that assigns negative attributes to people based on the degree of their perceived skin darkness. This prejudice operates on a spectrum, with darker skin tones often eliciting more severe forms of marginalization and dehumanization.

This book focuses on teaching African American students by white teachers, but that is not the only project that needs a full examination. Being strategically essential allows for a focused approach to this one area. Still, the intersectionality of sexual orientation, colorism, sexism, anti-indigenous, and a multiplicity of other oppressions also impacts students and their teachers. However, as with all analyses, the questions I wrestle with in this book narrow the focus. This is an examination of the phenomenon of white teachers in classrooms of mostly African American students, but many other foci also need to be explored. The goal is that the theory herein will apply to many contexts.

So much of whiteness is taken for granted as normal or the only acceptable way of doing things, making it critical to explore and implement strategies that further its decentering and eventual disintegration (Michael et al., 2017). Consequently, whiteness may be understood as the intersection of privilege based on the perception of being a member of the white race and the assumption of normality that being white has in the United States. Part of my project is to uncover whiteness and separate it from normativity so that teachers will be equipped to enter into relationships of Caring

Solidarity with their Black students. That is only possible if white people see their whiteness and develop what Helms (1990) referred to as a positive white racial identity.

The framework of Caring Solidarity addresses both the mindsets that allow a person to move toward solidarity and the skills of empathy, alliance, and being an accomplice. As Katsarou et al. (2010) stated, "To truly teach in solidarity with schools and communities requires of teachers both specific mindsets and skill sets" (p. 152). This theory addresses critical perspectives on solidarity that include white allies (Patel, 2011), false empathy (Delgado, 1996; Warren & Hotchkins, 2014), and white savior syndrome (Straubhaar, 2014).

Caring Solidarity is also situated in second-wave white teacher identity studies (Jupp et al., 2016) and is applied to students and teachers. Much of the theoretical work is based on scholarship by African American scholars in elementary settings, and the insights of these scholars are crucial to constructing the theory and are quoted and cited widely in this book. This theory aims to delve deeply into the mechanisms, conditions, and mental commitments necessary to do that work.

This theoretical work also relies on Culturally Relevant and Sustainable Pedagogies. It seeks to be an extension or precursor needed for white teachers to build solidarity and a mechanism for integrating these frameworks fully into daily teaching. Caring and solidarity have been explored separately and tangentially in education for decades, but have not been combined to describe the effort of teachers who work across the color line.

The Equation: Black and Brown Kids and White Teachers

From August to June, teachers meet young people in schools to teach them the ideas, skills, and knowledge needed to become successful in the wealthiest, most powerful society ever created by humankind. The responsibility is awesome. With the mechanisms teachers provide, these students will vote, earn a living, raise a family, and leave their legacies on society. The work teachers do in the classroom every day shapes the future. Many jobs pay more and carry more prestige, but it would be difficult, if not impossible, to find a job with as much influence over more people than being a teacher.

Teachers' profound influence in shaping the future is undeniable, but it is essential to recognize that the context in which they work is far from equitable. While educators strive to prepare students for success, the systems they navigate are deeply entrenched in racial segregation and dominated by whiteness at every level. These systemic realities shape not only students' experiences but also the composition of the teaching force itself, which remains overwhelmingly white and female, even as the student population grows increasingly diverse. To fully understand the role and responsibility of teachers in this landscape, we must use data to examine these disparities and their impact on education.

For example, even seventy years after the *Brown v. Board of Education* decision, integrated schools remain largely aspirational rather than a reality (Ma, 2024). According to the National Center for Education Statistics (NCES), the American teaching force is 80 percent white, middle-aged, and middle-class (Feistritzer et al., 2011; Loewus, 2018; Taie & Lewis, 2022; Taie & Goldring, 2017). That is slightly down from 82 percent in the last survey in 2012. About 77 percent of teachers are women. In pre-k through sixth-grade schools, 90 percent are women; women make up around 56 percent in high schools. Thus, it is safe to say that most teachers are white women. Nine percent of all teachers identify as Hispanic, a slight increase, and 6 percent of all teachers who identify as Black is down slightly since 2012.

In 1972, the first year the US Department of Education collected demographic data for the newly desegregated schools, students of color accounted for 22 percent of total enrollments, and teachers of color constituted 12 percent of the teaching force, a 10-percentage-point gap between the two groups. A decade later, the disparity had grown to 17 percentage points, with students of color making up 27 percent of total enrollments and teachers of color accounting for only 10 percent of the workforce (p. 283).

The US Department of Education's Institute of Education Sciences (IES) predicted that by 2015, only 46 percent of K-12 students would be white, a prediction that came true, and by 2022, 45 percent of K-12 students identified as white (Musu-Gillette et al., 2017). In 2017, students of color made up 40.6 percent of the total US public school population. By 2022, this percentage had increased to 66 percent, with higher proportions in the largest cities (Ingersoll & May, 2011). According to the NCES, 49.5 million students were enrolled in public schools in 2022, including 7.4 million (15 percent) Black students and 14.4 million (29 percent) Hispanic students.

Given the overwhelming percentage of teachers who are white, many students of color spend their entire school day being taught by white educators. This fact highlights the importance of addressing the ideology, behavior, and role of white teachers in structuring schools to meet the needs of all students.

The Quick Fix?

Systems and their leaders look for quick fixes to intractable problems. One answer put forth to desegregate schools and increase the buy-in of students of color is to bring more teachers of color into the classroom. Education leaders work to bring new teachers from racially and ethnically diverse backgrounds into the profession, but their efforts have not been enough. Once teachers of color are in schools, they face challenges from students and adults, and schools of education are often not ready to aid teacher candidates of color in dealing with the micro and macro aggression that will come at them but research has indicated that Black students who have even one Black teacher in their schooling experiences in low-income schools will have 29 percent greater interest in school and are 39 percent less likely to drop out before completing high school (Gershenson et al., 2017). However, as Milner (2006) explained, simply having a Black teacher in the classroom is not the solution it is often assumed to be unless that teacher is culturally competent and actively avoids deficit-based thinking.

Additionally, the assumption that Black students only need role models is inadequate, as it shifts responsibility away from white teachers and fails to address their critical role in supporting Black students (Brown, 2012; Milner, 2006; Williamson, 2011). It is imperative to approach the problem of students' disenfranchisement from schools from as many angles as possible. As the number of students of color continues to outpace the pool of teachers of color, increasing the number of teachers of color in our schools is an essential and aspirational goal (Stotko et al., 2007; Villegas et al., 2012).

For the foreseeable future however, white teachers will remain the predominant demographic in schools, and it will take many years before there are enough teachers of color to alter that reality (Milner, 2006). Therefore, white teachers must play a central role in dismantling the barriers that hinder the success of students of color (Sleeter, 2001). While schools urgently need more counselors, more inclusive and effective multicultural curricula, and increased numbers of teachers and administrators of color, these changes cannot happen quickly enough to impact the current generation. To address these barriers to students' success, white teachers must recognize whiteness across all areas of the curriculum, pedagogy, and school structures. This can only be done by working in solidarity with communities, parents, and colleagues of color. If done well, it will result in changes to all students' and staff's schooling experiences. It is a profound and systemic shortcoming that our schools remain so deeply influenced by white supremacy and entrenched in systems of whiteness. This entrenchment has left generations of students marginalized, disenfranchised, and under-resourced, with some even losing their lives due to the unwillingness to reimagine an inclusive and equitable society. The prioritization of comfort and position by those in power has come at a significant cost, often overshadowing the need to ensure that all students have an equal opportunity to thrive and share in America's promises.

The New Generation of Teachers: Same as the Old Generation?

Scholars have noted that white teacher candidates wrap deeply held racism in the language of care. In this mindset, teachers will state that students of color do not value education and need to be motivated to learn with external reward systems like prizes, candy, or money. These preconceived deficit notions often range from clinical, pathology-based explanations of students' perceived shortcomings, to wholesale condemnation of students' cultures, to arguments that students must learn whiteness in order to succeed (Osei-Kofi, 2005; Payne, 2013; Valencia, 2010). When candidates enter the field, these stereotypes are often reinforced through teacher talk, a lack of understanding of what they see in classrooms, and a lack of awareness of their biases (Sleeter, 2005).

The cycle is perpetuated from candidacy to teaching to mentoring, and even as teachers join the professorate in schools of education, many still cling to their deficit models and seek to help candidates get *good placements*, meaning wealthy white schools in the suburbs, and do not ask the larger questions about oppressive structures (see Mervosh, 2019). As Valencia (2010) clarified, "deficit thinking typically offers a description of behavior in pathological or dysfunctional ways—referring to deficits, deficiencies, limitations, or shortcomings in individuals, families, and cultures" (p. 14). These models are the default for many teachers and teacher candidates, and they blame students for a lack of success in the classroom (Boucher & Helfenbein, 2015; Gorski, 2006; Osei-Kofi, 2005).

Teachers live in the gap between theory, practice, societal forces, and economic realities, and are always in the creation process. The data is clear that white teachers see students as a bundle of deficits or as a threat to the learning environment. Britzman (2003) explained that teachers come to the profession with *chronologies* negotiated through their classroom lives both as students and as teachers. Teachers negotiate their socialization differently depending on their many interactions with culture and identity, combined with their frames around *power, knowledge, dependency, and negotiation*. While teachers enter the profession as caring individuals, their models of care often miss the aspects needed by Black students: solidarity with them and a deep knowledge of who they are, culturally, racially, and individually. According to Eslinger (2013), teachers also fall victim to a savior mentality and a white supremacist belief structure that must be quelled to create a culturally responsive classroom.

Britzman rejected the notion that there is one monolithic culture of teachers, stating, "Within any given culture, there exists a multiplicity of realities—both given and possible—that form competing ideologies, discourses, and the discursive practices that are made available to them" (p. 70). The ability to transcend racial divisions is not embedded in the potential teacher as an innate talent. Instead, teachers develop these skills in a process that can take years, depending on their understanding and experiences. However, with the need for white teachers to stand in solidarity with students of color, teachers must be portrayed in our discussions as able to learn to move into anti-racism and solidarity, no matter where they start. Casey (2016) extended this caveat,

> We often make the mistake of treating white people who have little experience thinking through issues of race and racism as resistant racists rather than as learners. We would never fault someone who had not taken geometry for not being proficient in their first efforts in a geometry course; why do we insist on faulting white people for not being proficient in their first efforts to understand what it means to be white in a white supremacist society and what this means for them as social actors? (p. 96)

The ongoing challenge is the need for solidarity and antiracism in education. Awareness of the world is essential to be truly educated, especially as an effective educator. Through writing, activism, and political action, people of color and their white allies are working to ensure that ignorance of racism, privilege, and white supremacy is no longer justifiable or acceptable. Consequently, white teachers are responsible for actively seeking out and learning from the perspectives of individuals who hold valuable *funds of knowledge* within their students' communities (Moll et al., 1992).

This is especially true for those white teachers who teach across the color line. If a teacher were to avoid all discussion of race and whiteness while interacting with Black students, that would mean they are not listening to their students and are finding ways to avoid the onslaught of information on the current state of affairs. Thus, rather than approach teachers as racists to be cleansed as a default position, I approach white teachers as learners who are more or less resistant to the understandings that must be achieved (Jupp et al., 2016).

A New Paradigm

Several elements to becoming a teacher in solidarity have emerged from my research and, more importantly, the research from the myriad of scholars of color who have generously taught me over the years and are cited throughout this book. While working toward solidarity with students, it is vital to contemplate the ebb and flow of this journey. Each individual who undertakes the transformation I envision will encounter different obstacles that could derail their choice to dismantle systems from which they benefit. The Caring Solidarity framework is designed for teachers seeking to build solidarity with their students and for researchers aiming to analyze and describe the practices of teachers who engage in this work. It was created to be both descriptive and aspirational. It can be used to describe teachers in the field currently working in caring solidarity with their students, and it can be used to train or develop teachers who intend to work toward caring solidarity. While the diagram in Chapter 6 and the chapters provide a structured path toward Caring Solidarity, the layers within the diagram should be understood as flexible and interconnected. Although they represent distinct stages or processes, their boundaries are permeable, allowing for overlap and movement, with varying levels of resistance or density depending on the context or individual journey.

Caring Solidarity offers a pathway or guide for white teachers on their journey toward more advanced and transformative pedagogies like Culturally

Sustaining Pedagogy (Paris & Alim, 2017) or Abolitionist Pedagogy (Love, 2019c). Recognizing that everyone starts from a different place in their understanding and practice, Caring Solidarity provides a practical and conceptual roadmap for teachers committed to evolving their teaching practices but may not yet feel equipped to embrace or implement frameworks that require deep personal interrogation. The journey toward creating an equitable and humane classroom is complex and challenging. It is a process marked by reflection, discomfort, learning, and unlearning. The path is winding and long, requiring consistent effort and a willingness to engage deeply with race, power, and privilege. However, the goal, a classroom environment where all students are seen, valued, and supported, is worth the struggle.

Therefore, the purpose of Caring Solidarity is to illuminate the path forward, helping teachers adopt pedagogical approaches that sustain and affirm their students' cultural identities while also working to dismantle oppressive systems. It acts as a map, pointing the way toward frameworks like Culturally Sustaining Pedagogy and Abolitionist Pedagogy while acknowledging that teachers need time and guidance to integrate these approaches into their practice.

Discussion Questions for Chapter 1

1   What events and movements in the past decade have propelled race from a "taboo topic" to a central issue in social discourse, as discussed in the chapter?

2   Why are current conversations on race in schools often unproductive, and what changes does the chapter suggest could lead to more meaningful outcomes?

3   Discuss why schools should be "gardens of democratic thinking" rather than "marketplaces"? How does this perspective shape his vision for teachers' roles in a racially just society?

4   What is the role of white teachers' in promoting racial justice in schools? How might a framework like Caring Solidarity help white teachers engage more meaningfully with African American students?

5   Why is strategic essentialism introduced as necessary for discussing race? How does it differ from essentialism as applied in frameworks like white supremacy?

Actionable Classroom Practices for Teachers from Chapter 1

- **Engage in Self-Reflection and Interrogate Personal Biases**

  Reflect on your positionality and examine your assumptions about race and privilege. Commit to ongoing personal growth in understanding racial dynamics. Here are six other books to support self-reflection and understanding of race and privilege.

  - *White Fragility: Why It's So Hard for White People to Talk About Racism* by Robin DiAngelo
  A foundational text that helps readers explore how white defensiveness can perpetuate racism and offers strategies for engaging in honest self-reflection about privilege.

  - *So You Want to Talk About Race* by Ijeoma Oluo
  This book is a practical guide to discussing race and privilege. It explores how systemic racism manifests in everyday life and challenges readers to examine their own complicity.

  - *Me and White Supremacy: Combat Racism, Change the World, and Become a Good Ancestor* by Layla F. Saad
  A workbook-style resource designed to guide readers through self-reflection exercises, helping them uncover unconscious biases and take actionable steps toward anti-racism.

  - *How to Be an Antiracist* by Ibram X. Kendi
  This book combines personal narrative with historical analysis to explore what it means to actively combat racism, encouraging readers to think deeply about their role in perpetuating or dismantling it.

  - *The Racial Healing Handbook: Practical Activities to Help You Challenge Privilege, Confront Systemic Racism, and Engage in Collective Healing* by Anneliese A. Singh
  A hands-on guide for individuals seeking to explore their biases, confront privilege, and work toward healing and justice within themselves and their communities.

  - *Between the World and Me* by Ta-Nehisi Coates
  Written as a letter to the author's son, this powerful memoir reflects on the personal and systemic impacts of racism in America, prompting readers to consider their place in the racial landscape.

- **Challenge Deficit-Based Thinking**
  Make stickies and posters to help both you and your students avoid framing students in terms of what they lack and instead focus on their strengths and the cultural knowledge they bring to the classroom. Challenge your administration to do the same.
- **Center Student Voices in Curriculum Design**
  Include student experiences, interests, and cultural backgrounds in lesson planning, allowing them to see themselves reflected in the content.
- **Address and Dismantle Racist Structures in Schools**
  Create a workgroup with colleagues and administrators to identify and challenge inequitable policies, practices, and curriculum materials in your school.
- **Participate in Professional Development on Anti-Racism**
  Seek out workshops, readings, and discussions to deepen your understanding of culturally relevant pedagogy and anti-racist practices.
- **Empower Students to Actively Engage in Equity Work**
  Encourage students to recognize and address injustices in their communities. Provide them with tools to advocate for themselves and others. Here are four resources to empower students to engage in equity work.
  - **Learning for Justice (Formally Teaching Tolerance)**
    Website: learningforjustice.org
    This site provides free resources, including lesson plans, student tasks, and professional development materials, designed to help educators help students understand social justice issues and take action.
  - **Youth Activism Project**
    Website: youthactivismproject.org
    It offers tools, stories, and workshops to empower young people to lead change in their communities. Its focus is on civic engagement and grassroots advocacy.
  - **Facing History and Ourselves**
    Website: facinghistory.org
    A resource hub for educators looking to teach about equity, history, and social justice. Facing History provides case studies, discussion guides, and activities that encourage students to analyze the world and take informed actions critically.

○ **Action Civics Toolkit by Generation Citizen**
  Website: generationcitizen.org
  This toolkit equips teachers and students with a step-by-step guide to identifying community issues, developing action plans, and participating in local civic processes to create change.

2 Race, White Supremacy, Whiteness, and Schools

As discussed in chapter one, to understand the gap between Black students and their white teachers, it is essential to center race as a concept and address it directly. Achieving solidarity requires acknowledging the differences in lived experiences and social-historical positions between these groups. The journey begins with white teachers recognizing that their lived experiences differ from those of their students and that these differences are rooted in race.

Race has been a defining feature of American life, shaping relationships, societal structures, and access to power and resources. Yet, despite its overwhelming influence, race is a myth, a socially constructed concept with no biological basis (Kolbert & Hammond, 2018; Painter, 2010). Minor differences in facial structure, hair texture, and skin color have been imbued with significance to justify the dehumanization and exploitation of people, often in ways so shocking that they are rarely discussed in schools or mass media. The reality of America's treatment of colonized and enslaved peoples is relegated mainly to books and films, where even factual accounts of historical atrocities are considered unsuitable for polite public conversation or political discourse. Europeans and Americans assigned meaning to superficial physical differences to create the concept of race, using it to justify their roles as colonizers and enslavers (Kendi, 2016; Painter, 2010).

Although skin color has no biological relevance, Americans frequently attribute moral, intellectual, and behavioral characteristics to pigmentation and sustain discrimination and inequality based on it. The construct of race wields vast power, shaping Americans' perceptions and interactions while supporting foundational institutions such as employment, the justice system, health care, real estate, and education. Race is not merely a descriptive category; it has functioned as a tool to distribute power and privilege and to reinforce systems of oppression. At its center, race is about power. It has been weaponized to justify slavery, segregation, and persistent inequities, perpetuating the false narrative of white superiority as a societal norm (Painter, 2010).

In contrast, culture refers to the shared institutions, norms, and practices that define human communities. Culture is expansive and inclusive, enriching human life through language, rituals, art, and technologies (Kohl, 1992). Unlike race, which is exclusionary and divisive, culture has the potential to strengthen our shared humanity. However, the conflation of race and culture often allows racism to persist, as race becomes a proxy for marginalization under the guise of cultural critique.

The Legal Construction of Whiteness in America

American legal history reveals how whiteness has been defined, redefined, and weaponized to maintain systems of privilege. Landmark court cases have played a critical role in shaping the concept of race, determining citizenship, personhood, and participation in society.

Dred Scott v. Sanford (1856): Denying Citizenship to Black Americans

The Supreme Court declared that Black people, whether enslaved or free, could not be citizens under the US Constitution. Chief Justice Roger B. Taney wrote that Black people "had no rights which the white man was bound to respect." This ruling enshrined a racial caste system into American law, using race to exclude an entire group from the protections and privileges of citizenship.

Post-Civil War

The Civil Rights Cases (1883): Permitting Private Discrimination

These cases struck down the Civil Rights Act of 1875, which sought to prohibit racial discrimination in public accommodations. The Court ruled that Congress had no authority to regulate private acts of discrimination, effectively legalizing systemic racism in private sectors and allowing segregation to flourish unchecked.

Plessy v. Ferguson (1896): Establishing "Separate but Equal"

In this landmark decision, the Supreme Court upheld a Louisiana law requiring separate railway cars for Black and white passengers, affirming the doctrine of *separate but equal*. Justice Henry Billings Brown, writing for the majority, argued that racial segregation was constitutional as long as the separate facilities were of equal quality. This decision legitimized racial segregation in virtually all aspects of public life, from schools to transportation, and provided the legal foundation for Jim Crow laws. The case entrenched institutionalized racial hierarchy in American society and remained a legal precedent until it was overturned by *Brown v. Board of Education* in 1954.

Ozawa v. United States (1922): Excluding Japanese Americans from Whiteness

Takao Ozawa argued for naturalization based on his skin color and cultural assimilation, claiming to be white. The Court rejected his petition, defining *white person* according to the principles of eugenics, excluding Japanese immigrants from whiteness and the privileges of citizenship.

United States v. Thind (1923): Rejecting South Asians from Whiteness

Bhagat Singh Thind argued that as an Indo-Aryan, he was *Caucasian* and eligible for naturalization. The Court dismissed this claim, emphasizing that whiteness was defined by *common understanding*, not scientific taxonomy, further manipulating racial definitions to exclude South Asians.

Lum v. Rice (1927): Affirming Racial Segregation

The Court upheld the exclusion of Chinese-American student Martha Lum from a white school in Mississippi, expanding segregation laws to include other racial and ethnic groups. This case reinforced legal definitions of race used to marginalize populations beyond Black and white dichotomies.

Mendez v. Westminster (1946): Challenging Ethnic Segregation

This case successfully contested the segregation of Mexican-American children in California schools, with the Court ruling it violated the Equal Protection Clause. Although focused on ethnicity, it set a legal precedent for challenging racial segregation and influenced *Brown v. Board of Education*.

Shelley v. Kraemer (1948): Prohibiting Racially Restrictive Housing Covenants

This Supreme Court case struck down the enforcement of racially restrictive housing covenants, which had been used to prevent people of color, particularly African Americans, from purchasing homes in specific neighborhoods. While private agreements to restrict property ownership based on race were still technically allowed, this decision prohibited courts from enforcing them, marking a critical step in challenging systemic housing discrimination.

Hernandez v. Texas (1954): Expanding Equal Protection

This case was pivotal in recognizing Mexican Americans as a distinct class entitled to equal protection under the Fourteenth Amendment. The Supreme Court ruled that systematically excluding Mexican Americans from jury service in Texas violated the Constitution. This case broadened the interpretation of race and ethnicity under the law, acknowledging discrimination beyond the Black-white binary.

Brown v. Board of Education of Topeka (1954): Declaring School Segregation Unconstitutional

This landmark decision overturned the *separate but equal* doctrine of *Plessy v. Ferguson* (1896), declaring segregation in public schools inherently unequal and unconstitutional. The ruling signaled a significant step toward dismantling institutionalized racism in education.

Brown v. Board of Education of Topeka II (1955): Mandating Implementation of Desegregation

After declaring school segregation unconstitutional in *Brown v. Board of Education* (1954), the Supreme Court issued Brown II (1955) to address its implementation, instructing local authorities and courts to desegregate schools "with all deliberate speed." While it emphasized the need for action, the decision's vague language allowed for significant delays and resistance, with many districts exploiting the ambiguity to stall integration. Despite these challenges, Brown II reaffirmed the Court's commitment to dismantling segregation and highlighted the complexities of translating legal rulings into practical, systemic change, underscoring the ongoing struggle for racial equity in education.

Loving v. Virginia (1967): **Dismantling Laws Against Interracial Marriage**

The Supreme Court struck down state laws banning interracial marriage, declaring them unconstitutional. This decision underscored that racial classifications were inherently discriminatory and violated the principles of equality.

Swann v. Charlotte-Mecklenburg Board of Education **(1971): Enforcing Integration**

The Court upheld busing as a legitimate tool for achieving racial integration in public schools, highlighting the necessity of active measures to address systemic racial inequities.

Regents of the University of California v. Bakke **(1978): Affirmative Action and Racial Quotas**

This case addressed the legality of affirmative action in higher education. The Supreme Court ruled that while race could be considered as one of many factors in admissions, strict racial quotas were unconstitutional. This decision significantly influenced the discourse on race-conscious policies, balancing efforts to redress past discrimination with concerns about "reverse discrimination."

Race, Power, and the Law

These cases demonstrate that race is not a fixed concept but a fluid one shaped by social and political forces. Legal definitions of race and whiteness have been manipulated to enforce hierarchies, deny citizenship, and marginalize communities of color. Over time, the courts have also been critical in challenging these inequities, illustrating the potential for legal systems to dismantle structural racism. However, despite these advancements, systemic racism remains deeply entrenched in American life. Legal victories often represent incremental progress rather than the wholesale elimination of racial inequities. Moreover, the persistent conflation of race and culture continues to mask racism under the guise of cultural difference.

Richard Rothstein's work (2017), *The Color of Law: A Forgotten History of How Our Government Segregated America,* delves into the systemic and deliberate policies that established and perpetuated racial segregation in the United States. Rothstein challenged the narrative that segregation results from personal choices or private prejudices, arguing instead that government policies drove it at the federal, state, and local levels. He documented practices such as redlining, exclusionary zoning, discriminatory lending practices, and the construction of racially segregated public housing. Rothstein illustrated how these policies were not merely accidents of history but were intentionally designed to enforce racial hierarchy and prevent African Americans from accumulating wealth and accessing opportunities for upward mobility.

Acknowledging race as a social construct does not diminish its impact; it emphasizes the need to address the systems of oppression built around it. The evolution of race in American law and policy demonstrates both the harm caused by racial constructs and the potential for dismantling them. Combating racism requires actively naming and challenging these constructs, confronting their historical roots, and addressing their enduring consequences. As Coates (2008) noted, addressing injustice begins with stopping the harm; if someone is actively stealing from you, the first step toward resolution is to stop the theft.

Defining Terms: Racism

According to Solorzano (1997), racism is defined using these three touchstones: "(1) one group believes itself to be superior; (2) the group which believes itself to be superior has the power to carry out the racist behavior; and (3) racism affects multiple racial/ethnic groups" (p. 8). This definition highlights that racism is not limited to individual acts of hatred or violence—though these can also be racist—but is fundamentally about the exercise of power within structures and institutions that exclude people based on immutable traits like skin color. It encompasses both the belief in the superiority of the people designated as white, their culture, their ways of being, and their ability to enact policies that reinforce and reflect that belief.

Until recently, most white people assumed that racism was under the strict purview of backward, unsophisticated degenerates who burn crosses, sympathize with Nazi Germany, and march with tiki torches. While that is all true, the small acts of segregating oneself from racially different people, racial jokes, financial barriers to school and college admission, the whiteness of the curriculum, and teachers' deficit thinking about students are all racism. All institutions are structured by individuals, and individual decisions support and maintain them, but there is no way to point to any one subgroup or socioeconomic level and say that they, alone, are racist and the rest of society is not. Although race is a social construct, it is made real through beliefs, ideologies, and actions, and influences societal structures and personal experiences.

Many white people struggle to recognize how deeply their thinking is shaped by race. Nice white people often seek to avoid being labeled as racist and emphasize their desire to find common ground (Renkl, 2018). However, white people's feelings have consistently dominated conversations about race, which has hindered efforts to dismantle white dominance in society. People who tiptoe around their sensitivities are complicit in upholding systems of whiteness. While most white Americans do not see themselves as racists, overwhelmingly, they continue to support policies and leaders that consolidate power and privilege within white communities. In America, the implicit expectation is that people of color should accept this imbalance of wealth, power, and privilege to maintain harmony. Anyone who demands racial justice is labeled as divisive, so when African Americans march, kneel, protest, or demand recognition, these actions are seen as a threat to white privilege, even though they aim to achieve equity, not division.

Defining Terms: Alethophobia

Alethophobia refers to a fear of or aversion to truth. In the context of racism and racial justice, alethophobia manifests as a reluctance to confront the structural and institutional truths that underlie white supremacy. This fear is not only about acknowledging the existence of racism but also about grappling with the uncomfortable realities of one's complicity within these systems. For many white Americans, the truth about American racism challenges their self-perception as *good* people and disrupts the narrative of meritocracy that suggests success is purely the result of individual effort. Alethophobia often leads to defensive reactions when racism is brought to the forefront. For instance, phrases like *I don't see color* or *All Lives Matter* are commonly used as shields to avoid engaging with the complexities of racial inequality. These statements, while seemingly innocuous, deny the specific experiences of people of color and obscure the systemic nature of racism. This aversion to truth prevents meaningful conversations about race and perpetuates the status quo.

Moreover, alethophobia reinforces the dominance of white feelings in discussions about race. When conversations about race provoke discomfort, white people seek to redirect the focus away from systemic issues to their own emotional distress. This shift in focus further marginalizes people directly affected by racism.

The refusal to confront truths also perpetuates the myth of neutrality in schools. Policies and practices that are portrayed as *race-neutral* maintain existing power dynamics because they fail to address the inequalities that disadvantage people of color. Alethophobia hinders progress by allowing individuals and institutions to remain passive in the face of injustice. It demands that people of color tolerate microaggressions, systemic exclusion, and inequitable treatment for the sake of social harmony. This reluctance to engage with the truth ultimately prioritizes preserving white comfort over pursuing equity and justice. Addressing alethophobia requires a willingness to confront brutal truths and a commitment to dismantling the systems of power that perpetuate racial inequality.

Defining Terms and Naming the Unmentionable: White Supremacy

White supremacy is one of those terms that has a simple meaning: the assumption that white people are better than others, but it is often avoided because it has been used in the social context to describe the most violent and detestable section of society. Any phrase's power to hurt others does not come from its sound or surface meaning, and the meanings of words and their social context are crucial (DiAngelo, 2018). The ideology of white supremacy is found in every corner of American history and life, from the first Conquistadores and Pilgrims to the founding of the nation that espoused liberty but still protected slavery. It includes Jim Crow, Juan Crow, crime bills that caused mass incarceration, crowds calling for a wall, and *mass deportation* on the southern border. Allen and Liou (2018) have explained whiteness as being "rooted in the active pursuit of white racial interests through the creation of institutional norms framed by the white supremacist social structure and its related normalized systems of practices" (p. 679).

The term *white supremacy* conjures racist hate groups, and most educated people disavow that version of white supremacy. Yet, white supremacy pops up again and again. As hooks (2013) explained, while people usually associate racism with overt "acts of aggression by whites against blacks," white supremacy, as a way to understand social structures, "addresses the ideological and philosophical foundations of racism" (p. 177). Sociologist Robin DiAngelo (2018) has written extensively about the term:

> White supremacy captures the all-encompassing centrality and assumed superiority of people defined and perceived as white and the practices based upon that assumption. White supremacy is not simply the idea that whites are superior to people of color (although it certainly is that), but a deeper premise that supports this idea—the definition of whites as the norm or standard for humans and people of color as an inherent deviation from that norm. (p. 129)

The ideology of white supremacy is the most divisive, cancerous, and self-defeating mental and social construct of our time, and yet it has largely gone unnoticed in the telling of US history. Allen and Liou (2018) explained:

> Whites are what people of color are not, or so the logic of Whiteness goes. If Whites depict people as culturally backward and deprived, then that means Whites are, by default, depicting themselves as culturally progressive and enlightened. If the controlling image depicts people of color as lazy and unintelligent. In that case, Whites are, by default, constructing themselves as smart and hardworking. (p. 686)

White supremacy was the driving force behind colonial rule across the globe, and in the post-colonial era, efforts to dismantle this ideology have become part of a broader, worldwide movement challenging colonial mindsets. Colonized peoples are deconstructing white dominance ideologically while also manually dismantling its influence in their historical narratives and systems. For example, students at University College London (UCL) launched the campaign "Why is My Curriculum So White?" in 2014 (Peters, 2015; Suissa & Chetty, 2018), and South African students demanded #RhodesMustFall in 2015 (Bosch, 2017). This global movement to dismantle the structures of white supremacy established during colonization spans the planet, as few countries on any continent were spared subjugation and reorganization by European powers. While the removal of symbols of white supremacy is only the beginning, it is an essential first step. As DiAngelo (2018) further explained:

> White people raised in Western society are conditioned into a white supremacist worldview because it is the bedrock of our society and its institutions. Regardless of whether a parent told you that everyone was equal, or the poster in the hall of your white suburban school proclaimed the value of diversity, or you have traveled abroad, or you have people of color in your workplace or family, the ubiquitous socializing power of white supremacy cannot be avoided. The messages circulate 24–7 and have little to do with intentions, awareness, or agreement. (p. 129)

Racism has its deep heritage in white supremacist ideology. Allen and Liou (2018) explained:

> In describing white supremacy as a social system, we are referring to a larger society that, despite times of what may seem like racial progress (e.g., the Civil Rights Era or Reconstruction), is fundamentally arranged to ensure that Whites remain in control of society, as they work to unjustly and immorally construct a higher social status over people of color. (p. 687)

DiAngelo (2018) challenged all white people to name the real issue in our politics and to begin the work of dismantling white supremacist ideologies in ourselves and the culture:

> Naming white supremacy changes the conversation because it shifts the problem to white people, where it belongs. It also points us in the direction of the life-long work that is uniquely ours; challenging our complicity with and investment in racism. Yes, this work includes all white people, even white progressives. None of us have missed being shaped by the white supremacy embedded in our culture. (p. 33)

Simply put, white supremacy is the belief system that assumes people who are not considered white are inherently inferior to those who are. It manifests in the perception of whiteness as the default standard by which all others are measured, positioning it as the norm against which *diversity* is defined. Within this framework, whiteness is seen as neutral, ordinary, and desirable, while all other racial and cultural identities are considered deviations. The ideology of white supremacy allows white people to justify their lack of faithfulness to God, the democratic ideals of the founders, and their moral principles, and its purpose remains to define white people as superior. As hooks (2013) explained, white supremacy is a sickness, and we all have symptoms:

> It is living in a culture of white supremacy that is often an unconsciously debilitating force diminishing the spirit. This is not new news for most black folks. From slavery to the present day, black folks have known that dealing with traumatic exploitation and oppression based on race creates life-threatening stress and concomitant illness that comes in its wake. (p. 185)

Sociologists and the Census Bureau will continue to argue about when and if the US white majority will be outnumbered, but what is clear is that schools and the country are becoming more multiracial, more multicultural, multilingual, less dominated by Christianity, and more cosmopolitan (Pew Research Center, 2015). However, that does not automatically lead to a power shift in favor of our students and families of color.

Thus, this problem of white supremacy is not a problem of a few crackpots but a worldwide norm that is being challenged across the globe, and disrupting it is the moral imperative of our age. Once recognized, white supremacy becomes visible in nearly every aspect of society, including the education system. It shapes the structure and functioning of schools, influencing everything from curriculum design to disciplinary policies and teacher expectations. From the earliest years of preschool to high school graduation, white supremacy has been baked into the foundations of American education, perpetuating inequities and reinforcing systemic barriers for students of color.

Requiring Whiteness as Normality

As discussed earlier, whiteness is the intersection of white normality and white privilege, and American society was explicitly constructed to increase the privilege of white people. To understand the influence of whiteness, we must further define it. According to Frankenberg (1993), there are three dimensions to whiteness. First is the "structural advantage" of the white power structure and its accompanying privileges. Second is the "standpoint" or positionality of being white and seeing the world through that lens. "Thirdly, it carries with it a set of ways of being in the world, a set of cultural practices, often not named as 'white' by white folks but looked on instead as 'American' or 'normal'" (p. 54).

McIntosh (2001) observed that there are unearned privileges given to white people based on the fact that they are white in a country where whiteness is normalized. While this concept causes discomfort for many white people, especially new teachers (see, e.g., Michie, 2007), it is not surprising to people of color where whiteness has always been a part of daily life.

This powerful concept of normality allows white people to assume that their activities are expected and that all others are abnormal or diverse. Bonilla-Silva (2010) explained that there is a pervasive practice referred to as "color blind racism" that allows white people to claim that they are not racist by denying that race matters (p. 2). "I don't see a person's race" is a common phrase that teacher candidates will state at the beginning of their programs. Oftentimes, this comes from their own constructs of justice and integrity because they equate racism with overt acts of discrimination and hate, something that they vow they will never do.

Just as it is unjust to treat all kids the same, it is also harmful to approach students as though they are deficient or in need of fixing. The refrain *kids are kids* is often heard in conversations with teachers and even within teacher preparation programs. However, research shows that students are not all the same. They differ racially, ethnically, and culturally from their teachers in ways that profoundly shape their experiences. Consequently, white teachers often experience difficulty connecting with their students and engaging with their identities beyond the limits of the teachers' own socialization and upbringing. While students are individuals, they are also members of identity groups, families, and communities. The race-evasive mindset of *treating all kids the same* overlooks these differences. It avoids acknowledging how students exist within social and cultural groups that may feel unfamiliar or inaccessible to their white teachers.

However, even when individuals share the same racial identity, differences in economic status, age, social groups, and the influence of social media create significant variations in their experiences, further confounding an already complex dynamic. Social media, in particular, has intensified these divisions in ways that many teachers are unaware of as they engage with their students. This complexity makes statements like *kids are kids* overly simplistic, allowing adults to avoid taking the responsibility to understand and engage in nuances of student life. If there is no difference in kids, then there is no need to meet the different needs of students. Bartolomé (1994) explained that this *kids are kids* approach to children's learning has been skewed by the mentality that frames adults as whole and some kids as broken. By assuming that some kids need fixing, we ask the wrong questions and are then frustrated by our lack of answers. This kind of essentializing is not strategic (as discussed in Chapter 1) but is a lethargic shorthand to avoid issues that need addressing.

Part of helping white teachers create solidarity with students is helping them understand the power of whiteness as a concept and as a force in the classroom. James Baldwin pointed out that whiteness is an illusion, yet that illusion has shaped all we do in schools (Coates, 2015). Whiteness allows white people to assume that all others are abnormal or diverse and that their diversity from the norm is pathology. Often, a cure is sought through the education system and manifests itself in many ways. As Levine-Rasky (2000) explained:

> Traditional solutions to inequitable educational outcomes for racialized groups of students have been directed to the putative problems of these racialized others ("them") and to the challenges in implementing culturally sensitive pedagogy (the space between "us" and "them") rather than to the workings of the dominant culture itself. (p. 272)

This division between *us* (white, middle-class, legacy-educated, dominantly cultured) and *them* (anything not on the list above) is the reasoning behind structures of white supremacy. The rationale becomes, "*We* have an obligation to help *Them* be more like *Us*." This is the essence of deficit models like Ruby Payne's (2013) *A Framework for Understanding Poverty* (Gorski, 2006). Thus, instead of designing curricula and structures around student populations, schools work to create pathways to bring these students into whiteness. Levine-Rasky (2000) continued:

> There is a willingness, for example, to increase the skills of marginalized groups through programmes catering to "their needs," such as special education, remedial reading, and segregated behavioural classes. There is a concomitant failure to penetrate the source of marginalization for these

identified groups, and thus, little commitment to providing these students with the same possibilities as those available to dominant groups. Indeed, the need for special programmes and the student failure observed in them continues to be explained by problems residing with the students and their families. (p. 272)

This cycle perpetuates the very inequities it claims to address, reinforcing the idea that marginalized students must change to fit into dominant norms rather than challenging the systemic structures that uphold white supremacy in education.

One prominent example of how whiteness manifests in education is through the enforcement of Standard English in classrooms. Teachers who insist on the exclusive use of Standard English often believe they are helping their students succeed by preparing them for a world where the norms and values of whiteness dominate. From this perspective, they may view themselves as caring educators equipping their students with the tools needed to navigate society. However, as Matias and Zembylas (2014) explained, this approach is rooted in a colonial mindset that conflates caring with acculturation into a white supremacist worldview. Rather than fostering a relationship of solidarity with students, it enforces assimilation and reinforces systemic inequities. Acts of white supremacy, such as enforcing linguistic conformity, are often hidden within what white teachers perceive as caring behavior, making these mental frameworks challenging to recognize and address (Gaztambide-Fernández, 2012; Gray, 2019).

The debate surrounding African American Vernacular English (AAVE) illustrates this tension. Scholars such as Gay (2010) and Seltzer (2019) have noted that discussions of AAVE remain contentious among educators and researchers. Godley et al. (2006) found that many teachers hold negative attitudes toward AAVE, viewing it as deficient and stigmatizing students who speak it. This deficit thinking leads to lower expectations for students who use AAVE, perpetuating harmful stereotypes and inequities. However, this perspective overlooks the reality that AAVE is not a deficit but a linguistic and cultural asset. It serves as a *fund of knowledge* and a vital tool for communication within African American communities (Moll et al., 1992).

Moreover, teachers can play a pivotal role in helping students navigate linguistic diversity without enforcing assimilation. As Delpit (2006) explained, teachers in solidarity with their students adopt a strategy that respects AAVE as a legitimate linguistic form while helping students code-switch between

AAVE and the dominant register. This approach equips students with the skills necessary for navigating spaces where Standard English is expected, such as in professional or academic contexts, without devaluing their cultural and linguistic heritage. By contrast, insisting on Standard English as the only acceptable form of communication in the classroom perpetuates anti-Blackness. It alienates teachers from their students, undermining the development of relationships of solidarity (Souto-Manning, 2013).

Ultimately, understanding and addressing language and race issues in education requires educators to confront uncomfortable truths about American history and societal norms. Love (2019b) explained:

> Teachers who disregard the impact of racism on Black children's schooling experiences, resources, communities, and parent interactions will harm children of color. This ignorance is not just a painful sign of a blatant lack of information—a function of racism is to erase the history and contributions of people of color—it is a dangerous situation as these teachers go on to take jobs in schools filled with Black and Brown children. This turns schools into places that mirror society instead of improving it. The hard truth is that racism functions as a "superpredator" of Black and Brown children within our schools. (online)

Until race is centered in the conversations about white teachers, there can be no progress toward a more inclusive curriculum or pedagogical framework (Sleeter, 2005). Until educators at all levels begin the project of dismantling white supremacist structures in schools and then the larger society, there will be no progress toward the multicultural goals they espouse. The current discourse of inclusion has proved insufficient to meet the challenges of today's versions of white supremacy. More is needed, and more is required from white teachers to solve the most significant problems in American education.

Centering Race Versus Not Talking About Race

To recap, McIntosh (2001) observed that there are unearned privileges given to white people based on the fact that they are white in a country where whiteness is normalized. Bonilla-Silva (2010) explained that there is a pervasive practice in schools referred to as "color-blind racism" (p. 2). This tendency allows white teachers to blame Black students for their failure, and Black parents can be ignored for not attending to their child's schooling. Ideological color blindness is a major force in the larger society (DiAngelo, 2018). As Hayes and Juarez (2012) explained, "Holding on to a color-blind framework allows people to address only the egregious forms of racism" (p. 7). It allows white people to be blind to "the very knowledge of culturally responsive teaching and social justice that is needed to transform the whiteness of education" (Hayes & Juarez, 2012, p. 7). In multicultural classrooms, centering race and culture is an exercise in freedom for both the teacher and the students. If race and culture are not in the open but left unsaid, secret, taboo, and untouchable, the messages conveyed to students reinforce oppression and privilege and devalue students of color (DiAngelo, 2018).

It can seem counterintuitive to white people that talking about race is the best way to combat racism. Broadly, the avoidance of race talk derives from a misunderstanding of race combined with an unwillingness to begin dismantling white supremacy in individuals and structures. *Not* talking about cancer did not lead to a cure for cancer. *Not* talking about a subject has never solved it. For example, Arizona has a troubled past and present when it comes to race and culture in the classroom, even banning Ethnic Studies courses in 2010. While much of the ban has been reversed, the climate of fear that surrounds schools in many states when talking about race and culture means that when teachers do engage in discussions, they risk infuriating white parents and legislators (Palos & McGinnis, 2012). Yet, when they do NOT have these conversations, students will act out in ways that reflect their lack of understanding.

As an example of these effects and the alethophobic reaction, in 2016, the senior class of Desert Vista High School in Ahwatukee, Arizona, near Phoenix, made black T-shirts with one gold letter per shirt spelling out "BEST*YOU'VE*EVER*SEEN*CLASS*OF*2016" in large, gold letters. After the picture, six white female students stood together laughing and photographed themselves with their shirts spelling out a racial slur using the letters and asterisks from the previous photo formation. This photo went viral on social media, creating a storm that enveloped the students and the school. The students were immediately punished with five-day suspensions, and one student gave a public, tearful apology for the *offense* while insisting that she was *not racist* (White & Ruelas, 2016).

When the students apologized for their offense, they did not understand that while their actions were indeed offensive, they were offensive because these students were both disrespectful and dismissive of the history of that word and its use as a tool of oppression. They tried to explain that it was a *bad word* to them and that they were breaking the rules of etiquette, not trying to subjugate their classmates or neighbors. They equated the word as a vulgarity on the same level as swear or curse words they cannot use in school. They refused to see that this action was different. It was an act of oppression, and the administration reinforced that impression through inaction.

The language around offense places the blame on those who receive the disrespect, not on those who wield words as weapons. In schools and in our social discourse, we have dealt with the language, not the reasons for it. These students argued that their actions were not racist because their white privilege allowed them to avoid seeing that they were not only being offensive but also oppressive. These personal actions were not understood by them as racism because, to them, only bad people are racist, and they did not perceive themselves as bad people. Instead, this was a professed act of rebellion, using a *bad word* they knew was taboo. The students were disrespectful and oppressive, not just to their classmates but to the entire community. In the investigation that followed, the tearful apologies were accepted, and the students returned to school. However, the administration did not ask the most critical question: *Against whom was this a rebellion?* The rebellion was against the idea that, as white people, there is something that is forbidden for them to say and do.

In the effort to paint racists as bad without dealing with the roots of white supremacy, schools have made oppressive language a forbidden fruit that can only be experienced among trusted associates. By avoiding race and the history of colonial oppression from Arizona's founding, the school's approach fed racism and pushed white students toward white supremacy rather than extinguishing it. White America's unease and denial about race, the history of race, and white supremacist structures create the ability to be *bad* in safe contexts. When used in these contexts, these words are supposed to be fun, festive, or risqué. These spaces function as outlets where white people express anger over what they perceive as transgressions against white supremacy. As white supremacy is increasingly challenged, many white people feel disoriented, believing they can no longer navigate the world according to the norms and expectations they were educated to rely upon.

Alethophobia has been a common theme in the last few election cycles. During the 2024 presidential campaign, the vice-presidential candidate referenced his previous Senate race, where he had assured Ohioans that their support for racist policies did not make them racist. In his 2022 campaign ad, he asked, "*Are you a racist?*" and "*Do you hate Mexicans?*" He then stated, "The media calls us racist for wanting to build Trump's wall. They censor us, but it doesn't change the truth" (Kilander, 2022). This framing aimed to neutralize accusations of racism while defending racist immigration policies. Another member of the inner circle of the campaign, disgraced media commentator Tucker Carlson, explained to a group of young white people at an event,

> The first [thing about this election] is that every person in this room needs to understand—you are not in a despised minority. You are in an incredibly gentle and tolerant MAJORITY who put up with this crap for way too long! As they insulted not only you but the memory of your ancestors who died for this country! They tore down statues to their memory! People who never built anything in their lives! They went out of their way to humiliate you and spit on you and the graves of your ancestors! And that is not an exaggeration; they did that! But this country is so nice. It's so polite. It's so thoughtful and, empathetic, and sweet. It's the kind of country that loves dogs and gives directions to strangers that we put up with it for four years … but not anymore! (Carlson, 2024)

As most white people do not want to be thought of as oppressors, rather than interrogate their position, the alethophobic reaction is to lash out at the people pointing out historical realities. White people have shown over the decades that they cannot imagine a world where they are not in charge. To them, equality with people of color is an apocalyptic nightmare. To illustrate, most white Americans in a poll described that they felt like they were the ones subject to discrimination because they felt like they were not allowed to say whatever they wanted to and about people of color without social consequences (Gonyea, 2017). People like Carlson have been invading the discourse where teachers and administrators have retreated. Their narrative is that people of color are undeserving of the status that white people have earned through hard work and ingenuity, erasing the contributions of all minoritized people and propagating the lie that only white people represent civilization and goodness.

Ultimately, by not teaching explicitly about racism, oppression, and race, schools are perpetuating the worst of it. The failure to explicitly address racism, oppression, and race in schools and society perpetuates the structures and ideologies that sustain white supremacist structures. The unwillingness to confront these issues fosters a dangerous cycle in which oppressive language and behaviors are treated as rebellious acts rather than clear manifestations of systemic racism. This avoidance reinforces privilege by shielding white students from accountability and prevents meaningful progress toward equity. The examples of Arizona's Ethnic Studies ban, the Desert Vista High School incident, and the racial rhetoric in political campaigns illustrate how race is mishandled in education and society at large. Instead of challenging white supremacy, these instances reveal how white privilege allows individuals to avoid examining their role in oppressive systems. The resistance to discussing race stems from a deep discomfort with sharing power and a fear of losing dominance. Yet, as Hayes and Juarez (2012) explained, addressing race and culture directly is essential to transforming education and society. Ignoring race conversations leaves students ill-equipped to navigate in a democracy, leading them to support ending it rather than embracing being equal members of society without the privileges of whiteness.

Discussion Questions for Chapter 2

1   The chapter emphasizes that race is a socially constructed concept with no biological basis. How does understanding race as a social construct influence how educators and policymakers should approach racial inequities in education?

2   The chapter states that "race is about power." Discuss how the concept of race has been historically used as a tool for power distribution in American society. How does this understanding challenge the notion of a "color-blind" approach in education?

3   Reflect on the legal cases discussed. How have legal definitions of race been used both to uphold and dismantle systems of racial oppression? What lessons can educators learn from this legal history?

4   The chapter introduces the concept of alethophobia, or the fear of confronting uncomfortable historical truth. How does this phenomenon manifest in schools and classrooms, and what strategies can educators use to address it effectively?

5   The chapter critiques deficit-based perspectives. How can educators shift their mindset to view cultural and linguistic differences as assets rather than deficits, and what impact might this have on their relationships with students?

6 The chapter argues that white supremacy is embedded in many aspects of the education system, from curriculum design to teacher expectations. What specific steps can educators take to recognize and disrupt these structures in their own classrooms and schools?

Actionable Classroom Practices from Chapter 2

- **Acknowledge and Celebrate Cultural Assets**

  Recognize and affirm students' cultural and linguistic backgrounds, such as African American Vernacular English (AAVE), as strengths rather than deficits. Encourage students to share their unique cultural perspectives.

- **Teach Critical Legal History**

  Incorporate the actual texts of legal cases like *Brown v. Board of Education* and *Plessy v. Ferguson* into the curriculum to illustrate the systemic nature of racial inequities and their historical context.

- **Address and Challenge Deficit Thinking**

  Avoid framing students of color as "needing to be fixed" in meetings with other teachers and administrators. Focus on their strengths and the systemic barriers they face rather than individual shortcomings.

- **Model and Teach Code-Switching**

  Teach students how to navigate between their cultural vernaculars and Standard English when necessary, without devaluing their primary linguistic identity.

- **Decenter Whiteness in Curriculum Design**

  Include diverse authors, perspectives, and historical narratives in lessons, ensuring that curriculum materials do not reinforce whiteness as the "norm."

- **Incorporate Anti-racist Practices into Classroom Policies**

  Critically examine classroom rules, grading systems, and disciplinary practices to ensure they do not uphold white supremacist norms.

3 "Gaps" and School-to-Prison Pipeline

After lifting the veil on the white supremacist structures in schools and society, they become impossible to ignore. The next step in addressing the structures that inhibit student success is to examine the classroom, punishment, and procedural structures that create what has been dubbed the school-to-prison pipeline (Hirschfield, 2008). *Reforms* such as zero-tolerance policies have created a pipeline directly from the schools to the correctional system for Black students (Fuentes, 2012; Hirschfield, 2008; Kim & Geronimo, 2009; Morris & Perry, 2016; Wald & Losen, 2003). This pipeline is created and maintained through laws and policies at every federal and state level and implemented through the individual actions of teachers and principals (Bryan, 2017). According to Wald and Losen (2003), a lack of effective behavioral interventions, harsh school removal policies, and a *get-tough* discipline system in schools and juvenile facilities have coalesced to create a pipeline from the school to the prison. This school-to-prison pipeline criminalizes childish behaviors and, according to Hirschfield (2008), has created a system of school governance where teachers and administrators have ceded authority to "criminal justice professionals" (p. 93). Hirshfield explained that this move to criminalization has been driven by fear of people who are not white and middle-class, combined with pressure to have all students perform on standardized measures.

Solidarity with students begins with the teacher's understanding of these structures and then the refusal to become part of the problem. This radical act of saying *no* is the next step in building relationships that lead to Caring Solidarity.

Origins of the Gap

Scholarship has long documented the persistent disparity in academic achievement between white and African American students, referred to as the *achievement gap* (Ladson-Billings, 2006, 2007, 2008). This gap is evident across all measurable metrics—test scores, graduation rates, and college admissions—and begins as early as preschool, extending through college (Haskins & Rouse, 2005). Despite decades of research and initiatives aimed at addressing this inequity, the gap remains deeply entrenched in American schools (Howard, 2010; Kuhfeld et al., 2018). It pervades both public and private education systems in urban, suburban, and rural settings, contradicting the assumption that it is solely an urban issue (Bradbury et al., 2015).

The definition of *success* itself plays a crucial role in perpetuating the gap. Beginning with the 1966 Coleman Report (Equality of Educational Opportunity), scholars and educators focused on explaining disparities in standardized test performance between Black and white students. While the report rightly attributed much of the gap to segregation, it oversimplified the solution by recommending that integrating Black students into majority-white schools would close the gap (Coleman, 1966). However, as discussed earlier, segregation persists in various forms, and the gap remains irrespective of the level of integration or segregation within schools. The desegregation efforts of the 1970s, initially successful, were gradually reversed in the 1990s as white communities adopted new methods to re-segregate schools. These strategies included a shift toward *community schools* and the intentional division of districts to separate students by race (Nazaryan, 2017). Reports reveal that US schools are now as segregated as they were during the Coleman era, with structural inequities baked into the system (EdBuild, 2016; Kucsera, 2014; Orfield et al., 2014).

Historically, segregation in America served a dual purpose: separation and subjugation. The underlying structure of whiteness, designed to concentrate power, has remained largely intact, even as overt segregation has become less socially acceptable. The racial makeup of classrooms is not the root cause of the achievement gap; instead, it is the systemic inequality embedded in the schooling system and perpetuated by the decisions of individual educators and administrators.

Ladson-Billings critiqued interpretations of the Coleman Report, which called for school integration but was misread by many as evidence of Black cultural inferiority, with exposure to white schools seen as the remedy. She reframed the gap as an educational debt owed to students of color, encompassing both market and non-market effects of systemic racism. For instance, historically, Black segregated schools received significantly less funding than white schools, a disparity that persists today. Regardless of whether Black students attend predominantly white schools or majority-Black schools, they face systemic barriers. In majority-white schools, Black students are less likely to graduate, attend college, or achieve competitive test scores compared to their white peers. Similarly, these outcomes persist in segregated, majority-Black schools.

Given that information, people must choose. Do they believe (1) that Black kids are naturally inferior to white students, or (2) that the entire education system is stacked against Black students? Given the evidence, it is either one or the other. Simply put, the answer is 2. If teachers and school officials are willing to set aside their sense of normality and look at the historical record, any fair-minded person would reach the same conclusion.

From the first day that Black students walk through the doors of the school, they face a labyrinth of roadblocks, challenges, insults, large and small, and doors closed. When Black students enter the school system, systemic obstacles, including implicit bias, inequitable resources, and micro- and macro-aggressions, stand in their way of achieving within the system. These barriers are not the result of individual students' abilities but are rooted in the historical and structural inequities of the education system. As Love (2019c) argued, effective teaching across racial lines requires rejecting the assumption that students are damaged by their Blackness or their communities. Instead, educators must recognize the real source of harm: the white power structures that perpetuate oppression.

Despite these challenges, African American students demonstrate extraordinary resilience, navigating a system stacked against them with courage and determination. Their success is a testament to their strength and perseverance. Yet the reality remains that too many students are unable to overcome these barriers, reflecting systemic failure rather than individual limitations. This ongoing tragedy underscores the urgent need for systemic change. The hope that *this year, this school, this teacher might be different* reflects the enduring faith of students, families, and communities. Change is possible, but it requires a fundamental shift in how students are treated, how schools are structured, and how educators conceptualize their role.

The ~~Achievement~~ Opportunity Gap

The concept of the achievement gap inherently assumes deficiencies in students, families, and communities of color. However, this perspective overlooks alternative ways of understanding the gap. Education professionals generally acknowledge that a quality education fosters opportunities and success in life. Many who enter the teaching profession were themselves successful in school and wish to recreate those positive experiences for their students (Britzman, 2003; Danielewicz, 2001). This personal history, coupled with the belief that education is a pathway to success, often leads teachers, especially white teachers, to view existing educational practices as both normal and desirable (Solomona et al., 2005).

The assumption of white normality, combined with the belief that tests, graduation rates, and college admissions are neutral benchmarks, creates a framework that neglects the lived realities of Black students in schools. Ladson-Billings (1995) argued that the language surrounding the achievement gap reinforces a deficit-oriented view of students and fails to interrogate the neutrality of the standards themselves (2006; 2007; 2008).

In response, scholars have worked to shift the research and policy narrative from an *achievement* gap to an *opportunity* gap, highlighting the systemic inequities faced by students of color (Darling-Hammond et al., 2014; Ladson-Billings, 2006, 2007, 2008; Love, 2019c). Ladson-Billings argued that equitable funding for schools serving predominantly Black and Brown students, alongside investments addressing social issues such as low wages and food deserts—would help reduce the educational debt and, by extension, the achievement gap. The educational debt is also tied to the exploitation of Black labor, both historically and in the present. Ladson-Billings noted that the wealth generated by enslaved Black people built the US economy and continues to do so through exploitative practices, such as prison labor (Browne, 2007). Today, incarcerated individuals, disproportionately African American, produce goods under conditions subsidized by taxpayers, perpetuating economic inequities. Against this backdrop, it is ridiculous for researchers to focus on an achievement gap without addressing the broader context of systemic exclusion from economic, educational, and civil rights since the nation's founding.

Reframing the achievement gap through critical questions can reveal the systemic inequities that perpetuate it:

- What if tests and curricula are not neutral but are instead components of a system designed to advantage white students and disadvantage Black students?
- What if the gap exists not because students are failing in schools but because schools are failing the students?
- What if this failure stems from white assumptions of normality and white inherent goodness?
- How might teacher behaviors change if schools and systems were understood to be failing students rather than students failing within these systems?
- What if teachers' ability to meet their students' needs is considered the gap to be addressed, rather than students' performance on normed assessments?

These questions prompt educators to critically examine structures that white teachers often take for granted. Scholars advocate for shifting the focus from student deficiencies to the lack of opportunities, resources, and support systems. Despite this, indicators such as income, race, and geographic location remain the strongest predictors of academic success, and the measures employed by school systems to close the achievement gap have predominantly targeted Black children.

Grit

Educators frequently perceive themselves as benevolent actors, resistant to acknowledging their complicity in perpetuating inequities. Ullucci (2012) observed, "The challenge arises in helping teachers come to terms with the ways whiteness and privilege function within these systems and how they can either be complicit with or rupture these mechanisms" (p. 90). White educators often use the achievement gap to critique students, parents, and communities rather than to see it as an opportunity to reimagine curricula and the educational environment (Crocco & Costigan, 2007). The popularity of *grit* as an organizing principle for understanding students of color falls into this category (Love, 2019a).

The concept of *grit*, as explained by Duckworth et al. (2007), has gained traction as a way to describe and then build resiliency in students. According to Duckworth, *grit* describes the traits of students who work "strenuously toward challenges" and can sustain that effort over the years despite "failure, adversity, and plateaus in progress" (p. 1088). According to this theory, high achievement does not come to those who are the smartest or even most talented but to those who persevere, especially against great odds. The theory is that their *grit* is evidenced by that success. Duckworth also includes that *grit* is connected to self-discipline and the ability to deny immediate gratification for long-term success (Love, 2019a).

At first glance, *grit* sounds like the kind of resilience that schools should instill in all students. It is the ability to stand in the face of adversity and trudge on when the going is difficult. However, this concept is more often used to fault those who do not succeed rather than to commend those who do. The thinking often goes that those without *grit* are somehow unworthy of success and that the educator's job is to create *grit* in their students (Love, 2019a; Stokas, 2015). In her book *We Want to Do More Than Survive*, Love (2019c), explained that a company called *The Character Lab* produces materials and friendly research studies on *grit* and relates it to everything, including the young adult novel *The Hunger Games*. But Love asked why students are expected to navigate a racist system and, when they rebel, are seen as somehow deficient in *grit*. The Character Lab insists it is interested in building skills to help students achieve their long-term goals. Love asked, however, "But what if your long-term goal is fighting racism? Is four hundred years long enough? We have rebelled, fought, conformed, pleaded with the courts, marched, protested, boycotted, created timeless art that reflects our lives, and become president of the country that disposes of us with little to no relief from our oppression. Is that not *grit*" (pp. 72–73)? Love explained that good teaching is "To abandon teaching gimmicks like 'grit' that present the experiences of dark youth as ahistorical and further pathologize them and evoke collective freedom dreaming" (p. 12).

It is a testament to the deep faith in America and their children's potential that parents send their students to schools that, generation after generation, disrespect and devalue those children (Duckworth & Quinn, 2009). Thus, some schools may even go far in equipping students for life in a white supremacist society, but seldom are they equipping students to dismantle it. As Love (2019a) explained,

> pedagogies that promote social justice must have teeth. They must move beyond feel-good language and gimmicks to help educators understand and recognize America and its schools as spaces of whiteness, white rage,

and white supremacy, all of which function to terrorize students of color. (p. 13)

Students build resilience out of the struggles that people with privilege do not have to endure, but schools act as though that struggle is the ordinary course of the life of students of color without asking why (Ris, 2015).

The Discipline Gap

Continuing to work on seeing the structures of white supremacy and the school-to-prison pipeline, attention should also turn to the unequal disciplinary actions taken against Black students in schools. The ideology of the achievement gap pervades schools where African American students attend. Methods to close the gaps have primarily focused on Black children themselves and have not treated it as an opportunity to change perceptions of race and the measures used to qualify success. Instead, the solution is often to treat the gap as a pathology afflicting Black students. In an attempt to improve test scores without changing how students are taught, school bureaucracies use deficit models and interventions that constrain the curriculum, eliminate the arts, enforce strict disciplinary codes, and focus on holding teachers and students accountable for raising test scores (Crocco & Costigan, 2007).

Love (2019c) explained, "For too many, suspension is a birthright of being young and Black" (p. 5). The research is clear that the pipeline begins early in the educational careers of Black students. According to a 2016 report by the US Department of Education, the gap in discipline and punishment of African American students begins before students are five years old. The report states that Black public preschool students (two–four years old) were 3.6 times more likely to be suspended from school than white preschool children, and while Black students make up 19 percent of enrollments, they make up 47 percent of out-of-school suspensions. "Black boys represent 19% of male preschool enrollment, but 45% of male preschool children receive[ing] one or more out-of-school suspensions. Black girls represent 20% of female preschool enrollment, but 54% of female preschool children receive[ing] one or more out-of-school suspensions" (CRDC, 2016).

Exclusion from school has real consequences for Black students' achievement over their educational lives. Morris and Perry (2016) found that African American students in a large Kentucky school system were suspended from school, excluding them from the learning process, at a rate of nearly six times that of their white peers. They further explained that segregation of Black students within the district can account for about 12 percent of out-of-school suspensions. Not surprisingly, the schools with the highest rates of African American students had the highest suspension rates. However, even in schools that were more integrated, "Each additional percentage of the student body that is black is estimated to increase the annual number of school suspensions by about ten, controlling for school size and socioeconomic composition" (p. 76).

Their analysis of exclusion from school and achievement tests of excluded students highlights the effects of segregation and disciplinary bias.

> The suspension disparity operates at both the school and individual levels, such that black students are more likely than white students to attend schools that employ higher levels of exclusionary discipline, and black students are also more likely to be suspended than their white peers within the same schools. In turn, racial and ethnic minorities underperform on reading and math achievement tests relative to white students in this school system. (Morris & Perry, 2016, p. 81)

They concluded that the "effects of suspension are long-lasting, setting into motion a trajectory of poor performance that continues in subsequent years, even if a student is not suspended again. Indeed, our results show that academic growth drops precipitously after one early suspension" (p. 82). Skiba et al. (2011) monitored the disciplinary practices of 364 middle and elementary schools, finding that African American students received harsher and more frequent discipline than their white peers. These exclusions are placed on Black students despite the fact that the behaviors are perceptibly similar to those of white students who did not receive the same types of punishment (Monroe, 2005).

Skiba et al. (2002) found:

> no evidence that racial disparities in school punishment could be explained by higher rates of African American misbehavior … White students were significantly more likely to be referred to the office for smoking, leaving without permission, obscene language, and vandalism. In contrast, black students were more likely to be referred to the office for *disrespect, excessive noise, threat, and loitering.* (emphasis added; p. 334)

Evidence overwhelmingly points to implicit bias, fear and suspicion of Black children, a lack of knowledge about cultural differences, and the structures in place that impede students of color from wealth and mobility, added to pressure for all students to perform on standardized tests, has pressed schools to exclude Black students, rather than teach them (Morris & Perry, 2016; Okonofua & Eberhardt, 2015; Skiba, Peterson, & Williams, 1997).

Gregory and Weinstein (2008) argued that the disproportionate number of suspensions of African American students, specifically males, leads to lower achievement and, therefore, a more negative attitude toward school, which can display itself in self-destructive or defiant behaviors, leading to more suspensions. This cycle can quickly lead to students being referred to the justice system and eventual incarceration (Gregory & Weinstein, 2008). A 2024 Report from the Government Accountability Office (GAO) tried to sound the alarm, but it was drowned out by a presidential campaign where the candidate for president constantly lied about immigrants eating dogs and cats; thus, the report on the state of Black girls in American schools received little media coverage. The report found that Black girls were 5.2 times more likely to be suspended than their white peers for similar or the same infractions.

> Black girls received harsher punishments than White girls, even when the infractions that prompted disciplinary action were similar. For example, Black girls had higher rates of exclusionary discipline compared to White girls for similar behaviors such as defiance, disrespect, and disruption. The data also show that in every state in the U.S., Black girls are disciplined at higher rates. When they also had a disability, exclusionary discipline rates of Black girls grew larger. (GAO, 2024)

These are only a tiny sample of the numerous studies that show the detrimental effects of educational exclusion and its causes rooted in whiteness and white supremacy. These effects snowball as students grow into adolescence, so it seems logical that the practice would be abandoned, yet it keeps going.

The problem of suspensions in preschool and elementary schools has caught the attention of some administrators. In Minneapolis, the Superintendent banned suspensions for all preschool, kindergarten, and first-grade students for the 2014 school year (Matos, 2015). However, the ban lasted only one year, after teachers and administrators complained that it left them without options for addressing student behaviors they found unacceptable (see Chapter 9 for an update).

Preschool students excluded from the learning environment fall behind and become elementary students who are suspended, who then fall further behind. Students who are slightly behind in elementary school, without purposeful intervention, become far behind in middle and high school. This cycle of suspensions, low scores, and more suspensions leads to behaviors that further disrupt the classroom focused on raising test scores. When a student comes in contact with police resource officers in middle or high school, the consequences of boredom, low achievement, low self-confidence, and the constant drip of failure in school can wash students into the justice system.

How the Pipeline Is Built and Maintained

While no one is saying that all preschool and elementary teachers are purposefully targeting Black youth for exclusion in the education system, there is overwhelming evidence that white teachers perceive Black students as a threat to the learning environment of their classrooms (GAO, 2024). Love (2019b) described her perceptions of white teachers, "Let me be clear: I do not think white teachers enter the profession wanting to harm children of color, but they will hurt a child whose culture is viewed as an afterthought" (online). Administrators are complicit in making that perception the basis for individual actions. This perception of threat by white teachers is the entryway to the school-to-prison pipeline. Teachers who lack the ability or desire to prevent students from entering the pipeline by inspiring them with a thought-provoking curriculum and classroom instruction in self-regulation create a self-fulfilling prophecy that students of color are unmanageable (Annamma et al., 2016).

As demonstrated by the school-to-prison pipeline and the uneven success of students based on race, schools are not neutral but instead are heavily biased in favor of white teachers and white children. The whiteness of school spaces is part of the curriculum as much as are the ABCs and students of color are continually disinvited to participate as equal entities. They are welcome to be in school as long as they are willing to follow the rules, and those rules are in service to white supremacy. Classroom teachers cannot afford to have students disrupt classroom procedures, as they must adhere to strict timelines dictated by administrators. Therefore, any behavior that diverts the teacher from the daily plan is labeled disruptive and results in action. The proliferation of School *resource officers* arresting students has moved from being the discipline of last resort to a primary disciplinary strategy in school buildings. These resource officers have come under increased scrutiny as student videos of officers in South Carolina, Texas, and Florida show officers slamming students as young as twelve to the ground, even dragging them across desks.

Videos are continually emerging of students being thrown up against walls and ripped from school chairs. Police officers in schools have led to a pattern where students of color are assumed to be guilty and that they are the problem. Black students have a reasonable assumption of unfair treatment by police, causing a complete breakdown of any social contract between the administration, the teachers, and their students. Instead of learning to be citizens in a democracy who trust and value the system, kids learn that their futures are filled with harassment, arrest, and violence from authority figures (Couvson, 2016).

It should horrify every American that innumerable children have been and are being handcuffed to chairs, desks, or by the elbows as their tiny hands are too small for the handcuffs to be effective, being led away by police officers (Malik, 2017). Most are children with disabilities, and some are white, but Black students take the brunt of disciplinary regimes.

As Goff et al. (2014) found, an "atmosphere of dehumanization" has pervaded school discipline (p. 10). Part of what they found was that police officers overestimated Black children's ages and perceived them as 4.53 years older than they were. They concluded that Black children, in contexts of that dehumanization, are prematurely treated as adults, leading to an increased use of violence to control behavior and an assumption of guilt. The 2024 GAO report corroborated this. The reasons for an increased suspension rate are especially disturbing and confirm what researchers have been saying for decades.

> For example, one study found that adultification—a form of racial and gender bias in which adults view Black girls as older and more promiscuous than their same-age peers—leads to harsher punishments for Black girls. Another study found that colorism—a form of racial bias against those with darker skin—is a factor in the disproportionate discipline of girls. (GAO, 2024)

Rather than school officials or educators working to keep students in schools, they have handed over discipline to police officers, who become the conduit introducing Black students to the school-to-prison pipeline for either major or minor incidents (Couvson, 2016). Hirshfield (2008) explained, "Teachers and administrators often perceive little choice but to summon repressive means to swiftly remove disruptive students from the classroom and the school" (p. 93).

This attitude, when added to the many cases each year of police abusing students in schools, shows that any good that comes from having an armed police officer in schools is outweighed by the negative impact their presence has on teaching, administration, and student well-being. The reasons for the suspension rates are varied. White teachers without the capacity to culturally connect with their students are more likely to depend on police officers, suspension, and exclusion as a form of punishment. Also, with more reliance on testing to measure teacher performance, educators are less likely to invest in students whose test scores are lower. Because of recent punitive *reforms*, teachers are increasingly accountable for student achievement on standardized tests. Yet, teachers' incapacity to meet the demands placed upon them has created the perception that harsh methods are needed to control student behavior. Added to that mix, schools with higher minoritized populations use a narrower curriculum that focuses almost exclusively on math and reading to meet those testing targets. Teachers are increasingly unable to use exploratory projects that build interest in learning.

This drill curriculum lowers interest in classwork and creates boredom for students, causing them to act out. To deal with these behaviors that disrupt the drill-test learning environment, teachers increasingly turn over authority to administrators and law enforcement in a futile attempt to force students to meet imposed academic standards (Fallis & Opotow, 2003). While this situation has become the norm throughout the United States, it is hardest felt in large cities, where high percentages of Black students are increasingly introduced to the correctional system at an early age by being pushed out of the school systems (Bowditch, 1993; Fuentes, 2012; Hirschfield, 2008; Wacquant, 2001). Bowditch (1993) found thirty years ago that students with lower grades and attendance were systematically encouraged to drop out of high school through the disciplinary process.

> The activities of the discipline office, which routinely identified "trouble-makers" and "got rid of" them through suspensions and involuntary drops, may be one important but largely unacknowledged mechanism through which schools perpetuate the racial and class stratification of the larger society. (p. 506)

Yet administrators have only increased their reliance on these methods. Hirshfield (2008) explained, "Teachers and administrators often perceive little choice but to summon repressive means to swiftly remove disruptive students from the classroom and the school" (p. 93).

Cuellar and Markowitz (2015) found a significant jump in the probability that students who are suspended out of school will become involved in the judicial system when they are not in school: "Being suspended out of school on a school day is associated with a more than doubling of the probability of offense" (p. 105). Further, they explained that "school suspension policies designed to handle problem behavior in school may contribute to overall crime rates out of school, highlighting a significant potential disadvantage of using out-of-school suspension as part of a school disciplinary policy" (p. 105). These and other studies show that there is a bias toward harsher discipline in schools for students of color and that when students are excluded from the school environment, they are more likely to end up incarcerated either during the school years or shortly after.

Pane and Rocco (2014) explained:

Exclusionary school discipline is commonly practiced when teachers perceive heightened misbehavior and classroom discipline, combined with the fear of losing control in the classroom. Exclusionary school discipline practices include the referral of disruptive students out of the classroom and their subsequent suspension and expulsion from school. (p. 29)

They clarified that the pipeline begins with referrals for disruption from individual teachers, then suspension from administrators, school failure, dropping out or expulsion, juvenile incarceration, and then adult prison (Losen & Skiba, 2010).

According to the ACLU, 90 percent of schools in the United States do not have enough counselors and social workers to meet the needs of students as schools are increasing their police presence. The ACLU report titled Cops and no Counselors: How the Lack of School Mental Health Staff Is Harming Students (2017) found in a nationwide survey:

- 1.7 million students are in schools with police but no counselors
- 3 million students are in schools with police but no nurses
- 6 million students are in schools with police but no school psychologists

- 10 million students are in schools with police but no social workers
- 14 million students are in schools with police but no counselor, nurse, psychologist, or social worker (Whitaker et al., 2017, p. 3).

The ACLU also found:

- Students with disabilities were arrested at a rate 2.9 times that of students without disabilities. In some states, they were ten times as likely to be arrested than their counterparts.
- Black students were arrested at a rate three times that of white students. In some states, they were eight times as likely to be arrested.
- Pacific Island/Native Hawaiian and Native American students were arrested at a rate two times that of white students.
- Latinx students were arrested at a rate of 1.3 times that of white students.
- Black girls made up 16 percent of the female student population, but were 39 percent of girls arrested in school. Black girls were arrested at a rate four times that of white girls. In North Carolina, Iowa, and Michigan, Black girls were more than eight times as likely to be arrested than white girls.
- Black and Latino boys with disabilities were 3 percent of students but were 12 percent of school arrests. (Whitaker et al., 2017, p. 5)

The evidence is overwhelming that American schools, especially secondary schools, routinely fail African American students. Instead of preparing young people for full participation as educated citizens in a democracy, these schools operate as racialized gauntlets, where even the slightest misstep can lead to disaster (Love, 2019a; b; c). Love (2016) refers to this slow, deliberate, daily process of dehumanization, disenfranchisement, and criminalization of African American youth as *spirit murdering*. While schools are admittedly facing unprecedented challenges, adults are tempted to try and meet them by changing student populations rather than changing their pedagogy. The resulting handover of authority, combined with the economic incentive to post improved test scores, has resulted in a consistent trend toward using the juvenile justice system to divert students from school systems unable to meet student needs (Fuentes, 2012).

The process that moves students from classroom to cellblock begins with behaviors that, in the past, would not have resulted in a suspension or a parent meeting but now result in criminal charges and confinement, introducing students to the justice system that can lead to adult incarceration (Cuellar & Markowitz, 2015). These interventions or altercations can include police officers trained in school discipline but often are not. Either way, the goal of officers in schools is to maintain student compliance, not to keep students in the learning environment. According to Wald and Losen (2003), harsh school removal policies resulted from the inability to create behavior interventions that would de-escalate situations. Instead of more humane structures that take time and resources, schools created zero-tolerance and get-tough policies that led to more suspensions and juvenile detentions.

The lack of cultural awareness and competency has made control the foremost goal of schooling and has made law enforcement officials the first, rather than the last resort, for controlling student behavior. With an attitude of confrontation, uniforms, and deadly weapons at the ready, police are embedded into the disciplinary structure, often without training in education. For these students and the rest of society, the loss of academic achievement, the expense of a system of monitoring students, increased police presence, incarceration, and the shattering effects on individuals and families are not justified by the outcomes. Are we more educated and secure as a nation because lives are lost and futures are ruined? What is the advantage? What are we gaining from the current system that does not fulfill the most basic mission to care for and educate children? What do we gain by more police, more incarceration, more rules, and more exclusion of students?

Black Teachers Are Not the Only Ones Responsible to Dismantle the Pipeline

Duncan's (2018) research highlights the critical and often unrecognized labor that Black teachers undertake to protect and empower their students in the face of systemic racism in schools. This labor involves not only resisting overt and covert racism but also actively creating spaces where Black students can thrive despite the structures around them. However, while Duncan's work underscores the transformative impact of Black teachers, it also raises an essential question about equity in the distribution of responsibility: Why is the onus for dismantling white supremacy in schools disproportionately placed on teachers of color?

Relying solely on Black teachers or other teachers of color to confront and address racism is neither practical nor just. This expectation not only perpetuates inequities but also risks burnout among educators who are already navigating the emotional toll of systemic oppression themselves. The work of dismantling white supremacy in schools must be a shared responsibility, requiring active and intentional participation from white teachers, who make up the majority of the teaching workforce in the United States.

White teachers must recognize their complicity in upholding structures of oppression and take deliberate steps to disrupt these systems. Adopting a stance of Caring Solidarity with students of color demands more than superficial commitments or performative allyship. It requires an unflinching examination of one's biases, an openness to discomfort, and a willingness to engage in transformative practices that challenge the status quo. This includes calling out and addressing racist practices among colleagues, advocating for equitable policies, and reimagining curricula and pedagogy to center the voices, experiences, and histories of marginalized communities.

Moreover, the stakes of inaction are too high to ignore. The pervasive school-to-prison pipeline is a stark reminder of how educational systems can and do function as mechanisms of oppression. It is not enough to implement *inclusive* curricula or adopt culturally responsive teaching methods if those efforts do not directly confront and dismantle the systemic factors that criminalize and marginalize students of color. White teachers must actively stand in opposition to these systems, not just rhetorically, but through concrete actions that challenge disciplinary policies, standardized testing practices, tracking systems, and other structural barriers that disproportionately harm students of color.

Dismantling the school-to-prison pipeline is a moral imperative. To continue teaching within a system designed to oppress while refusing to act against it is to be complicit in its harm. White teachers have a unique responsibility and opportunity to leverage their privilege to advocate for systemic change by partnering with their colleagues of color and committing to the ongoing work of dismantling white supremacy. This is not only a professional obligation but a fundamental act of humanity and justice.

Discussion Questions for Chapter 3

1 How do zero-tolerance policies and the increased presence of school resource officers contribute to the school-to-prison pipeline? What alternative disciplinary strategies could schools implement to disrupt this cycle?

2 The chapter critiques the concept of the achievement gap and suggests reframing it as the opportunity gap. What are the key differences between these perspectives, and how might this reframing change how educators approach inequities in education?

3 What role does bias play in the disproportionate disciplining of Black students? How can teachers and administrators address these biases in their day-to-day practices?

4 The chapter highlights disparities in discipline, such as higher suspension rates for Black students starting as early as preschool. How do these inequities impact long-term student outcomes, and what steps can schools take to create more equitable disciplinary practices?

5 The chapter critiques the concept of grit, particularly as it relates to students navigating a racist education system. How does framing success as a matter of grit obscure systemic barriers, and what are the implications for educators?

6 The chapter emphasizes the shared responsibility of all educators, particularly white teachers, in dismantling the school-to-prison pipeline. What specific steps can educators take to ensure their classrooms are part of the solution rather than the problem?

Actionable Classroom Practices from Chapter 3

- **Adopt Restorative Practices**
  Implement restorative justice techniques, such as peer mediation and restorative circles, to resolve conflicts and address disciplinary issues without exclusionary measures.

- **Critically Examine and Revise Discipline Policies**
  Advocate for removing zero-tolerance policies and replacing them with equitable disciplinary practices prioritizing student support over

punishment. Create an interdisciplinary project that examines the issue using data from your district.

- **Build Culturally Responsive Classroom Management**

  Create a computer folder of culturally competent strategies that affirm students' identities and minimize misunderstandings based on cultural differences. Each break, commit to incorporating several of them in the following school term lessons. Give this folder to other teachers and student teachers.

- **Develop Positive Relationships with Students**

  Foster trust and solidarity by creating a safe, supportive classroom environment where students feel valued and understood. Two resources are listed here.

  - **Responsive Classroom**
    Website: responsiveclassroom.org
    This research-based approach emphasizes social-emotional learning and practical tools for building trust, fostering respectful communication, and creating a positive classroom community.

  - *Culturally Responsive Teaching and the Brain* by Zaretta Hammond
    This book provides strategies for building authentic relationships with students by understanding their cultural contexts, promoting trust, and leveraging those relationships to support academic success.

- **Reduce Reliance on School Resource Officers**

  Advocate for reducing or eliminating police presence in schools and reallocating resources to hire counselors, social workers, and psychologists. Run for school board to begin reversing oppressive practices in your community.

- **Incorporate Social Justice Education**

  Design lessons that analyze and address the school-to-prison pipeline using data from your community and district.

- **Collaborate with Families and Communities**

  Volunteer and partner with students' families and community organizations to understand their needs and perspectives, ensuring inclusive and equitable support systems.

- **Track and Analyze Disciplinary Data**

  Regularly review and graph classroom and school disciplinary records to identify patterns of inequity and adjust practices to address disparities.

The Inadequacy of Multicultural Education as Implemented

Since the 1970s, Multicultural Education (MCE) has been the framework on which all efforts at education across difference are draped. Multicultural education, as envisioned by James Banks (1995), the venerable scholar and educator, is an outgrowth of the Civil Rights Movement and seeks to integrate those ideals into the teaching practices of all students (Payne & Welsh, 2000). Banks' work with schools, textbooks for teacher education, and scholarly mentorship are directed toward the goals of creating a school system where everyone is included, valued, and part of the learning community. Banks traced the origins of the multicultural movement back to the early twentieth century, with W. E. B. Du Bois and Carter G. Woodson (1933). Both Du Bois and Woodson argued for the end of segregation from a political and humanitarian standpoint. Du Bois asked why the basic standards of humanity were not applied to Black people,

> What do we want? What is the thing we are after? … We want to be Americans, full-fledged Americans, with all the rights of other American citizens. But is that all? Do we want simply to be Americans? Once in a while through all of us there flashes some clairvoyance, some clear idea, of what America really is. We who are dark can see America in a way that white Americans cannot. And seeing our country thus, are we satisfied with its present goals and ideals? (Du Bois, 1926/1994, p. 290)

Writing in 1933, Carter G. Woodson blamed the education of African Americans as a contributing factor to the mindset of segregation, stating that inferiority was drilled into people in almost every class and "in almost every book" (p. 2). He explained that the school curriculum was not a tool for enlightening and questioning his current situation but to engrain white supremacy and Black inferiority into the minds of Black children, thereby ensuring their continued oppression. Woodson asked,

> to handicap a student by teaching him that his black face is a curse and that his struggle to change his condition is hopeless is the worst sort of lynching … This crusade (for a curriculum that advances Black people) is much more important than the anti-lynching movement because there would be no lynching if it did not start in the schoolroom. Why not exploit, enslave, or exterminate a class that everybody is taught to regard as inferior? (p. 3)

Banks explained that during the 1960s, as a response to the Civil Rights Movement and the Women's Movement, educators sought to add other voices and experiences to the curriculum. "Sometimes in strident voices, African Americans, frustrated with deferred and shattered dreams, demanded community control of their schools, African-American teachers and administrators, and the infusion of Black history into the curriculum" (Banks, 1995, p. 18). Throughout the 1970s and 1980s, with leadership from scholars like Banks and Geneva Gay, amid limited success and frequent lapses, schools have worked to become less of a melting pot where everyone is invited in to become like the white majority, but more like the salad bowl, where all people are invited to become part of the new American culture and still retain their individuality (Gorski, 1999).

Banks (1997) included these goals for a multicultural curriculum, paraphrased here:

1 Help students view the curriculum from diverse cultural and ethnic perspectives.

2 Contribute to a healthy nationalism and national identity.

3 Develop students' abilities to make reflective decisions about ethnicity and culture, take personal and social responsibility, and become active in creating a more just world.

4 Help students to understand their own cultures and reduce self-segregation.

5 Help students understand that all people have cultures and that one is not superior to another.

6 Help students develop important school skills while also learning about culture and being human (Payne & Welsh, 2000, pp. 25–28).

Gay (2010) explained that culture matters in educating students of color. She rejected the proposition that *cultural blindness* creates equality in the classroom and positioned that there are notions that construct this framework in the minds of teachers. Cultural neutrality is a fallacy that educational reform be grounded only in "positive beliefs about the cultural heritages and academic potentialities of these students [of color]" (p. 23). Gay explained that teachers should see culturally different students as assets to the classroom to create a validating curriculum and called for instruction based on learning styles that incorporate multicultural materials into schools. In Gay's discussion of the comprehensive approach of culturally responsive teaching, a teacher who practices it will mediate curriculum and educate the "whole child" (p. 32). She argued that academic success can best be attained through the teacher's cultural awareness and the use of collective effort rather than competition. Gay's description of the multicultural curriculum as multidimensional advocates for a comprehensive approach to teaching. Curriculum, climate, instruction, and assessment can all be combined under the umbrella of one common set of goals. She explained, however, that "to do this kind of teaching well requires tapping into a wide range of cultural knowledge, experiences, contributions, and perspectives" (p. 34).

However, Banks and Gay's laudable and democratic goals are perceived as a threat to white supremacist Conservatives. Critiques of multicultural education, especially in popular books by authors on the right, share a common theme. In their imaginings, multicultural curricula weaken our national unity forged in Europe (Sleeter, 2001a). As discussed in earlier chapters, US schools are becoming increasingly diverse and concerned about culture (Fry, 2009). Unfortunately, they are also doing all that they can to address that diversity while, at the same time, avoiding discussion of race (see Chapter Two) (Kobayashi & Peake, 2000). The need for a multicultural framework for US schools did not spring from a lack of awareness that other people exist. It came from the need for people of color to gain and hold power.

Multicultural Education Does Not Go Far Enough

In 2001, noted multicultural writer and teacher educator Christine Sleeter seemed to predict the future when she explained:

Conservatives hope to destroy public support for multicultural education and mobilize public opinion to endorse a conservative definition of how young Americans will be taught to view the United States in its diversity, and the positions of the United States and European Nations within a hierarchical, capitalistic, global order made up of diverse people. (p. 89)

These definitions include the Conservative belief that schools are not the place for cultural expression and should only be intellectual spaces where culture is an unnecessary add-on. They advocate that education should be a tool for assimilation, making attendance to culture a diversion from the American project. Also, Sleeter explained that because most teachers do not know enough about non-European cultures to help students broaden their worldviews, they are more likely to do more harm through their ignorance. (See Chapter 11 for a discussion on the Conservative attacks on books, curriculum, and pedagogy).

Paris (2012) explained that, before Multiculturalism, teachers saw all aspects of culture that were not part of whiteness as deficits to be overcome through education.

Deficit approaches to teaching and learning, firmly in place prior to and during the 1960s and 1970s, viewed the languages, literacies, and cultural ways of being of many students and communities of color as deficiencies to be overcome in learning the demanded and legitimized dominant language, literacy, and cultural ways of schooling. (p. 93)

Trying to do what is best for students and responding to their own notions of what good people do, schools have worked to infuse a sense of multiculturalism while strategically avoiding asking white people to change their own framework about race. They have sought to accomplish this monumental task, to infuse tolerance or appreciation of other races and cultures, without disrupting white supremacist ideas and frameworks (May, 1999).

Seldom does the curriculum critique the narrative that worldwide colonization was a net good. It does not question the inherent goodness of colonial actors, nor does it tell the complete story of the victims of that colonization. It does not implicate the Christian Church, Capitalism, or the Enlightenment for their roles in conquest and genocide from the fifteenth century to today. There are resources available, such as Zinn's (1980/2015) *A People's History of the United States*, *The Zinn Education Project* https://www.

zinnedproject.org, *Rethinking Schools* https://rethinkingschools.org, and Dunbar-Ortiz's (2014/2019) *An Indigenous People's History of the United States*, that are all extremely helpful, accurate, and challenging to the curriculum of white supremacy. They are part of very few curricula, even in advanced high school courses (however, we always used them at Minneapolis South when I was teaching there. Zinn was compelling and transformative for students).

Especially now, there is little question that these Conservative designs exist in education, are prevalent, and are constantly pushed in the debate of how best to teach children. If these conceptions are to be rejected as ineffectual or harmful, then they need a replacement that will inspire teachers and students to adopt a more democratic mindset. A more relevant critique of multiculturalism than one offered by Conservatives is that MCE has not gone far enough to change the narratives of Americans from the racial hierarchies of the past. In short, MCE still reinforces whiteness to avoid conflict with Conservatives as much as possible.

The *Foods and Festivals* Approach

MCE practices have undoubtedly improved students' educational experiences. Still, they have not gone far enough to change how white teachers, or the majority culture, see people who look different from them. Every single day, schools, teachers, and communities still tell students of color that their cultural and racial selves are not normal and that their expressions of cultural identity are not welcome.

To be multicultural, teachers must move beyond deficit thinking and a condensed, essentialist view of the cultures in their classrooms. In practice, multicultural approaches that should have critically examined the power of whiteness have instead devolved into a superficial *parade-of-cultures* model of multiculturalism. Criticized as a shallow dip into other people's cultures or the cultures of people who are not considered white, in this approach, clothing, foods, language, and other characteristics are *celebrated* without the assumption that there will be any deep understanding or solidarity with the cultures on parade. Teachers often use what Ladson-Billings and Tate (1995) called the *foods and festivals* approach to celebrating diversity (p. 61). For example, the culture of Mexico is paraded with food and clothing from southern and central Mexico, but there is no assumption of an understanding of the political struggles of the Mayans against the Mexican government or the United States' involvement in the destruction of Honduras that has led to migration through Mexico to the United States. Instead, teachers, ignorant of other places and cultures from their own, depend on their own stereotypes and social media to create lessons that instill racism into their students rather than steer them away from it.

For example, even in 2021, a teacher dressed up with paper feathers and danced around the room to give students a mnemonic device to remember a trigonometry function. Other teachers, even teachers of color, dressed in stereotypical Mexican dress and posed before a brick *wall* to celebrate Cinco de Mayo. Helfenbein (2003) explained that educators should avoid essentializing students to a static version of cultural identity: "Culture plays a role in the construction of human reality, but only a role. Any static notion of cultural relations fails to recognize the complexity of social interactions and reifies misconceptions, stereotypes, and prejudice as truth" (p. 11). An additive approach to multicultural curriculum allows teachers to feel like they are inclusive in the curriculum that they are doing their part, but these essentialized images are doing little to educate white students about their diverse world, do not address the power of whiteness, nor do they empower students of color to see themselves as anything but *the Other* in the classroom.

Hoffman (1996) referred to this as "hallway multiculturalism" when she explained the trip down the hallway of her teaching college covered with multicultural posters made by education students (p. 547).

> As an anthropologist of education, I knew I ought to applaud such efforts at fostering multicultural awareness. Yet, whenever I walked down the hall, my instinctive reaction was far from positive. I was not sure exactly what bothered me, but it seemed somehow that the overall effect was one of ideological conformity—as if the students had all been programmed to think in exactly the same way, with the same images and same words. The very fact that the "lessons" of multiculturalism were so codified seemed to undermine the essential multicultural theme—an inherent openness and flexibility … It seemed to me all too pre-packaged, a parroting of the "right" themes—a lesson, in a sense, too well learned. (p. 547)

When there is no attempt to interrogate the power dynamics of the classroom, adults assume they are *the norm* and have *perfect knowledge*. This *perfect knowledge* assumes that white teachers' understandings and communication pathways are above question. Helfenbein (2003) was concerned about this attitude,

A common mistake, seen clearly in the revitalization of the standards movement in education, suggests that knowledge can be communicated directly from transmitter to receiver. This model ... assumes that the cultural identities of both parties are closed systems and that no mediation of the message occurs in the process of communication. (p. 11)

As May (1999) explained, "In effect, essentialist racialized discourses are 'disguised' by describing group differences principally in cultural and/or historical terms—ethnic terms, in effect—without specifically mentioning 'race' or overtly racial criteria" (p. 13). A genuinely multicultural education would interrogate whiteness, seek to de-power it, and create a classroom where everyone is part of the diversity. It would deepen understanding of the nature of culture as fluid, dynamic, and rich. According to Helfenbein (2003), this knowledge would lead to "new possibilities and better truths" (p. 11).

Schools Reinforce White Supremacist Structures

While MCE works to include all people in the curriculum, it has not succeeded in decentering the white majority's hold on the schooling structures or the curriculum. Culturally Relevant Pedagogy and Multicultural Education have been part of staff development and studied by educators in university programs for decades. Bulletin boards in hallways celebrate difference, and days are set aside for ethnic celebrations. But, looking at white students, have these efforts made them any smarter about race? As evidenced by the current conversations about race and who Americans elect, lessons on tolerance, acceptance, and inclusion did not advance white Americans' thinking about race.

What would school look like if Black students' lives really, truly mattered?[1] How would our schools be different? What would our school days be like? What would the curriculum look like? The buildings? The halls? How would our teaching be different?

As discussed in Chapter 2, schools in the United States are segregated by race, even in school districts with diverse populations. Schools within these districts are segregated along racial and socioeconomic lines. According to the Pew Research Center (2015), students of color now outnumber white students nationwide. However, this is not the experience for most children (Krogstad & Fry, 2014). While the aggregate numbers indicate an increase in the percentage of students of color, segregation and other demographic patterns mean that white students are still the majority in most districts where they reside. Even with that segregation, the language and concepts of inclusion and multiculturalism have permeated the curriculum and school culture in the United States. There is no doubt that, in innumerable ways, MCE has changed teaching. Teachers now look beyond *Dick and Jane* to teach reading and beyond the white presidents for heroes to depict on their walls. Including other people's stories and depictions of browner faces became imperative in the classroom. However, the fundamental structures have changed little, as the names and faces in the curriculum were changed (Krogstad & Fry, 2014).

There is a gap between the multicultural commitments of schools and the follow-through on those understandings when students graduate. School systems have worked to implement Culturally Responsive Pedagogy (CRP) into practice and conducted hours of professional development. Yet, the main indicators of success have not been moved. Critics who study education contend that multicultural education has not been a complete failure nor a complete success. If multicultural education had succeeded, the United States should have gone further regarding racial equity and access to capital, law, and education (Kanpol & McLaren, 1995).

The persistence of inequities in our schools, even amidst adopting MCE and CRP, signals that a more profound, more systemic transformation is required. If Black students' lives truly matter, schools would not merely integrate stories and faces of color into existing frameworks but would radically rethink their foundations. Buildings would reflect cultural pride and community empowerment; hallways would resonate with a sense of belonging and safety. The curriculum would center marginalized groups' histories, contributions, and perspectives, challenging dominant narratives rather than merely adding to them. Teaching would prioritize liberation, critical thinking, and joy over compliance and standardization.

Such schools would measure success not only by test scores but also by the thriving of all students, dismantling systemic barriers, and cultivating equity and justice. Change demands a shift from performative inclusion to transformative practices that disrupt the roots of inequality. This vision challenges us to confront the uncomfortable truths about segregation, power, and privilege that persist in our educational systems. Only when we are willing to dismantle these structures can we create schools that honor the inherent worth and potential of Black students and, by extension, all students.

Moving Beyond Multiculturalism: Critical Multiculturalism

While schools have been tasked with the democratic responsibility to build a multicultural society, they have failed to help white people gain a democratic identity that would ward off the assault of racists and white supremacists. The toxic stew of bigotry on cable news cannot bear all the blame for dismantling American's commitment to democracy and multiculturalism. The implementation of MCE has not demanded necessary identity work from white students, so they can easily throw off all their multiculturalism with their graduation caps. It is inevitable that, when they leave the warm embrace of schools, white people become vulnerable to anti-democratic ideologues, fearmongers, and racists.

As we are seeing now, this halfway integration and multicultural education has not been enough to eliminate white supremacist ideology among the white US population. According to a Wall Street Journal poll in 2015, "only 34% of Americans believe race relations in the U.S. are fairly good or very good, down from a high of 77% in January 2009, after the election of Barack Obama as America's first black president" (Nasaw, 2016). Before the Obama inauguration, Conservatives and Liberals hailed the election of an African American President as proof that America had moved past racial divisions and dropped old prejudices to create a new, cosmopolitan future: a new *post-racial* society.

However, things have only gotten worse. In a 2017 poll by the Pew Research Center, 70 percent of Republicans (86 percent of whom were white) stated that white people face *some* or *a lot of* discrimination. As these poll numbers illustrate, white people feel that they do not have a stake in a multicultural society. Racist language has now reached a fevered pitch. Even the use of blatantly racist language and outright slurs against racial minorities has become commonplace, even in the highest echelons of power (Sondel et al., 2018).

School buildings are built for children, but adults shape and structure them. Some of these adults are committed to multiculturalism, and others are not. Teachers have built social justice into schools' mission statements but have failed to address the causes of students' disenfranchisement. If schools were equipping their students with the tools of democratic life, there would be no market for the anti-Black and anti-immigrant sludge that is the steady evening diet of too many white people. It would not exist. The appeals of racists wanting to be elected to power would not even resonate. The last decade has made it clear that these former children were not equipped to combat falsities, conspiracy theories, or false equivalencies, nor were they schooled in democratic sensibilities.

The children in classes since the 1970s have learned the lessons of multicultural education, but, as adults, they disparage it as nothing more than political correctness or *wokeness*. The reasons for this have been explained by bell hooks (2013), "Structural racial integration with no fundamental change in white supremacist thinking and values has simply meant that black people, though 'integrated' into various areas of mainstream life over time, were and still are seen as inferior" (p. 178). Even in schools where students share the same space, the social construction of white supremacy is a primary hidden curriculum for students of color.

For decades, there have been calls for a more critical approach to the MCE curricular reform movement (Goldberg, 1995; Kanpol & McLaren, 1995; May, 1999). According to May (1999), the critical multicultural approach works to avoid some of the problems with multicultural education while addressing the criticism that MCE's critics do not give a plan to address the white supremacist structures in schooling. May worked to decouple the concepts of race, the socially constructed and ever-shifting categories based on skin color, with culture, the deeply human ways of being in the world that define how we live and act toward each other. Helfenbein (2003) opened a new way of looking at multicultural education, calling for a more extensive discussion of the "untidy elements of culture" and asking whether identity can be better explored through "creolization, mestizaje, and hybridity" (p. 13). This take on critical multiculturalism asks students to deeply explore not only others but themselves and their cultural influences. The problem is that race and the historical reasons for race in this country and around the world must be part of that discussion.

Paris (2012) called for a more robust approach to curriculum and pedagogy. He explained that the terms used to discuss the teacher's role around culture in the classroom do not do enough to help teachers see themselves as more than just instructors who "tolerate" the differences of language and culture in their classroom but actually advocate for the needs of their students. "I question the usefulness of "responsive" and "relevant"— like the term "tolerance" in multicultural education and training, neither term goes far enough" (p. 95).

He continued, "Relevance and responsiveness do not guarantee in stance or meaning that one goal of an educational program is to maintain heritage ways and to value cultural and linguistic sharing across difference, to sustain and support bi-and multilingualism and bi-and multiculturalism" (Paris, 2012, p. 95). As Love (2019b) explained,

> White teachers need to want to address how they contribute to structural racism. They need to join the fight for education justice, racial justice, housing justice, immigration justice, food justice, queer and trans justice, labor justice, and, above all, the fight for humanity. (online)

Two problems with the implementation of MCE are often seen in classrooms. First, the term culture in MCE frequently stands in for race in common discussions; thus, Crayola crayons that reflect various skin colors were marked as multicultural. People conflate race and culture and improperly use physical characteristics as if they were indicators of culture. That conflation also led to a furthering of racism because it imparts traits to people based on skin color. The issue with so much of how multiculturalism is practiced is that these two concepts are conflated because of a discomfort with discussing race and the role of white people in defining race, creating racial categories, and oppressing people who are not considered white. The discussion of race makes people cringe, so they imbue culture with the talk of race to avoid discomfort. This version of MCE teaches and reinforces white racial and cultural supremacy as an ideological construct in the minds of all children. Returning to Woodson's point that schools are created to teach Black students inferiority, the conflation of race and culture actually intensifies rather than breaks down racism. This is the process that critical multiculturalism seeks to avoid and is the focus of much of its critique.

Multicultural education theorist Sonya Nieto (1999) explained that multicultural education must be anti-racist education, "teaching does not become more honest and critical simply by becoming more inclusive" (p. 4). The curricula are set so that they do not challenge racism, so that they do not ask students to see themselves as members of a society built upon racism, and they avoid making students feel like they have a stake in tearing down the structures that have been put in place specifically to benefit white people.

Critics, including May, argue that MCE often essentializes the cultures it seeks to represent, reducing them to oversimplified traits or practices. This approach is frequently used either to teach white people about non-white cultures or to reinforce narratives of white goodness and the superiority of whiteness. These methods encourage students to view cultural practices as uniform within a group, reinforcing stereotypes and fostering perceptions of other cultures as exotic or inferior. Consequently, rather than cultivating genuine appreciation for diversity, such practices perpetuate harmful assumptions and hierarchies.

Thus, instead of creating people who appreciate cultures, we develop people who see everyone else's culture as exotic and inferior. Neither multicultural techniques nor the assumptions behind them expect the teacher or students to think critically about the power dynamic in the classroom, white communities, or the United States, where whiteness is experienced as the norm. Therefore, it is reasonable to ask whether MCE has accomplished only part of its mission and to seek an alternative to essentialist ways of thinking about culture.

While the pillars of our multicultural teacher education programs— Multicultural Education (Banks & Banks, 2016), Culturally Relevant Pedagogy (Ladson-Billings, 1995), Culturally Responsive Teaching (Gay, 2010), and Culturally Sustainable Pedagogy (Paris, 2012)—are all excellent frameworks for teaching all students, the groundwork needed before implementation is seldom done, and schools are not addressing the gross disparity in the daily treatment of students of color. Love (2019b) challenged white teachers to go beyond the MCE curriculum,

> So, the question is not: Do you love all children? The question is: Will you fight for justice for Black and Brown children? And how will you fight? I argue that you must fight with the creativity, imagination, urgency, boldness, ingenuity, and rebellious spirit of abolitionists to advocate for an education system where all Black and Brown children thrive. I call this abolitionist teaching. To love all children, we must struggle together to create the schools we are taught to believe are impossible: Schools built on justice, love, joy, and anti-racism. (online)

Schools have spent years continually trying *this* technique and *that* strategy. Teachers and administrators, exhausted and ill-equipped, place blame on anyone but themselves. Despite the years of scholarship, teaching in colleges of education, and in-service training of the teaching force, there has been little change in the attitudes of white people about race in America. When solutions are sought, the adults and their behaviors, attitudes, or mental models are not considered as causes or even as variables. When blame is passed out, it goes to the students, communities, and parents. Whether that blame is in the form of a *culture of poverty*, as in Ruby Payne (2013), or false caring based on white supremacy, teachers who are not in solidarity with students blame parents and communities for their perceived inadequacies (Smiley & Helfenbein, 2011).

Multiculturalism, with its worthy and reachable goals of curricular inclusion, has not done the work that many had hoped for in dismantling the structures of racism in our schools. To have a multicultural curriculum that does not grapple with colonialization and slavery flattens the narrative and essentializes the people under study. The goal should be to complicate the narratives and to build students' identities to include culture, race, ethnicity, gender, and sexual preference, and let all of our students explore their identities and to become open to the identities of others.

A New Paradigm Is Needed

Too often, educators only go so far as to blunt the sting of racism without challenging its cause. Creating a just and equitable world for students requires confronting the root problem of white supremacy woven into school structures. Teachers who are ill-equipped to work with Black students try to overcome, overpower, and overtalk their students. To those teachers, the purpose of their classroom is to train the students in proper behavior, not in the content. In other words, these teachers try to bend their students to their whiteness and acculturate their students into that system. This often affects how new teachers think and talk about *respect* and the *real world*. They see the real world as the world run and maintained by white people for the benefit of white people. To them, that is not a troubling notion but a comfortable one. These teachers perceive it as a goal for their students to be successful in that white world without disrupting it.

Milner (2010) described the positioning of a teacher-participant and listed four elements that allowed a white male teacher to succeed with students who are racially different from him: (1) learn from the students and adjust practices accordingly; (2) develop a "deeper understanding of the impact of race;" (3) develop relationships with students that "transcend cultural boundaries;" and (4) understand how to take advantage of opportunities to learn from students (p. 46). However, helping teachers connect their whiteness to their classroom practice is a difficult task.

Thus, a new paradigm is needed to meet the needs of students in diverse communities, even though multicultural education has been the norm since the 1970s. Multitudes of phenomena, including mass incarceration, the rise of white supremacist groups and terrorism, and the election of populists and xenophobes across the globe, show two things: (1) the multicultural curriculum enacted since the 1970s has not produced the desired effect of eliminating white supremacy as an ideology for a significant percentage of the population, and (2) the level of threat to students of color has ramped up so the response must be much more robust than has been done before.

Returning to the question, *what would school look like if Black students' lives really, truly mattered?* Teachers would stand in solidarity with students by interrogating their whiteness and dismantling the oppressive, white supremacist structures in their schools, classrooms, and communities (Keating, 1995). They would stand up for their Black students, demanding they be treated as full citizens and human beings in all areas of society. That is the goal of Caring Solidarity.

Teachers will say they have chosen a life with children because they want to have a positive, transformative impact on students' lives (Duncan-Andrade, 2007). They just need the tools to do so. Great teachers defy their detractors and inspire their students to see themselves for who they are, not how others paint them. If the conversation is framed away from the perceived deficits of students of color to areas where those teachers need to deeply reorient their own self-perception and actions in the communities of color they serve, white teachers can begin to build the needed mindset to move beyond multiculturalism to solidarity.

Great teaching changes lives. Great teachers shape the future. Great teachers carry with them into the classroom a healthy mixture of defiance and devotion. That mix is most especially on display when great teachers work with students who are the most marginalized. To demolish the structures that impede our students' educations, white teachers must make a daily commitment to interrogate and dismantle the power of whiteness. If teachers are going to cross the color line and teach Black students effectively, they must do more than *tolerate* the diversity of the students in the classroom (Paris, 2012). To be successful, the teachers who commit to this work must make a clear decision to do so with understanding, empathy, and solidarity with students. While dismantling these structures is a challenge and not a threat, some cannot tell the difference. The work will be hard. It will cost. It will have failures. But for those who persevere, the rewards will be beyond measure.

Discussion Questions for Chapter 4

1   How do *food*, *festivals*, and *hallway multiculturalism* approaches limit students' and teachers' potential for racial and cultural understanding?

2   Why is it important for white teachers to interrogate their own whiteness when teaching in diverse classrooms, and what are the consequences if they fail to do so?

3   What is the role of the teacher in either reinforcing or dismantling white supremacy through their pedagogical choices and classroom practices?

4   How can teachers effectively incorporate critical perspectives on colonialism, slavery, and white supremacy into their curriculum without alienating students or communities?

5   What steps can schools take to ensure that MCE initiatives move beyond performative gestures to achieve transformative change for students of color and their communities?

Actionable Classroom Practices from Chapter 4

- **Engage in Identity Work:** Keep a self-reflection journal to understand how whiteness and privilege influence your teaching practices. Encourage other white teachers to join in a discussion of these journals.

- **Integrate Diverse Perspectives:** Comb through your curriculum to find places where you can center marginalized groups' histories, contributions, and voices and challenge dominant narratives.

- **Build Solidarity:** Go out of your way to attend community celebrations outside your white identity. Develop authentic, empathetic relationships with students and other adults, acknowledging and celebrating their cultural identities.

- **Challenge Racism Openly:** Address issues of race and racism explicitly in the classroom to dismantle stereotypes and foster equity. If necessary, seek expert help.

- **Utilize Transformative Resources:** Incorporate texts like *A People's History of the United States* and resources from organizations like the Zinn Education Project and Rethinking Schools.

- **Collaborate with Communities:** Partner with community organizations, students' families, and communities to better understand their needs and perspectives.

Note

1 Thanks to Denise Taliaferro Baszile and Boni Wozolek for giving me the time and space to explore this question at AERA.

5 **The Asset Pedagogies**
Caring, Allyship, and Solidarity

After laying out the issues and the imperative to move beyond multicultural education and more robustly respond to the current crises facing Black students, it is important to examine the pedagogies that are making positive changes in schools and children's lives. These pedagogies are often called *asset pedagogies* because they view children of color as assets rather than assuming language, racial, and cultural differences as deficits.

Charged with helping districts follow the law after *Lau v. Nichols* (1974), the federal government established a mandate to teach English to non-proficient students. Cazden and Leggett (1976) called for schooling that was "more responsive to cultural differences among children" (p. 3). They explained, "School systems are asked to consider cognitive and affective aspects of how different children learn so that appropriate teaching styles and learning environments can be provided that will maximize their educational achievement" (p. 3). Since then, as Paris and Alim (2017) pointed out, "collaborations between researchers and teachers proved deficit approaches untenable and unjust" (p. 87). Paris and Alim (2017) used the term *asset pedagogies* to explain the approaches that lift students up as resilient, inquisitive, and knowledgeable about themselves and their communities and not as others have typically cast them: as deficient intellectually or culturally (Payne, 2013; Valencia, 2010).

In her 1994 book, *The Dreamkeepers*, Gloria Ladson-Billings challenged teachers and researchers to reject deficit models and recognize the inherent strengths of African American children. She explained that culture should be at the center of pedagogy in multiracial and multicultural classrooms and discussed "principles at work" that combine high expectations and awareness of African American culture to create a classroom where "culturally relevant pedagogy" (CRP) could take place (p. 17). She outlined an approach resting on three criteria: (1) students must experience academic success; (2) students must develop and maintain cultural competence; and (3) students must develop a critical consciousness through which they challenge the status quo of the current social order (p. 160). Her subsequent work, especially her (1995) article, *Toward a Theory of Culturally Relevant Pedagogy*, has been a hallmark of asset-based pedagogical research and practice.

Elements of CRP include identification with and commitment to the African American community, viewing students as extended family members, stressing mastery of math and literacy, and judicious use of authority in the classroom. To move past strictly linguistic differences or passive cultural asynchrony as explanations for Black students' lack of achievement in classrooms, Ladson-Billings (1994) explained culturally relevant teaching this way:

> [It] uses student culture in order to maintain it and to transcend the negative effects of the dominant culture. The negative effects are brought about, for example, by not seeing one's history, culture, or background represented in the textbook or curriculum or by seeing that history culture, or background distorted. (p. 17)

In her other writings, Ladson-Billings' (1995) explanation of CRP echoed that of other theorists who have called for a more humane and democratic approach to teaching by tapping into the cultural strengths of students (Brown-Jeffy & Cooper, 2011; Hermes, 2005; Phillippo, 2012; Shevalier & McKenzie, 2012). Called "culturally responsive teaching" by Gay (2010), the current body of literature uses both terms. Both Ladson-Billings and Gay have argued that through culturally appropriate interactions and relationship building, teachers learn to raise expectations as students rise to meet them.

Paris (2012) called for a new term and a paradigm change to reflect a newer era in thinking about multiracial classrooms. Minoritized language and ways of knowing, Paris argued, are still assumed to be deficits, as race and culture are statically linked. Such assumptions "have led to the unfortunate simplification of resource pedagogies as solely about considering heritage and traditional practices in teaching and not also about considering the shifting and changing practices of students and their communities" (p. 93). He was concerned that the terms teacher educators use to discuss teachers' roles in culture in the classroom do not adequately support teacher candidates or, by extension, students in elementary and secondary classrooms.

Paris (2012) also called for students to be treated in ways that use culture as an asset in learning, but he asked that teachers go even further to embrace and sustain culture and language plurality in classrooms. Teachers are not explicit enough in their support for students to "support the linguistic and cultural dexterity and plurality necessary for success and access in our demographically changing U.S. and global schools and communities" (p. 95). Paris challenged teachers to go beyond the learning of cultures and the simple essentializing of culture to truly embrace all cultures in the classroom and help students preserve their cultural identities.

In a later work, Paris and Alim (2017) sought to reposition the discourse on the research, pedagogy, and curriculum applied to and provided to students of color. This demographic and linguistic approach confirmed that the United States will become increasingly diverse and that centers of power will shift away from white cultural norms and Dominant American English (DAE) as people of color increase and other forms of English, along with other languages, grow. They also pushed those who claim to be culturally relevant to become more political and show a deep commitment to students and their communities. They explained that efforts to impose English-only laws constituted an attack on students of color, demanding a response from teachers to blaze a path toward increasing students' political and academic power. Paris (2012) explained that Culturally Sustaining Pedagogy "seeks to perpetuate and foster-to sustain linguistic, literate, and cultural pluralism as part of the democratic project of schooling" (p. 95).

Geneva Gay, in her book *Culturally Responsive Teaching: Theory, Research, and Practice* (2000/2010), reasoned that teachers' understanding of their students' cultures would lead them to a better ability to tailor curriculum and pedagogy to students' needs.

> For example, teachers need to know (a) which ethnic groups give priority to communal living and cooperative problem solving and how these preferences affect educational motivation, aspiration, and task performance; (b) how different ethnic groups' protocols of appropriate ways for children to interact with adults are exhibited in instructional settings; and (c) the implications of gender role socialization in different ethnic groups for implementing equity initiatives in classroom instruction. This information constitutes the first essential component of the knowledge base of culturally responsive teaching. (Gay, 2010, p. 107)

McCarty and Lee (2014) posited that Indigenous students need even more than sustaining pedagogy, as explained by Paris. In their framework, called "Culturally Sustaining/Revitalizing Pedagogy (CSRP)," they argued that students on and off of tribal lands are "in a fight for cultural and linguistic survival" and that sovereignty, self-determination, and self-identification are a struggle that native youth experience against the backdrop of colonization and ethnocide. They identify three components of this framework: first, attention to power relations with the "goal of transforming legacies of the colonizer"; second, an emphasis on native language acquisition; and third, a focus on community, "respect, reciprocity, responsibility, and the importance of caring relationships" (p. 103). This framework, grounded in indigenous pedagogy, is instructive for all work with colonized and oppressed communities.

Beyond the questions of demographic or moral appeals to multicul- turalism, and despite the popularity of Gay's, Ladson-Billings', and Paris's work among educators and teacher educators, the prevalence of deficit models and white supremacy in schools and society as dominant ideologies have not abated. The evidence shows that schools are still places of trauma for students of color, from the suspension of preschoolers and early elementary students (Malik, 2017) to the suspensions of African American middle and high school students (Monroe, 2005; Skiba et al., 2011), the rounds of bullying of minoritized students that has taken place since 2016 (Southern Poverty Law Center, 2017) and the continued existence of the school-to-prison pipeline that washes students from schools into the justice system (Wald & Losen, 2003). The urgency of the need has only increased since the development of these frameworks.

Caring for African American Students and Warm Demander Pedagogy

Gay (2010) described caring as an essential part of teaching in multicultural classrooms. "Caring is one of those things that most educators agree is important in working effectively with students, but they are hard-pressed to characterize it in actual practice" (p. 48). To Gay, caring focused "on caring *for* instead of *about* the personal well-being and academic success of ethnically diverse students … Caring for is active engagement in doing something to positively affect it. Thus, it encompasses a combination of concern, compassion, commitment, responsibility and action. (p. 48)

According to Gay (2010), for teachers to care for students, they need to celebrate students and enjoy their differences, while still expecting a great deal from them. "Teachers who really care for students honor their humanity, hold them in high esteem, expect high performance from them, and use strategies to fulfill their expectations" (p. 48). Gay argued this is a type of "authentic caring" where teachers and students develop "sustained, trusting, respectful and trusting reciprocal relationships" (p. 49). Trust is difficult to build across the color line. So many students have trusted only to be betrayed by teachers who say one thing but do another. A teacher in solidarity must build trust and help students unlearn reasonable distrusting behaviors through consistency and care.

Ware (2006) explored ways in which white teachers form bonds and achieve success with African American students. She identified a type of teacher who uses what she calls "warm demander" pedagogy (see also Gay, 2010, p. 75; Kleinfeld, 1975). This term refers to a set of highly organized, discipline-oriented, caring teachers who use culture as a tool for connections with their students. The white teachers Ware described adopted what she perceived as an African American cultural identity to better communicate with their students (p. 45).

Coined by Kleinfeld (1975), warm demanders are first concerned with the classroom climate and building rapport with students, but are also deeply committed to student achievement. To accomplish both, warm demanders use a combination of adopted cultural norms along with school structural and cultural values to build relationships and move students toward academic achievement (Ware, 2006). Love (2019c) described her third-grade teacher who fits the warm demander profile,

"Mrs. Johnson did not just love her students, she fundamentally believed that we mattered. She made us believe that our lives were entangled with hers and that caring for us meant caring for herself" and the classroom where Love learned and felt valued, "It was a collective spirit of accountability, love, and purpose. She genuinely listened to us, took up our concerns in her teaching, and made sure each voice in the classroom was heard" (pp. 47–48).

Cooper (2003) observed teachers who used culturally relevant pedagogy in the classroom and examined the conceptual beliefs of successful white teachers of Black elementary children. The teachers had high expectations for their students, a well-developed work ethic, were able to reflect on their performance, and viewed themselves as effective teachers. Cooper also found that the teachers she interviewed had a developing racial consciousness, defined as being "involved [in] specific articulation of race matters, including racism in the teacher's personal and professional lives" (p. 423). Further, Cooper included respect and commitment to the Black community, empathy for Black children, and a willingness to learn from the Black community. Yet, despite their own feelings and knowledge of racial issues, these same teachers did not discuss race or bring up racial issues in their classrooms. They were hesitant to purposefully address the concept of racism with their students.

Ladson-Billings (1994) and Cooper (2003) similarly described how successful teachers of Black elementary children use techniques described as "authority" in the classroom and that they are "second mothers" to their students (p. 414). The authors noted that this function is beyond what many would consider the role of a teacher. Teachers in these classrooms monitor every aspect of a student's well-being, care, and feeding during their time in school. These teachers are quick to correct students and praise them as the situation dictates. They use sharp voices to point out infractions but use terms of endearment like "Sweetie" or "Baby" when praising (Cooper, 2003, p. 423).

The ethic of caring, as defined by Noddings (1984), also sheds light on the discussion. It is related to, but distinct from, the description given by Ladson-Billings (1994), Gay (2010), and Cooper (2003). According to Noddings (1984), the current system's masculine orientation has failed to foster the kind of ethical citizenry democratic-minded individuals seek. It creates people who compete rather than care. Noddings believed that schools could teach students to care about each other, themselves, the world, right action, and their academic subjects.

To Noddings, "The primary aim of every educational institution and of every educational effort must be the maintenance and enhancement of caring" (p. 172). Noddings theorized that caring involves engrossment, where one person's attention is entirely taken up by another person, and motivational displacement, in which one person's goals and success are the main reasons for the relationship with the other (Noddings, 1984). Noddings' belief that schools should be places where people take care of one another emotionally has its roots in the feminine ethic of caring. She explained that caring is central to teaching and parenting. Noddings (1995) explained six ways that schools can become more caring.

1   Be clear about the goal of schooling that is to produce competent, caring, loving people.

2   Take care of needs for affiliation with peers and adults.

3   Worry less about control of students.

4   Eliminate the hierarchies of programs and curriculum.

5   Give part of the day to "themes of care" where spiritual and emotional needs are met.

6   Teach the students that caring means they are competent (p. 368).

Noddings' (1984) ethic of caring represents a distinct approach to relationships within the educational environment, emphasizing a way of being that contrasts with traditional expectations of teacher-student interactions. This framework highlights a divergence between the cultural competencies required of teachers, particularly in school settings, and the ways marginalized students often require expressions of caring that differ from Noddings' conceptualization. These differences extend to how teachers enact care, with culturally responsive approaches requiring teachers to understand and adapt to their students' unique needs, experiences, and contexts. Noddings' (1984) approach was gentle, and Gay's (2010) was empathetic, whereas Howard (2002), Cooper (2003), and Ladson-Billings (1994) described caring teachers who have a sharper tone. However, part of that difference is that Howard, Cooper, and Ladson-Billings identified a deeper need for teacher intervention in students' lives, and they also displayed a depth of investment in students' success that is lacking in Noddings' caring narratives.

Coleman (2007) and Bidwell (2010) found similar trends in their studies of Black teachers of Black middle school students. Coleman found that students value teachers whom they term nice, describing Black students' perceptions of their academic success as attributable to what teachers thought of them. They valued teachers who demonstrated that they cared, communicated with students personally and academically, gave affirmative feedback, and simplified and explained content matters (Coleman, 2007). Bidwell found that three strategies were essential to the teachers' success with African American students: forming meaningful relationships with students, engaging students in racial conversations, and reflecting both individually and with colleagues.

In contrast, Howard (2002) interviewed African American students to record their understanding of what makes a successful teacher. From student interviews and observations, Howard identified terms students used to categorize an "effective" teacher (p. 429). First, teachers who students perceived as effective were able to structure their classrooms in ways that made the students feel like the classroom was a "home," and the members of the class felt like "family" (p. 431). Howard explained that this home feeling was built on relationships within the classroom and on the rituals and traditions that developed. One example, as part of the school curriculum, students took part in the "morning circle," during which they could speak to friends and develop interpersonal relationships (p. 432).

However, Howard described the other side of this family atmosphere as the use of shame as a method of behavior management. It was an essential part of one teacher's classroom culture that no student should "shame" the family (p. 432). Shame, sarcasm, and sternness were mixed with praise, community, and high expectations to create an atmosphere in which students did well, respected their teacher, and, in interviews, expressed that they were learning. Howard (2002) also identified "culturally connected caring" as a way to frame the student responses (p. 434). Howard explained:

> Culturally connected caring refers to a display of caring that occurs within a cultural context with which students are familiar. Behavioral expectations, nurturing patterns, and forms of affection take place in a manner that does not require students to abandon their cultural integrity. (p. 434)

Thus, Howard advocated for a caring deeply rooted in students' cultural understandings and communication styles.

Second, Howard found that a teacher's "passion" was an integral trait leading to success. He described the communication style and types of affirmation students reported showed teachers' caring for students, which included "hollering or yelling" (p. 437). Students reported that the teachers expressed their caring by asking about students' lives outside of school and demonstrating real investment in student success. "Students seemed to believe that teachers who were not as emotionally and passionately concerned with their learning were teachers who 'don't even care about us'" (p. 437).

Although the students Howard studied perceived the various ways teachers reacted to them as caring, it is important to note that this approach is not universally accepted within the African American community. In fact, Howard reported that several students said they did not respond to these techniques:

I don't like how she yells at people if they get a question wrong. She can ask a question we [students] don't understand then she yells and says, "listen to the question, listen to the question!" Then she'll get mad. (p. 440)

All the teachers in Howard's study were African American and expressed that they thought they were using culturally appropriate pedagogy to challenge and care for their students.

To attempt to bridge the gap between CRP and caring, Parsons (2005) and Eslinger (2013) have worked to integrate the two concepts to demonstrate a way of being in the classroom that most effectively meets the needs of minoritized students. Eslinger posited that the answer might come from culturally responsive caring. "A substantial part of white teachers' inability to adequately convey their care, I contend, is their resistance to addressing issues of race and racism" (p. 5). Eslinger explained that successful teachers interrogate their own whiteness and their *a priori* knowledge and attitudes about race, racial minorities, and their own privileged status. "White teachers need: (1) to develop a rich and culturally diverse knowledge base; (2) to interrogate their identities and the privileges associated with them; and (3) to critically examine curriculum and pedagogy" (p. 5).

Allyhood and Allyship

Before Ladson Billing's work in the 1990s, the conversation in education research about the schooling of African American students seldom focused on the adults who work in the buildings or structures where the schooling takes place. Instead, it often focused on the students themselves, their families, or some type of cultural deficit model. Addressing the inequalities of schooling must begin not with the students but with the adults and the structures that monitor, act upon, and cause that inequality (Harvey & Reed, 1996). Adopting strength-based techniques and CRP are helpful, but until white teachers who teach across the color line join in solidarity with their students to dismantle white supremacist structures in the classroom, school, and larger society, the *achievement gap* will continue, and most educators will blame the victims of racism for its effects (Ladson-Billings, 2006; 2007).

To move teachers into more direct acts of solidarity, some activists and researchers have embraced the concept of *allyship* to describe their work as advocates and allies of their students of color (Patel, 2011). During the time of desegregation in the 1970s, a great deal was written on white teachers employed in still-segregated or newly desegregated systems (Paley, 1979). In the twenty-first century, there has been a rise in the literature that uses the concept of *critical white allies*, *allyship*, and *allyhood* (Case, 2018; Patel, 2011; Reason et al., 2005; Waters, 2010).

The concept of allyship is rooted in a framework of social justice work and asks white people to "deconstruct cycles of privilege and oppression" through a cognitive understanding of the nature of privilege and interpersonal experiences with people of color (Waters, 2010, p. 6). But, as Utt (2013) pointed out, white privilege allows allies to pick which parts of the alliance they are comfortable with, "part of the privilege of your identity is that you have a choice about whether or not to resist oppression" (online). Allyhood is increasingly viewed as a step toward solidarity rather than an end in itself, as it remains a step removed from fostering genuine relationships of solidarity (Love, 2019c; Patel, 2011). As Masoom (2017) explained, allyhood, often expressed in white social justice culture, is

> perfectly contradictory to everything you'd expect the ideal "ally" to be. Just as both the privileges and oppressions we face don't take breaks, neither can true solidarity. Discussions regarding being an "ally" inherently imply choice—the choice to step back and not engage. (online)

Utt (2013) also explained, "As a White person, I have a responsibility to stand up to racism and work to bring White people into the anti-racist conversation in a way that they can hear and access." Under this definition, the white ally is more than someone who shows sympathy; they are active in their empathy. Yet, they still retain enough privilege to remove themselves at any time. While an allyship approach addresses some of the behaviors of successful white teachers, it is not adequate to explain teachers who build deeper, political relationships of solidarity with students in conditions that allow them to make a difference in their students' lives (Alonso et al., 2009; Duncan-Andrade, 2007; Wilde, 2007). Allyhood still allows for a white supremacist framework and can result in teachers who have a false empathy (Delgado, 1996; Patel, 2011; Warren & Hotchkins, 2014) or a white savior syndrome (Straubhaar, 2014).

Allyship, often described as a form of alliance, emerged in response to the growing need for action against Conservative attacks on people of color who have been demanding justice. It reflects an increasing awareness that white people must be part of the solution, but often stops short of recognizing white people and societal structures as central to the problem. Allyship allows white individuals to maintain comfort in their lives and privilege, continuing to benefit from white supremacist systems. While allyship is not wrong or harmful, it is insufficient to address the challenges our students face. Solidarity requires more than occasional acts of justice; white teachers cannot claim to be allies or in solidarity while simultaneously perpetuating both justice and injustice as part of their overall approach.

"Come with Me!"

An excellent metaphor on many levels, *Wicked*, originally a groundbreaking Broadway musical, became a 2024 blockbuster film. Directed by Jon M. Chu (2024) and featuring lauded performances by Cynthia Erivo as Elphaba and Ariana Grande as Glinda, the film explored the complex bond of friendship forged between two women from different backgrounds. Elphaba is a green-skinned outcast marginalized by society, and Glinda is privileged and popular. The two represent metaphorically and racially distinct characters. Their relationship becomes a lens through which the creators—author Gregory Maguire (1995) and screenwriters Winnie Holzman and Stephen Schwartz—expose hard truths about the formation, maintenance, and fragility of alliances.

In the film, there are many times when Galinda (Glinda) acts performatively in coalition with various characters, but a moment that captures the nature of Elphaba and Glinda's alliance occurs during the performance of "Popular." In this scene, Glinda outlines her plan to bestow her social privilege upon Elphaba. While Glinda frames it as an act of generosity, it reflects how she values political and social capital and deep investiture in her place in that hierarchy, stating at the end of the scene, "Just not as popular as me." Two other moments encapsulate the choices across lines of difference when Elphaba invites Glinda to "Come with me." The first occurs when Elphaba invites Glinda to join her in meeting the Wizard, promising "your heart's desire." Glinda eagerly accepts, but when the Wizard's corruption is revealed, and Elphaba must flee, harnessing her powers to "defy gravity," Glinda demurs. Rather than joining Elphaba in her rebellion, she symbolically supports her by handing her a cape to keep her warm as Elphaba escapes on a broomstick.

Cynthia Erivo's portrayal of Elphaba is unapologetically racialized, evident in her hairstyle and her refusal to obscure her facial features with a fake nose, for example. Her performance both entertains and challenges traditional notions of good and evil. This complexity is highlighted in a pivotal scene where the Wizard offers to change Elphaba's green skin, framing it as the solution to her struggles. She rejects his offer, asserting that her true "heart's desire" is not to alter who she is but to see the animals in Oz set free. The Wizard's response—"The best way to bring folks together is to give them a really good enemy"—reveals a harsh truth about societal power structures. Elphaba's solidarity with the animals, an oppressed and marginalized group under the Wizard's rule, immediately leads to her being labeled as "wicked" and cast as an enemy of the entire country. This metaphor encapsulates the work of allyship: aligning with the oppressed provokes greater ire from the powerful than the oppressed themselves ever could. In Broadway fashion, redemption at the end comes from an act of allyship by Glinda that allows for a happy ending without disrupting the power balances that created the wicked–good dichotomy. In the chapters that follow, I will delve deeper into the costs of solidarity and the concept of being a traitor to whiteness and white privilege.

In many ways, *Wicked* transcends its fictional setting to offer a self-aware exploration of privilege, marginalization, and the nature of allyship. The narrative interrogates the fantasies of allies and the limits of individuals' willingness to take risks or face consequences when their fates are not perceived as shared. By forcing audiences to reflect on their perceptions of power and identity, *Wicked* becomes a commentary on the complexities of standing in solidarity with racialized Others. It asks us to examine our readiness to engage in allyship and reflects white peoples' willingness to comply with unethical or corrupt powers and their fear of *getting into trouble* when the cost becomes real.

Solidarity

Until the first edition of this book in 2020, solidarity had been discussed in relation to teaching but had not been emphasized as a major factor in the ability of white teachers to connect with their African American students (Duncan-Andrade & Morrell, 2008; Gay, 2010; Milner, 2010; Paris, 2012; Sleeter & Soriano, 2012).

Gaztambide-Fernández (2012) observed that "solidarity is often mobilized as an expedient way of expressing certain political ideals without any concern for articulating what precisely is meant by solidarity, often confounding multiple meanings" (p. 46). Similarly, Wilde (2007) noted that the concept of solidarity has been "confined to the realm of rhetoric while serious theoretical work has concentrated on other aspects of political association such as democracy, nationalism, community, multiculturalism, and human rights" (p. 171). Wilde defined solidarity as "the feeling of reciprocal sympathy and responsibility among members of a group which promotes mutual support" (p. 171). Despite its connection to emotions such as love and friendship, solidarity has often been neglected as a central concept in educational literature, relegated to an assumed meaning or treated as a feature of cultural responsiveness and social justice. However, those who have discussed it have framed it from a more political standpoint in the context of teaching and pedagogy.

Bayertz (2013) traced the term solidarity back to Roman law, where it referred to the shared responsibility for common debts within a family. Over the centuries, it evolved into "a mutual attachment between individuals." Still, despite its frequent use in literature and political movements like unionization, solidarity has rarely been dissected or analyzed in depth, remaining largely a presumed concept (p. 3). Bayertz explained, "Although in everyday politics the term solidarity is freely used, as when required, in order to mobilize a readiness to act and/or make sacrifices, it has seldom been the object of elaborated theory" (p. 3). In his effort to define solidarity, Bayertz (2013) divided it into two levels: the factual level, which identifies common ground among individuals, and the normative level, which defines the mutual aid that humans extend to one another when necessary. He noted that solidarity is often conflated with related terms like community spirit or charity, making its meaning ambiguous. Bayertz worked to differentiate between four concepts of solidarity and explain their uses.

The first use of solidarity aligns with fraternity or kinship, rooted in the idea that all humans share a common origin. In this understanding, solidarity is possible when individuals set aside their differences and embrace the universality of humanity, a concept similar to *cosmopolitanism* as described by Appiah (2007). Secondly, solidarity can be understood as a device that explains the functioning of society as a whole. In this interpretation, people divide labor, adhere to social norms, and follow laws to coexist harmoniously, navigating daily life with minimal disruption from violence or crime. This surface-level solidarity is primarily driven by self-interest and hinges on the assumption that everyone is included in the benefits of society. When individuals or groups are excluded, solidarity breaks down, and self-interest can devolve into selfishness (see also Scholz, 2012).

As Bayertz (2013) described, the third form of solidarity involves groups uniting to stand against greater powers in pursuit of shared interests. On the positive side, this can manifest in collective efforts to correct injustices, such as protests or movements advocating for social change. However, it can also take harmful forms, such as criminal conspiracies, police unions protecting members despite pervasive wrongdoing, or mob violence targeting innocent individuals. This version of solidarity is often based on class, race, ethnicity, or other affiliations and is primarily motivated by achieving group-specific goals. Lastly, solidarity under the framework of the welfare state serves as a justification for redistributing resources to promote the greater good. Taxation and efforts to limit income inequality are central to this form of solidarity, emphasizing that the fruits of collective labor should benefit society as a whole (Bayertz, 2013).

Solidarity in Education

As Freire (2014) expressed it, *critical pedagogy* articulates a different form of solidarity with students and what that looks like. To Freire, solidarity begins with the "dialectical unity" of knowledge production, solidarity, and action. These three concepts form the basis for "praxis," which moves the educator to a higher ability to connect with students and a higher purpose of empowering the oppressed (p. 38). He explained that the oppressed are forced into a duality and, to survive, oftentimes internalize their own oppression. Solidarity, then, is a means to ending that oppression, but it is a fearful step.

> The conflict lies in the choice between being wholly themselves or being divided; between ejecting the oppressor within or not ejecting them; between human solidarity or alienation; between following prescriptions or having choices; between being spectators or actors; between acting or having the illusion of acting through the action of the oppressors; between speaking out or being silent, castrated in their power to create and re-create, in their power to transform the world. This is the tragic dilemma of the oppressed, which their education must consider. (p. 48)

This internalization of oppression allows for survival in an oppressive system but robs all of the people involved in the oppressive system of their humanity. Through relationships of solidarity, the oppressed can open up their humanity and throw off oppression, first within themselves and then in the world outside (Gaztambide-Fernández, 2012; Harvey, 2007).

Freire (2014) also addressed the oppressor. He explained that even if a member of the oppressor class begins to understand the oppression they have been inflicting, that does not necessarily mean that they will join in solidarity with those in the oppressed classes:

> Discovering himself to be an oppressor may cause considerable anguish, but it does not necessarily lead to solidarity with the oppressed. Rationalizing his guilt through paternalistic treatment of the oppressed, all the while holding them fast in a position of dependence, will not do. Solidarity requires that one enter into the situation of those with whom one is solidary; it is a radical posture. (p. 49)

Thus, when discussing teachers and students of color, teachers of any color may see the oppression of their students and still work to keep their students in the system. Rules about pants, hair, language, and other weapons of oppression are internalized not only by young people but also by the adults, so that sometimes even people of color will engage in assimilationist narratives with students rather than liberatory ones.

Once a person has acknowledged the humanity of the oppressed, the next step is to act and work to alleviate that oppression:

> True solidarity with the oppressed means fighting at their side to transform the objective reality which has made them these 'beings for another.' The oppressor is solidary with the oppressed only when he stops regarding the oppressed as an abstract category and sees them as persons who have been unjustly dealt with, deprived of their voice, cheated in the sale of their labor—when he stops making pious, sentimental, and individualistic gestures and risks an act of love. (Freire, 2014, p. 50)

Freire understood that these actions would engender risk. This risk can mean loss of status, income, respect from others in the same field or school, or loss of income. It could also mean losing a job. Standing in solidarity is more than mouthing the words; it is doing the actions that are required to pull down the structures of oppression that the privileged have enjoyed. Freire continued,

True solidarity is found only in the plenitude of this act of love, its existentiality, and its praxis. To affirm that men and women are persons and as persons should be free, yet to do nothing tangible to make this affirmation a reality, is a farce. (p. 50)

Love in action; action in concert *with* the oppressed, not *to* them, is the essence of Freire's solidarity. Action pedagogy is created when teachers go beyond instilling facts and testing standards to knowing, caring, loving, and acting on behalf of their students.

As Freire pointed out, "One cannot impose oneself, nor even merely co-exist with one's students. Solidarity requires true communication" (p. 76). And that it was a requirement in the pursuit of true humanity, but was only possible in "fellowship" and cannot "unfold in the antagonistic relations between oppressor and oppressed" (p. 76). To build trust, the person seeking a relationship of solidarity must work to be trustworthy before making the overture. To be trusted, the trustee must prove to be trustworthy.

Because of its all-encompassing and political nature, solidarity was seldom used to describe the behaviors of successful teachers in education. Teachers who advocate for students against systems of oppression are often ignored in favor of more technocratic descriptions of the act of teaching. Solidarity in education is often described as an emotional connection with students, however, the political aspect is equally important for teachers who cross the color line. Sleeter and Soriano (2012) explained that education theorists see solidarity as a step toward teaching for social justice wherein "teachers empathize with and care deeply about their students and therefore work with students' communities within the broader political project of identifying and eliminating oppression" (p. 4).

De Lissovoy and Brown (2013) delineated two models of solidarity in education: (1) a model that is based on a struggle, where people come together for a common cause or a movement to accomplish a task, and (2) a second model referred to as "solidarity as alliance":

Seeks to negotiate rather than overcome differences between partici-pating individuals or groups in order to achieve a strategic goal. This approach views differences not merely as obstacles but potentially as positive political resources. Pioneered in the civil rights movement, and more subtly worked through in more recent antiracist and gender equity advocacy, this paradigm is familiar to anti-oppression movements that recognize a basic division (among those involved in the struggle) between "target" and "ally" groups. (p. 7)

Gaztambide-Fernández (2012) summed up the concept,

First, solidarity always implies a relationship among individuals or groups, whether as a way to understand what binds people or brings them together for civic or political action. Second, solidarity always implies an obligation or a sense of duty regarding what is just or equitable, whether it is construed in relationship to some notion of human rights or a social contract or to commitments to struggles against particular forms of oppression. Third, solidarity always implies a set of actions or duties between those in the solidary relationship. (p. 50)

Drawing on the scholarship of feminist authors, Gaztambide-Fernández proposed a *pedagogy of solidarity* that seeks to break the colonial relationships between teachers and students and between students and the curriculum. His theory involves three modes of solidarity that can lead to an anti-oppressive, anti-racist, and decolonizing pedagogy.

Relational. This form of solidarity is expressed in a deliberate commitment to building a relationship based on mutual respect,

To think of the pedagogy of solidarity as relational is, first, to acknowledge being as co-presence, by deliberately taking as a point of departure that individual subjects do not enter into relationships, but rather subjects are made in and through relationships. (p. 52)

This conception of solidarity expresses itself in the ability to know as much as possible about the person with whom the relationship is sought. It leaves room for the creation of the self and the other, together and separately.

Transitive. This is about the act of doing solidarity; as Gaztambide-Fernández stated, a person can *Solidarizarse* with another person or group. This act of solidarity rises from Freire's concept of *praxis*, "the pedagogy of solidarity is about an action that also affects or modifies the one who acts—to solidarize oneself with" (p. 54). It also stands in contrast to a type of solidarity as a performance that seeks to aggrandize oneself rather than pull together in the interest of the marginalized and disenfranchised.

Creative solidarity aims to upend the relations that currently govern human interactions and asks those who seek solidarity to redefine identity, culture, and the relationships involved in those interactions. Creative solidarity "involves creatively engaging with others in unexpected and perhaps even inopportune ways that might rearrange the symbolic content of human exchanges by mobilizing that which always exceeds the very terms of the encounter" (p. 56).

Gaztambide-Fernández's concepts of solidarity nestle into Caring Solidarity to describe the project of white teachers who seek a deeper, more impactful teaching experience across the color line. As defined, solidarity is a crucial element of successful teaching in multiracial classrooms. However, building solidarity across the color line in classrooms takes commitment and patience and must be renewed each fall when a new set of students comes through the classroom door.

Only teachers in relationships of solidarity with their students will be able to fully implement Culturally Relevant Pedagogy, where teachers foster student success, maintain their own and students' cultural competence, and develop critical perspectives that challenge white supremacist and inequitable social structures (Ladson-Billings, 1995). To expect to implement Culturally Relevant or Culturally Responsive Pedagogy without first creating relationships based on caring and solidarity will result in teachers feeling like they are failing and are unable to reach African American students. It is like building a house on a foundation of sand.

Even if schools make concerted efforts to diversify school curricula, personnel, and pedagogy but keep the structures of white supremacy, they have not met their obligations as educators committed to justice. A multicultural school that still imposes white supremacy is no more liberatory than a school committed to segregation. Bettina Love (2019b) shared her own experience,

> For Black and Brown children in the United States, a major part of their schooling experience is associated with White female teachers who have no understanding of their culture. That was certainly my experience. My K-12 schooling was filled with White teachers who, at their core, were good people but unknowingly were murdering my spirit with their lack of knowledge, care, and love of my culture. (online)

Love explained that to stop this type of violence, the school system and the people who teach in it will need to undergo a personal and structural overhaul, requiring changes in how teachers see themselves in the classroom and in how schools are structured.

Specifically, there is a need for a school environmental and teacher commitment framework that addresses the needs of Black students taught by white teachers for the curricular framework of MCE and asset pedagogies to flourish. The literature on the relationships, power dynamics, and pedagogy across the divide of racial difference is vast. It has a long history, and scholars now address these power relationships using the counter-narratives of people of color challenging the paradigm of white supremacy (see De Lissovoy, 2010; Love, 2019a; b; Solorzano & Yosso, 2002).

Asset pedagogies such as Culturally Relevant Pedagogy (CRP) (1995) and Culturally Sustaining Pedagogy (CSP) (2017) offer transformative approaches to teaching that view students' identities, languages, and cultures as invaluable resources rather than obstacles to overcome. These frameworks demand that educators reject deficit models and engage in practices that affirm and amplify the strengths of students of color. Teachers must cultivate authentic relationships with their students, hold high expectations, and foster critical consciousness to empower students to challenge systemic inequities.

However, adopting these pedagogies requires more than theoretical understanding; it necessitates a paradigm shift in teacher preparation, school structures, and personal beliefs. White teachers must move beyond performative allyship and embrace the risks and responsibilities of solidarity, dismantling oppressive systems within and beyond the classroom. This work is difficult. It demands vulnerability, persistence, and a commitment to justice. Yet, as Freire reminds us, true solidarity is an act of love and a means to transform classrooms. Without a foundation of solidarity, even the best-intentioned pedagogical frameworks will fail to reach their full potential in supporting students of color.

In the next chapter, the Caring Solidarity framework fills a gap left by teacher education and professional development by proposing a theoretical and paradigmatic change in how successful white secondary teachers of African American Students are described. The purpose is to extend the conversation about teachers using multicultural curricula to create culturally relevant or sustaining classrooms, to describe teacher behaviors and commitments to develop relationships of solidarity.

Discussion Questions for Chapter 5

1 How do asset pedagogies, as discussed by Paris and Alim (2017), challenge deficit-based approaches to education? What are some practical ways educators can incorporate asset-based thinking in their classrooms?

2 Gloria Ladson-Billings (1995) outlined three criteria for CRP: academic success, cultural competence, and critical consciousness. Which of these criteria do you think is most challenging for educators to implement, and why? Can you provide examples of how these principles might look in practice?

3 How does Gay's (2010) concept of "authentic caring" compare to the "warm demander" pedagogy described by Ware (2006)? Do you believe one approach is more effective than the other, or are they complementary? Support your argument with examples from the text.

4 Freire (2014) emphasized the risks and commitments involved in true solidarity. How does this concept of solidarity apply to the relationships between teachers and students in racially diverse classrooms? What challenges might white teachers face in building solidarity with students of color?

5 The chapter contrasts allyship and solidarity, noting that allyship can sometimes allow white educators to remain within their privilege. What are the limitations of allyship as a framework for white teachers, and how does solidarity offer a more transformative approach?

6 The chapter emphasizes the need for educators to interrogate their own privilege and embrace culturally responsive and sustaining pedagogies. What specific changes would you propose to teacher education programs to better prepare teachers for multiracial and multicultural classrooms?

Actionable Classroom Practices from Chapter 5

- **Start Each Day with Relationship-Building Activities**

  Begin the school day with morning meetings, one-on-one check-ins, or community circles where students can share something about their lives, fostering trust and mutual understanding.

- **Set Individualized Goals and Celebrate Progress**

  Work with each student to set academic goals that reflect their potential, track their progress regularly, and celebrate small successes with positive reinforcement tailored to their interests (e.g., a certificate or a note home).

- **Create a Multilingual and Multicultural Classroom Display**

  Include posters, student work, and resources in students' native languages alongside visuals and quotes representing diverse cultures. For example, display a "cultural pride" bulletin board showcasing students' family traditions or heritage.

- **Journal Weekly About Bias and Classroom Dynamics**

  Dedicate fifteen minutes a week to reflect in a journal on any moments of bias or assumptions you may have made and analyze how you handled classroom power dynamics. Use this to plan improvements for the following week.

- **Incorporate Social Justice Projects into the Curriculum**

  Design a project where students research and present on a local or global issue they care about, such as food insecurity, climate change, or racial equity. Guide them to develop actionable solutions.

- **Use Positive and Direct Communication**

  When managing behavior, combine culturally familiar phrases with clear expectations. For example, instead of saying, "You're disruptive," use, "I expect you to refocus because I know you can excel here, and I want to help you succeed."

- **Avoid Labels Like "Struggling" or "At-Risk"**

  When discussing students with colleagues or parents, highlight their strengths and potential instead of focusing on deficits. For instance, say, "They show great creativity and resilience; we're working on tapping into that for their writing."

- **Stand Up for Students in Faculty Meetings**

  If a policy or discussion unfairly targets students of color, demand equitable changes. For example, propose alternatives to zero-tolerance discipline policies that disproportionately impact marginalized students.

- **Host a Community Day or Family Involvement Event**

    Plan a monthly event where families are invited to share their skills, traditions, or experiences. For instance, organize a cultural heritage day where families bring food, stories, or performances to the school.

6 A New Framework
Caring Solidarity

The Framework: Caring Solidarity

Caring Solidarity is a model that describes teachers working in solidarity with their students of color. It can also help teachers and teacher candidates move from solidarity with whiteness and deficit models to caring and solidarity with their students and communities. To give an overall description of the Caring Solidarity framework, it comprises two encompassing levels of action to create relationships of solidarity with students of color. They are (level 1) Empathy and (level 2) Caring Solidarity. Within the level of solidarity are two sublevels, delineating teachers' degrees of commitment and actions as advocates or accomplices. The framework has four commitments, two levels of care, and two deeper levels of solidarity. The commitments (recognition, proximity, interrogation, and action) are divided into two mindsets: love on one side and grace on the other. These commitments stem from caring for students and a desire to meet their needs.

I will explore each level in detail in the following chapters, examining its reasons, theoretical frameworks, literature, methods employed, and the motivations that drive it. To assist you in navigating this discussion, I recommend keeping a copy of the diagram on the next page readily accessible as a reference point throughout these chapters.

Teachers develop their commitments gradually as they interact with students and navigate the day-to-day realities of teaching. However, changes in circumstances—whether positive, such as students winning an award or receiving an influx of funding, or negative, like a school closure or a traumatic event within the school—can disproportionately hinder a teacher's growth in specific areas, even after they have achieved solidarity in other situations.

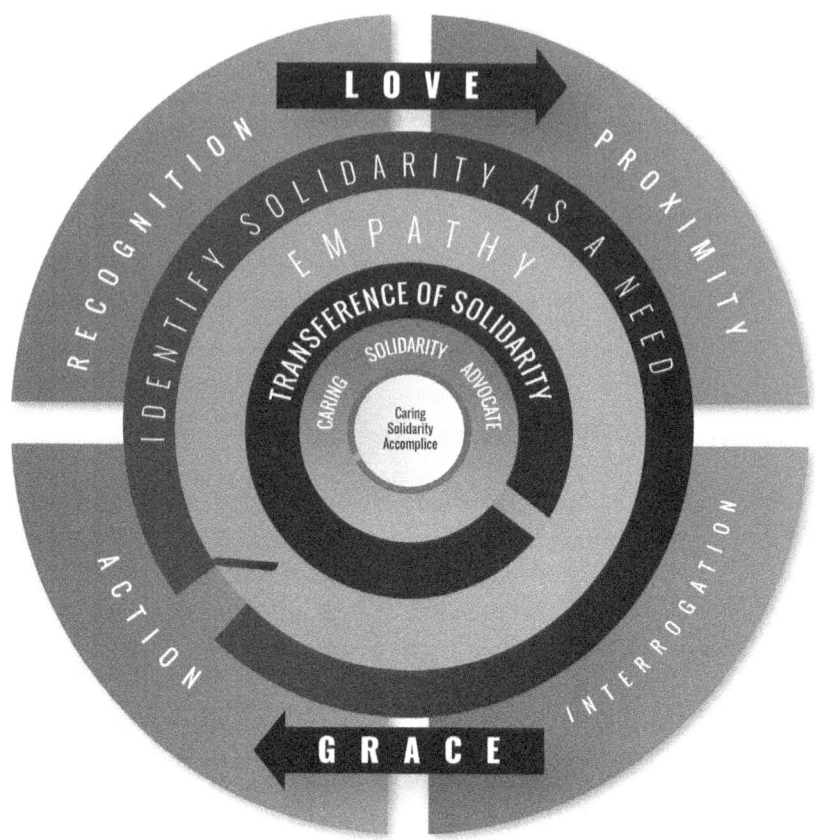

Figure 6.1 Caring Solidarity Diagram.

When white teachers engage with students of color, they begin to learn and grow into their roles as educators who cross racial lines. Their ability to advance in this journey depends on several factors, including their life experiences, the school environment, their curiosity and dedication, and the quality of mentorship and leadership they receive during their preparation and in their workplace. For instance, a teacher who is effective in a racially and culturally diverse school with a majority-white population may find new challenges if demographic shifts result in a majority-minority student body, requiring them to adapt to a different cultural context.

Adapting to a new situation requires personal growth, a renewed commitment to previous values, and the embrace of new ones. This process demands a deeper level of dedication and a fresh understanding of how meaningful relationships, rooted in solidarity, are built. The Caring Solidarity model provides a pathway to thriving and success for white teachers working in racially diverse settings. Caring Solidarity's commitments are (1) Proximity, (2) Recognition, (3) Interrogation, and (4) Action.

Two mindset conduits move teachers from one commitment to the other. The first is love, which moves people from recognition to proximity. The other is grace, which moves people from interrogation to action. To move to relationships of Caring Solidarity with students, the commitments are met at different levels. (Level 1) Empathy (Level 2), Caring Solidarity as an advocate (Level 3), and Caring Solidarity as an accomplice (Indigenous Action Media, 2014; Powell & Kelly, 2017).

It is important to note that the path to Caring Solidarity is not straightforward or automatic. Accomplices are not grown like trees. It is not a natural process. It is a set of decisions, and they have consequences. Sometimes, white people will choose to move and then retreat upon seeing the opposition until they are strong enough to return. Sometimes, they never make that choice. However, the choice to move toward Caring Solidarity comes with its own rewards. Not the least of which is a more successful classroom, school, and community.

The Commitments and Mindset Conduits

Commitment to Recognition. The first of the four commitments is a *commitment to recognition.* That recognition allows teachers to see their students as they are, not as they are in the teacher's imagination. As most white teachers do not have vast experience living with people of color before becoming teachers, the world of imagination is all that new teachers know about working in multiracial schools. Sometimes, that is informed by solid teacher preparation, but movies and the news are often the basis for new teachers' knowledge about the students they will meet.

As explained earlier, whiteness in media, schools, and the social world all reinforce a detailed curriculum of white normality, white supremacy, and anti-Blackness. So, being taught their whole lives that they are the standard of which all cultures, beauty, and behaviors should be measured, white teachers walk into classrooms of Black students and must unlearn the very paradigm of their existence.

When these new teachers meet their students, most white teachers bring little into the classroom that allows them to frame the experiences they will have from day one. If they are committed and stay with it, the white teacher will eventually begin to see the students for who they are and experience what can be referred to as the *shock of recognition*. In his 1850 essay "Hawthorne and his Mosses," Herman Melville summed up how people with no history can acknowledge one another, describing the impact of fellow writer, Nathaniel Hawthorne.

> Take that joy to yourself, in your own generation; and so, shall he feel those grateful impulses in him, that may possibly prompt him to the full flower of some still greater achievement in your eyes. And by confessing him, you thereby confess others, you brace the whole brotherhood. For genius, all over the world, stands hand in hand, and one shock of recognition runs the whole circle round. (Melville, 1850/1985, p. 1157)

New white teachers who come to schools without exposure to other races and cultures oftentimes come to these schools with the idea that they will become the white savior (Straubhaar, 2014). They have seen movies like *Dangerous Minds* (1995) and *Freedom Writers* (2007), where teachers make inspiring speeches that turn young ruffians into scholars (Cammarota, 2011; Hughey, 2010). As part of whiteness, white people think that their presence is an ostensible good (Applebaum, 2011; Sullivan, 2014). The stance of the missionary, or the fixer, allows them to perceive students as needing their values, not just guidance (Warren & Talley, 2017).

Recognition in Critical Theory

The Caring Solidarity model of recognition is rooted in the work of contemporary philosopher Axel Honneth (1995). Honneth's recognition provides a solid foundation in Critical Theory for Caring Solidarity as a framework for teachers encountering diversity for the first time in their lives. Honneth's recognition is more than a glance around the room; it is instead a commitment to a relationship built upon understanding the other person as a person, not for what can be done for one party or the other.

Recognition is not an exchange but the creation of a bond that can only happen when both parties are able to see beyond the external and acknowledge the humanity of the other person. To Honneth, solidarity is built upon the recognition of the status of others. The level of that recognition comes from the intersubjective *esteem* built between them (Blunden, 2003).

In his signature volume, *The Struggle for Recognition: The Moral Grammar of Social Conflicts* (1995), Honneth explained that the system of ethical life is based in struggle. Combatants struggle for recognition in the eyes of others, and there is no assumption of status without struggle.

Honneth's volume reconceptualizes the State of Nature, as explained by Hegel, Hobbes, and other social contract theorists of the Enlightenment. Using Hegel's work to reconceptualize Hobbes' concept of a mythical natural state before civilization, the question that has vexed philosophers is: "What happened at the exact point where people decided to abandon the rule of the strong, give up some of their rights as individuals, and bind together to create civilizations and society? Honneth explained that, for Hegel, the conflict arose between individuals over recognition, status, or esteem. The esteem that arises through conflict allows the parties to recognize each other legally, socially, and morally.

Recognition does not happen without conflict, and esteem does not come without cost. Recognition is an earned state, not a natural one. That conflict creates the conditions for recognition, and the esteem or respect that grows out of the encounter establishes the humanity of both individuals in the other's eyes. Extending Honneth's framework to classrooms, recognition is possible only when two entities with differences recognize each other's humanity and meet in a place where teachers can teach, and students can learn.

The *shock of recognition* is the moment when white teachers confront the inadequacy of the racialized assumptions they have been taught and come to recognize their students as fully human, complex individuals rather than flat abstractions. In the teacher–student relationship, there is a demand for respect from teachers and an equally strong demand for recognition from the students. New white teachers in classes with Black students assume that they will have authority based on economic, structural, and racial status. However, students often do not immediately hand over that status without the teacher proving their worthiness. As children grow into adolescence, the demand for recognition grows.

The longer recognition is withheld from students who are not truly seen, the more strongly they will withhold respect and recognition until the teacher earns it. This struggle, on the students' part, to be seen in all their humanity, and the teacher's struggle to be appreciated as an authority, is the root of the conflict between the white teacher and the Black student. Neither can do their jobs to their fullest potential until that conflict is resolved. Recognition involves a different way of examining interactions with white teachers and their students. The *shock of recognition*, if correctly negotiated, can set a teacher on the road to success across the color line and is the beginning of the process toward solidarity. While the *shock of recognition* is a momentary experience, the unlearning and learning that follow are a long and revealing process. To do it, a white teacher must be willing to spend the time, effort, and emotional labor to recognize the humanity of students who are racialized in both society and the mind of the teacher. Recognition is the act of seeing Black children (and all Black people) for who they are, not through the lens of whiteness.

Shibboleths as Signs of Recognition. After the initial stages of recognition, the white teacher seeking Caring Solidarity will begin to move toward the next stage. To do that, communication must become possible. However, many teachers do not come with the tools to speak with people who are racially and culturally different from themselves. As recognition progresses, words that will help teachers move into the group of students can be used. Language, gestures, and customary greetings are powerful ways humans communicate the recognition of another person. How individuals communicate with others reflects the level of respect, recognition, and value they attribute to them. Whether conscious or unconscious, language and tone serve as indicators of social positioning and interpersonal regard. The broader concept encompassing these linguistic choices and behaviors is known as a *shibboleth* (Du Bois, 1903/1994). A *shibboleth* refers to specific words, phrases, or speech patterns that signal group membership, distinguishing those who belong from those who do not. These verbal markers serve as gatekeeping mechanisms, reinforcing social boundaries and affirming shared identities within a community.

The use of the shibboleths by outsiders, if done respectfully and within an attempt at solidarity, can be accepted by the *in*-group. However, for white teachers, the use of shibboleths should be done as part of an overall expression of solidarity. If not, the teacher can be perceived as phony or even mocking. As Milstein (2015) reminded, "identity does not automatically mean solidarity" (p. 65). That sometimes manifests when outsiders misappropriate aspects of students' cultures into their own identity rather than respectfully using shibboleths to make connections.

Misappropriation occurs when an outsider, such as a new teacher, incorrectly assumes *in*-group status and uses *shibboleths* without permission or inappropriately. In some cases, teachers may deliberately adopt students' language, either to mock them or to assert dominance. This constitutes a misuse of shibboleths and does not foster solidarity; instead, it leads to rejection and deepens the divide between students and the teacher. This behavior should be actively avoided and called out when observed. Teachers should remain mindful of the colonial implications of linguistic misappropriation, recognizing that borrowing elements of students' culture for connection fundamentally differs from claiming or co-opting those behaviors and words as their own. White teachers who develop relationships of solidarity cultivate a nuanced understanding of cross-cultural communication to build authentic relationships in multiracial and multicultural classrooms. This requires self-awareness, humility, and a commitment to respecting students' linguistic and cultural identities.

There is a common argument that white students might feel alienated if a teacher uses a language other than Standard English in the classroom. However, this concern overlooks the ongoing alienation students experience in moment-to-moment interactions that often seek to erase their culture, identity, and uniqueness. Wouldn't all students benefit from developing a deeper appreciation for diverse languages and cultures? This type of pushback often stems from the assumption that centering other cultures inherently displaces white people—a perspective rooted in intolerance for these shifts. White supremacy perpetuates the belief that white students and teachers lack nothing in their monolingualism or monoculturalism. It resists any possibility that differences might hold equal or greater importance than whiteness. To these people, differences may be tolerated, but only as long as they do not challenge the primacy of whiteness. Consequently, complaints of unfairness when other cultures are given prominence are ultimately grounded in white supremacy. White teachers working in multicultural classrooms—especially those striving for solidarity—should be prepared to challenge this argument and educate white parents and colleagues about the necessity of decentering whiteness.

Successful white teachers who cross the color line immerse themselves in the culture of the school, the neighborhoods, and their students' cultural settings. They learn the community's language and exchange shibboleths. These shibboleths facilitate the exchange of ideas and enable teachers and students to trust one another. If done correctly, shibboleths are an outward sign of the commitment to recognition. They are a mechanism to show students they are being seen for who they are and not for their approximation to, or distance from, whiteness. The respectful, humble use of shibboleths to show respect is often welcomed, even if initially mistrusted, and is a way to show respect. If done with consideration for recognizing and owning the cultural differences between white teachers and students of color, the use of shibboleths can be part of building relationships of solidarity between teachers and students.

Love as a Mindset Conduit to Proximity. Love moves people from recognition to proximity. When people declare their love, they move in together, and sometimes they marry and make deep commitments. They establish lives together. Family members share homes, friends share bonds, and they often express love for one another. As bell hooks (2000) stated, "Only love can heal the wounds of the past. However, the intensity of our woundedness often leads to a closing of the heart, making it impossible for us to give or receive the love that is given to us" (p. xxvii). Love heals. Love permeates. Love envelopes.

Ask any teacher most days, and they will tell you they love their students. Sometimes secondary teachers are less likely to do so, as there are taboos around the language of love, but even they will declare their love for the job, school, or team. The love of one's students is an outgrowth of recognition. Without recognition, there can be no love nor solidarity, as there is no relationship. There are many ways to discuss love as a concept, but for this discussion, it is crucial to frame love as an action that moves a person toward solidarity with another. That kind of love, the political act of commitment to another outside themselves and their kin, is a commitment many say they have when entering the teaching profession, but in practice, they often fall short (Matias, 2016a; 2016b).

To frame the love that leads to solidarity, Frankfort School Critical theorist Erich Fromm's work *The Art of Loving* (1956) elucidates the active loving relationship of solidarity:

> Love is an activity; if I love, I am in a constant state of active concern with the loved person, but not only with him or her. For I shall become incapable of relating myself actively to the loved person if I am lazy, if I am not in a constant state of awareness, alertness, activity. (p. 118)

Being active and loving as a teacher means caring for students. It means that a teacher will put their students' needs first; they will do what is necessary for students to succeed and not hold students in contempt. It means the teacher does not belittle students. hooks (2000) explained that love is an action:

> To begin by always thinking of love as an action rather than a feeling is one way in which anyone using the word in this manner automatically assumes accountability and responsibility. We are often taught we have no control over our "feelings." Yet most of us accept that we choose our actions, that intention and will inform what we do. (pp. 12–13)

Love is a choice people make. It is not merely a feeling or a preference for one over the other, as in the love of ice cream. The love that leads to Caring Solidarity transcends the day-to-day feelings a person may or may not have. It is a commitment to love and to be with the other person or people. That is why it leads to proximity. Loving a community or an individual is possible only when a commitment to solidarity is also made (Matias & Allen, 2013).

To Fromm, the act of loving requires one to forego the selfish narcissism that is a hallmark of the young and grow into a person with the capacity to embrace faith in the one who is loved.

> The ability to love depends on one's capacity to emerge from narcissism, and from the incestuous fixation to mother and clan; it depends on our capacity to grow, to develop a productive orientation in our relationship toward the world and ourselves. This process of emergence, of birth, of waking up, requires one quality as a necessary condition: faith. The practice of the art of loving requires the practice of faith. (p. 112)

This act of growing up, of leaving the childish imaginary behind, is an important step. As Fromm explained,

> Thought and judgment are not the only realms of experience in which rational faith is manifested. In the sphere of human relations, faith is an indispensable quality of any significant friendship or love. "Having faith" in another person means to be certain of the reliability and unchangeability of his fundamental attitudes, of the core of his personality, of his love. (p. 114)

As discussed earlier, new white teachers often arrive with a set of imaginary students in their heads. However, if they are dedicated to their craft, they will experience the *shock of recognition*. That shock is a startling, waking experience that should move them away from the imaginary to the real people in front of them. Only through that recognition is love possible, and if correctly cultivated, it can move them toward solidarity.

The love Fromm describes is only possible if it is not an exchange, for example, *love in exchange for love back*. The love that leads to solidarity is based on caring for someone outside of oneself. It does not depend on conditions and is unconditional:

> Unconditional love corresponds to one of the deepest longings, not only of the child, but of every human being; on the other hand, to be loved because of one's merit, because one deserves it, always leaves doubt; maybe I did not please the person whom I want to love me, maybe this, or that—there is always a fear that love could disappear. (p. 39)

While privilege itself does not preclude caring about others, privileged status allows the choice of altruism as one of many alternatives and the reasons for choosing to teach (Danielewicz, 2001). However, when linked to privilege, altruism will impede Caring Solidarity because it will invariably ask for gratitude in return. Altruism is an exchange. One person is helping another, for at least the good feeling of doing good for another. That is not a relationship of solidarity.

Beyond the conditions, Fromm framed his concept of love that leads to solidarity as *respect*. This is not an authoritarian form of respect but a loving respect that rests on recognizing the other person's humanity and their ability to love unconditionally. It is a gift freely given as a free person, not a payment demanded:

> Respect means the concern that the other person should grow and unfold as he is. Respect, thus, implies the absence of exploitation. I want the loved person to grow and unfold for his own sake, and in his own ways, and not for the purpose of serving me. (p. 26)

Love that leads to solidarity, built on a foundation of recognition, is only possible between free people who love, not out of need but as an outgrowth of freedom and recognition of the dignity of the person loved. It is an act of loving that moves people toward a relationship of solidarity.

To Fromm, three elements of this kind of love needed to be in place for this respect to flourish. These three elements resonate with teachers and are certainly part of any teacher's identity and daily practice: discipline, concentration, and patience "throughout every phase of his life" (p. 102).

Discipline. As with anything one has to work at to become proficient, love takes discipline. Fromm equated the art of loving to learning to play an instrument or Zen archery. The discipline of love as an educator means that teachers will get up early to make copies, prepare activities, and grocery shop before school to ensure students have food.

Secondary schools often start before dawn, and teachers are there as soon as possible to get started on the day's activities. Sometimes, coffee in hand, grabbing food as they walk, or eating while driving through the snow to get to school and meet their students, teachers who display this type of discipline are love in action. After the students arrive, sometimes sleepy with oftentimes empty stomachs, teachers are there to care for them:

> It is essential, however, that discipline should not be practiced like a rule imposed on oneself from the outside, but that it becomes an expression of one's own will; that it is felt as pleasant, and that one slowly accustoms oneself to a kind of behavior which one would eventually miss, if one stopped practicing it. (p. 103)

Throughout the day, teachers distribute love through questions, answers, feedback, compliments, songs, stories, puns, and silly sayings. To be effective, these things do not come from mandates or canned lesson plans but from inside teachers' hearts and souls.

Great teachers recognize that disciplining themselves is necessary to teach students effectively. The undisciplined teacher will not plan for student learning effectively, will not create an environment conducive to learning, and will not build those relationships of caring solidarity because they are not secure on their own. Discipline brings the conditions necessary for love and success in the classroom.

Concentration. Fromm's concept of concentration was the ability to be alone with oneself; the ability to spend time without thinking about anything, which allows for rest. The ability to be alone allows a person to be independent of others and, therefore, is able to love. "If I am attached to another person because I cannot stand on my own feet, he or she may be a lifesaver, but the relationship is not one of love" (p. 103). For teachers, to be in relationships of Caring Solidarity with their students means that they must understand themselves and be confident in their pedagogy, practice, and who they are in the school and the world.

This cannot happen on the first day or, often, the first few years of a teaching career. Navigating and negotiating relationships across race and cultural barriers is hard work and takes a never-ending commitment to self-understanding as well as maturity in the position of the *teacher*. They must have a sense of who they are as white people in a school across the color line and have a presence that comes with time and concentration:

> To be concentrated means to live fully in the present, in the here and now, and not to think of the next thing to be done while I am doing something right now. Needless to say, that concentration must be practiced most of all by people who love each other. (p. 106)

To build Caring Solidarity relationships, teachers must possess a strong sense of self, enabling them to withstand the inevitable mistakes and setbacks of the teaching journey without losing resolve. This requires a unique kind of courage—not to confront an external adversary, but to face the internal enemies: the fear of imperfection, a fear of students, the fear of being wrong, looking foolish, or being misunderstood. Building relationships across difference takes the presence of mind, courage, and faith. As Fromm stated, this kind of concentration:

> requires courage, the ability to take a risk, the readiness even to accept pain and disappointment. Whoever insists on safety and security as primary conditions of life cannot have faith; whoever shuts himself off in a system of defense, where distance and possession are his means of security, makes himself a prisoner. To be loved, and to love, need courage, the courage to judge certain values as of ultimate concern—and to take the jump and stake everything on these values. (p. 116)

Successful teachers across the color line value their students and communities. They value and create curricula where students are recognized and represented. They value their students' cultures and do not consider their cultures superior to their students'. They are continually learning from their students and communities. Those values allow love to flow from the teacher to the students and then back.

Teachers who lack this ability to love will not receive love in return. While a teacher who does all these things may not receive love in return, they are guaranteed that love will not flow back if they do not. To give and receive love from students and communities, white teachers must have a firm grasp of pedagogy and content and the flexibility to concentrate on solidarity.

Patience. As with any art, Fromm's active loving must be patiently mastered over time. The act of teaching is not something that can be mastered in a course or a program. It takes time with students, with books, and with oneself in reflection. Fromm explained:

> Eventually, a condition of learning any art is a *supreme concern* with the mastery of the art. If the art is not something of supreme importance, the apprentice will never learn it. He will remain, at best, a good dilettante but will never become a master. This condition is as necessary for the art of loving as for any other art. (pp. 101–102)

The art of teaching across the color line also requires the practice of patience, a commitment to students, and, especially, a commitment to learning *from* students. The discipline needed is multifold, but among the most important is the ability to reflect on one's own standpoint. Great teachers are constantly revisiting their practice and their mental frameworks. They are willing to be challenged, even uncomfortably, and use that challenge as an opportunity to learn and grow. They are disciplined in their study of pedagogy, practice, and content. They are students of their students. In other words, they study their students and learn from them. They learn how to meet their students in Caring Solidarity through disciplined observation, interaction, and study.

Teachers in relationships of solidarity are willing to be patient with students and with themselves. They learn and grow with their students. They lead students to new understandings while also learning from them. White teachers who meet their Black students with patience, are secure in their own pedagogy and content knowledge, and are open to new understandings of race, power, and culture, can create a powerful, loving environment for students in which they feel valued, cared for, and cared about. In return, the students enliven the classroom and enrich the life of the teacher.

The Commitments—Commitment to Proximity

Many teachers' first critical commitment is the act of crossing the color line. For white teachers, this physical movement is often their first sustained interaction with people of color outside a context involving service or exchange, and it frequently represents the first time they are asked to care for children who do not look like them. However, most white teachers are not adequately prepared for this journey, lacking the cultural, emotional, and pedagogical tools to navigate the experience successfully.

According to Danielewicz (2001), teacher identity is structured around three interconnected areas:

1   *The ability to form bonds and personal relationships of solidarity with students* involves cultivating trust, empathy, and meaningful connections that transcend superficial interactions.

2   *The theory of their own practice* includes understanding why they choose to teach in a particular place with a specific population, shaped by their motivations, values, and goals.

3   *Their pedagogy* is deeply intertwined with their self-image as a teacher and their personal commitments, reflecting how they see themselves.

For many teacher candidates, crossing the color line means being thrust into diverse educational settings without prior life experience in communities of color or students outside their social class. These candidates often lack the cultural competence or self-awareness to engage effectively in these environments. Consequently, teacher educators play a crucial role in guiding them through this process. By fostering reflective practices and asking critical questions, teacher educators can help future teachers explore their own biases, positionalities, and assumptions. This reflection enables them to better understand their identities and roles in a multiracial and multicultural classroom.

However, not every teacher candidate possesses the temperament or mindset required to succeed in a multiracial classroom. Developing the skills and dispositions necessary for this work requires intentionality, effort, and a willingness to embrace discomfort. For those who do succeed in crossing the color line, the experience profoundly shapes both their professional and personal identities. It becomes the defining feature of who they are as teachers, embedding itself into their practice, pedagogy, and sense of self.

Once teachers can recognize their students, they can move closer to them and live, be, and exist inside the cultural parameters of their students' community. That becomes part of the process of creating a teacher identity. The identity will be shaped by the experiences of living, working, and moving in spaces that are not primarily defined by whiteness. Proximity begins with white teachers teaching in the school, but it cannot end there if they are to achieve relationships of solidarity (Harvey, 2007). Many teachers declare they are in solidarity with students but stop short of moving into communities where people of color live, shop, school their children, and participate politically. However, until a teacher is willing to be a member of the community, they will always have a distance between themselves and the students they teach.

This is not to suggest that white teachers who live apart from their students cannot be effective educators or even strong allies for them.

However, teaching in communities of color during the day while retreating to white enclaves at night reflects a disengagement that prevents the deeper relational work necessary to cultivate Caring Solidarity. Solidarity requires more than professional obligation; it demands a willingness to be in genuine proximity to the communities one serves, both physically and emotionally. Unless a person is willing to be in proximity to the one they declare they love, that love is hollow and, perhaps, not love at all. Relationships require presence, investment, and a willingness to navigate discomfort to foster trust.

Teachers who take positions in multiracial and multicultural schools without reflecting on what it means to teach across the color line can cause harm, whether through cultural missteps, unexamined biases, or an inability to foster inclusive and affirming learning environments. To be effective, successful teachers engage in ongoing self-reflection, actively seek relationships beyond the school, and commit to the lifelong work of dismantling racial hierarchies within themselves and the systems in which they operate.

As degreed professionals, teachers are aware that they have choices in life, and white teachers should make choices out of conviction. That conviction may or may not lead them to work with students who do not share their white identity. Those choices range from where to live to whom they want to teach. As McIntosh (2001) famously stated, "White privilege is like an invisible weightless knapsack of special provisions, maps, passports, codebooks, visas, clothes, tools, and blank checks" (p. 188). One of the privileges of whiteness is the ability to go anywhere and do anything that a person decides to do without restrictions based on race. When a white teacher takes a teaching position in a multiracial school, they should do so with the expressed intention of crossing race and class lines, effectively a choice to define their teacher identity. To be successful, they perform a conscious act. This proximity is a choice. Plenty of communities across the nation have only a few students of color attending, and teachers often earn more in these districts. So, no white teacher should work in multiracial schools without a commitment to bonding their identity to their students through recognition and then proximity. To do otherwise sets everyone up for failure.

The Caveat—Neoliberalism, Reform, and Gentrification

This concept has reasonable criticism. Gentrification, or the immoral displacement of people of color in neighborhoods that newly appeal to middle- and upper-class white people, has been a topic of scholarly and political discussion since the 1990s (Lipman, 2013; Wyly & Hammel, 2004). The displacement of already marginalized communities by white people is a consideration that must be taken by white teachers who want to teach in those neighborhoods successfully. Additionally, displacement will not engender solidarity relationships. However, without proximity, there will always be a distance that impedes the relationship. This causes a quandary that is important to explore.

As stated earlier, nice white people tend to believe that their presence is unquestionably good, and that tendency allows them to move into spaces that have been re-fit to meet white standards. Sullivan (2014) explained that white people are *ontologically expansive*. In other words, they tend to see themselves as the norm and assume that all spaces are theirs for the taking. She explained that white people have a "habit, often unconscious, of assuming and acting as if any and all spaces—geographical, psychological, cultural, linguistic, or whatever—are rightfully available to and open for white people to enter whenever they like" (p. 20).

When white teachers teach in places where Black kids are brought TO them, as in suburban magnet schools, charters, or private schools that are not rooted in communities of color, that is not the same kind of proximity that would bring about Caring Solidarity. That may lead to allyship or even advocacy, because that teacher may care deeply about their students, but Caring Solidarity involves moving oneself toward the people with whom solidarity relationships are sought (Milstein, 2015).

The issue is that teachers have already moved into these spaces. As pointed out in Chapter 1, white teachers are already teaching Black students in communities. The case is settled that white teachers will interact with communities of color. The question is how and to what degree. Teachers must know the communities where students live to succeed in advocacy and allyship with students.

The politics and implications of gentrification and place are real and challenging to navigate, so it may take time for some new white teachers to move into proximity with students while others are able to dive in from the first school bell. This privilege also extends to the choices white people are able to make about where to live and the type of lifestyle they wish to have (Lipman, 2013). The successful teacher who seeks to engage in Caring Solidarity must be committed to proximity. Allyship can mean proximity at school alone. However, to move to greater levels of solidarity with students, teachers in Caring Solidarity will live, possibly raise families, and become deeply involved in the neighborhood socially, politically, and culturally where their students live.

The Commitments—Commitment to Interrogation

The other commitments that can lead to Caring Solidarity are on the lower part of the diagram. Beginning with interrogation, Eslinger (2013) explained that successful teachers of students of color interrogate their own whiteness and their *a priori* knowledge and attitudes about race, racialized communities, and their own privileged status. "White teachers need: 1) to develop a rich and culturally diverse knowledge base; 2) to interrogate their identities and the privileges associated with them; and 3) to critically examine curriculum and pedagogy" (p. 5). According to Eslinger, teachers also fall victim to a savior mentality and a "white supremacist" belief structure that must be quelled to create a culturally responsive classroom (p. 8). Since, as has been explained earlier, most new teachers have limited interaction with people from outside their white enclaves, often, those decision-making frameworks lead to a colorblind ideology or a missionary mindset that sees students as deficient rather than whole beings, members of communities, and change agents. Understanding whiteness and why it matters involves examining the self, identity, and ideology. Individuals doing their internal investigation are practicing what Cochran-Smith (2003) described as *interrogation*.

For a white teacher to be successful in the hypercultural classrooms of today's schools, they need a deeper understanding than simple cross-cultural communication. As discussed earlier, whiteness is about power, privilege, and the ability to act with care about the feelings, positions, or standpoints of others not seen as white. Working to break down one's privilege can be difficult and frightening, and many abandon the project before it even begins. It is much easier to retreat from the day-to-day grind of holding oneself accountable and default to blaming students for their lack of middle-class sensibilities (Payne, 2013). Colorblind mentalities allow white people to be blind to "the very knowledge of culturally responsive teaching and social justice that is needed to transform the whiteness of education" (Hayes & Juarez, 2012, p. 7). Nearly every day, teacher educators hear someone express that *the kind of kids we get*, or *those kids*, are the problem, not the teachers' responses to differences, the structures of inequality that students endure, or their reactions to racism. Done correctly, this interrogation can lead to a *sensibility* that allows one to take risks in and out of the classroom (Love, 2014).

Cochran-Smith (2003) explained that several steps can aid a person to interrogate their whiteness. The first is to listen or read stories of people of color and work to hear and believe that those experiences, although different, are as valid and accurate as their own. Secondly, to begin to tell the person's own racialized story, they will begin to verbalize the differences and similarities between the stories of their lives and those of people of color. Singleton and Linton (2006) asked participants in conversations about race to *remain in the moment* and focus on the present when someone tells a story that challenges whiteness. These techniques that are part of *Courageous Conversations about Race* (2006) that can help white teachers begin the journey of interrogating their whiteness.

Four Agreements of Courageous Conversations

1 *Stay Engaged*

- Be fully present in the conversation, even when discomfort arises.
- Engagement includes active listening and genuine participation.

2 *Experience Discomfort*

- Acknowledge that discomfort is a natural part of addressing race and racism.
- Growth occurs in spaces of vulnerability and tension.

3 *Speak Your Truth*

- Share your authentic experiences and perspectives.
- Avoid generalizations or speaking on behalf of others.

4 *Expect and Accept Non-closure*

- Understand that these conversations are ongoing and often do not resolve immediately.
- Commit to continued dialogue and reflection.

Six Conditions of Courageous Conversations

1 *Focus on Personal, Local, and Immediate*
   - Start by reflecting on personal experiences and connections to race.
   - Avoid abstract or theoretical discussions that can distract from the immediate impact of race on people's lives.

2 *Isolate Race*
   - Center the conversation on race explicitly, rather than diluting it with other forms of oppression or issues.

3 *Normalize the Presence of Race in Conversations*
   - Acknowledge that discussing race is essential, routine, and necessary.
   - Move beyond discomfort to create an environment where race can be discussed openly.

4 *Monitor Agreements, Conditions, and Establish Parameters*
   - Regularly check in on the group's adherence to the Four Agreements and ensure respectful dialogue.
   - Set clear guidelines for the discussion.

5 *Examine the Role and Presence of Whiteness*
   - Address how whiteness and privilege operate within systems, institutions, and personal interactions.
   - Be aware of how whiteness shapes perspectives and conversations.

6 *Speak to the Heart and Mind*
   - Engage participants emotionally and intellectually to foster deeper understanding and empathy.
   - Use storytelling, personal experiences, and data to create holistic discussions. (Singleton & Linton, 2006)

Interrogating whiteness requires intentionality, vulnerability, and a willingness to embrace discomfort as part of personal and professional growth (Keating, 1995). By confronting deeply ingrained ideologies, such as colorblindness or missionary mentalities, white teachers can begin to dismantle the power structures and biases that impede culturally responsive teaching and Caring Solidarity. The Four Agreements and Six Conditions of

Courageous Conversations provide a structured framework for this work, emphasizing the importance of staying engaged, speaking the truth, and accepting the ongoing nature of racial equity work. By listening to and valuing the stories of people of color, sharing their own racialized narratives, and remaining present in difficult moments, white educators can challenge their assumptions and disrupt inequitable practices. This transformative journey, though challenging, is essential for creating meaningful change in education and beyond.

Positive White Racial Identity

The long-term purpose of interrogating one's whiteness is to come to an understanding of a positive white racial identity. In 1990, psychologist and scholar Janet Helms created a scale to identify stages that will lead a person from the position of white supremacy to a positive white racial identity. Her stages are summarized, updated, and applied here:

- *Stage 1-Contact*: the ideology of color-blindness indicates this stage (Bonilla-Silva, 2010). The person may deny that racism still exists or declare that white supremacy is a *hoax* or a liberal talking point (Friedersdorf, 2019). This person may deny that attacks on people of color are racially based or that police shootings of unarmed Black people are the result of white supremacy or anti-Blackness.

  - They will defend the Confederate flag and Southern pride as *heritage, not hate*. They may even acknowledge that racism exists but will deny that it is a problem that must be dealt with. They may even call people who identify race as an issue as the *real racists* against white people. They will demand that immigrants show *gratitude* for being allowed to stay in the United States.

  - White people are socialized into these ideologies from childhood, and this can come from a lack of contact with people of color. Add right-wing media to the mix, and this person will be on a long journey to build a positive racial identity. They will be able to move if confronted with the reality of the lives of people of color. This can happen if a grandchild of color is born into the family or if confronted for their non-racism stance by others they respect in the family, at work, church, or in other social situations.

- *Stage 2-Disintegration*: Ideally, when white people enter colleges and universities, they are confronted with stories, theories, and a new set of explanations for the world that will contradict the *common sense* they have been given in conservative white communities. There are, of course, ways to avoid this uncomfortable experience through strategic choices in private schools, college classes, or attending conservative universities that shelter white students from these new understandings.

  - When the white student is confronted with a deeper understanding of race, its impact on communities, and the appalling history of colonization and slavery, they can sometimes feel guilt or shame at what their ancestors or other white people have done. This guilt can be redirected to action and anti-racism. If that happens, a white person can move to the next stage. However, if left without help, a person in this stage can find plenty of websites and political groups that will support them regressing and tell them that everything they learned is either useless, not accurate, or, worst of all, a conspiracy to commit *white genocide.*

- *Stage 3-Reintegration*: In this stage, white people blame others for the effects of white supremacist ideology. While the description of this stage seems like backsliding, it is an essential part of the process. This is the (un)enlightened, *yeah, but* person who endures in social situations and college classrooms. People in this stage are willing to accept that white people have racial privilege and that those who are not perceived as white have been oppressed. However, they are annoyed when told that privilege has enabled them and their families to succeed, even when a specific person is mediocre.

  - They are the people who bring up the repression of the Irish or their own immigrant stories to show that their journey has been just as difficult as slavery. They will also use deficit models for the achievement gap and may blame a *culture of poverty,* a lack of parent interaction, or a lack of *role models* as reasons why Black students do not do as well as white students in schools.

  - I hear this often from my Latino students, who blame a lack of parent involvement with children for a long list of perceived deficits. I spend a portion of my class time helping my students understand the structural oppression they are currently under. The Texas education system has quelled discussion of colonization's impact or the violence that Latino communities have endured for centuries under Spanish, then Anglo rule in Texas, and many just do not know that things have ever been any different from today. When they ask their parents and *Abuelos* about the topics we discuss, the stories flood forth, and they come to me wide-eyed, sharing the experiences of their ancestors. This is my constant reminder that white supremacy is all-pervasive in colonized spaces like Texas and is not predicated on white identity.

- *Stage 4-Pseudo-Independence*: This is the stage where people will begin to have a positive and realistic white racial identity. They are ready to look to people of color to explain racism and accept that explanation. They do not question the narratives of racism they encounter. They seek out advice and counsel from people of color on matters of race. They do not assume that white people know best or that they will always be the ones in charge.

  - However, this stage is still developmental in that people seek to be non-racist and expect people of color to do the work of undoing racism. They do not see themselves as part of the solution nor the problem, and may still engage in what West (2013) called *hipster racism* or casual white supremacy when in social situations or when trying to be humorous.

- *Stage 5-Immersion*: In this stage, a person actively works to be an anti-racist. They may call out friends who use *hipster racism* or join in conversations as a white ally. They may join groups seeking to stamp out racism or participate in protests against racial discrimination. They will speak up in classes and ally themselves with people of color. At this stage, they are still developing a positive white racial identity, but they are becoming more comfortable with the idea that they are part of the solution to white supremacist structures and anti-Blackness.

- *Stage 6-Autonomy*: This last stage is characterized by a clear understanding and acceptance of a positive white racial identity. There is a clear understanding of the history of colonization, slavery, and segregation in America and the world. There is a desire to know more about the histories of people who are not perceived as white. There is a desire and a capacity to read literature by people of color, and this person has real friendships across the color line. From here, a person can engage in relationships of solidarity (Harvey, 2007).

Helms's work, rooted in psychology, has profoundly influenced scholars looking to understand the creation of a positive white racial identity. While this theory helps to understand many white people's experiences, it is difficult to reconcile that white teachers are thrust in front of children before reaching a certain degree of maturity, which comes with the autonomy stage. Therein lies the dilemma for professors of education and district educational leaders. The stages take time, study, reflection, and experience, all things that are in short supply when they hire freshly minted teachers from undergraduate programs or, more difficult, trainees from a fast-track alternative certification program. However, Black students cannot wait for their teacher to come around to recognizing their humanity, so white teachers must engage in creating relationships of solidarity, even before they are fully formed as autonomous anti-racists (Harvey, 2007; Helms, 1990).

Things to Consider

As this chapter illustrates, white teachers who seek to enter relationships across the color line based on Caring Solidarity must interrogate their whiteness. As Matias (2016b) stated, "It is not enough that white teachers are trained to be masters of cultural competency of the *Other* [if they] are never asked to interrogate their own whiteness" (p. 199). To be successful, white teachers who cross the color line immerse themselves in the long process of understanding the privilege of being white in the United States (McIntosh, 1988/2001). To that end, here are some steps, not in order, that are needed to interrogate whiteness.

Count the cost. White people must ask themselves what they are willing to lose by confronting truths that others already know. Truthfully, white people are deceived from birth. Although less than 10 percent of the global population is white, they hold the vast majority of economic and political power—a dominance built on a history of violence and brutality. Despite this, white children are taught that they and their ancestors are innocent, as though the world naturally fell into its current state without exploitation or theft.

This narrative perpetuates the false belief that their ancestors, communities, and cultural heroes are free from blame for the systemic theft and dehumanization of others. Such deception creates an identity rooted in untruths, and addressing these lies requires acknowledging *alethophobia*—the fear of truth— as discussed in Chapter 2. The first step is to decide whether the process of unlearning these falsehoods will be too destabilizing to endure. For some, this fear becomes a barrier to seeking the truth. However, stepping out of the shadow of these lies offers liberation for those with the courage to face them. While the journey can be daunting and overwhelming, it is essential for ethical growth. Overcoming *alethophobia* allows for a deeper understanding and freedom from the burden of deception, paving the way for a more honest and just existence.

Study, read, and reflect. The work of authors of color who have explored whiteness would take a whole other book to list, but the references in this book are a good place to start. Other books by white authors (like DiAngelo, 2018; Michael, 2015; and Irving, 2014) who are also interrogating whiteness are also great resources.

Ask questions. Ask questions of adults, yes, but it is important to ask questions of students. Seldom do students get asked anything of consequence and the adults in their lives are loathed to admit they do not know something. Sample questions for kids are "Why is that?" "What do you think of that?" "How do you cope with that?" Questions that, on the surface, are not about race are often the beginning of wisdom about race. It will be less effective if teachers ask about specific things they have just read or the latest new theory. Stop: listen, and things will be revealed in ways that are only possible when the hearer is ready. Returning to Honneth's *recognition* from earlier in this chapter, when teachers ask open-ended questions of students, they engage in acts of recognition that affirm students' cognitive and moral capacities, fostering their self-confidence and self-respect. These questions signal that students' perspectives matter, challenging traditional hierarchies in which adults are positioned as the sole bearers of knowledge and students as passive recipients. Through this process, teachers and students engage in mutual discovery, where listening and openness become pathways to uncovering truths and fostering solidarity.

Seek learning and professional development. Conferences, workshops, museums, and classes all allow white people to engage in learning about race, racism, and the effects of white supremacy on all people. Seek out experts, read, reflect, and think about whiteness and how to diffuse its impact on everyone, but specifically students. I cannot emphasize enough that, in these times, we need to join and strengthen unions and professional organizations such as the National Council for the Social Studies (NCSS) and the National Science Teachers Association (NSTA). If we are to stand against the misinformation and outright dystopian world authoritarians conceive of, we must have national organizations with the strength to advocate and, if needed, defy state and local governments that seek to oppress our students. Conferences, workshops, books, and articles are available to members and can serve as a lifeline when it seems there is no refuge for truth and oppression is the default strategy.

Engage in dialogue, but avoid explaining everything YOU know. Teachers must engage in critical dialogues about race, whiteness, and white supremacy, but they will not learn if they are in *teacher or telling mode*. Like people reformed from anything, reformed white people can be annoying and ridiculous to people who have lived race consciousness their entire lives. Instead, amplify what people of color say in meetings. These meetings can be with parents, colleagues, or both. Remember that, as a white person seeking to enter into relationships of solidarity, it is essential to listen, learn, and be taught. However, and this is VERY important, do not merely repeat a phrase or idea and take it as a possession. Instead, include the speaker, as in, "I agree with what *NAME* said. I think it is important that we hear that." Then, you can repeat the idea and check to ensure it was right. "Is that what you meant, *NAME*?" Then talk with the person who was amplified to make sure they are OK with it. If not, do not repeat (Case, 2018).

Helms (1990) and Tatum (1992) stated that the goal of this act of discovery is the autonomy stage, in which a white person can transcend their own feelings and form alliances with people of color. This alliance is preceded by what Tatum referred to as *antiracist behaviors*.

> The positive feelings associated with this redefinition energize the person's efforts to confront racism and oppression in [their] daily life. Alliances with people of color can be more easily forged at this stage of development than previously because the person's antiracist behaviors and attitudes will be more consistently expressed. (Tatum, 1992, p. 17)

This alliance, or a relationship of solidarity, becomes possible through antiracist behaviors. However, achieving antiracist behaviors requires a white person to interrogate their whiteness by critically examining the privilege it affords. When undertaken with sincerity and determination, this process can be profoundly liberating, breaking free from the prison of whiteness. Freire (2014) articulated this journey toward liberation, stating:

Liberation is thus a childbirth and a painful one. The man or woman who emerges is a new person, viable only as the oppressor-oppressed contradiction is superseded by the humanization of all people. Or to put it another way, the solution of this contradiction is born in the labor which brings into the world this new being: no longer oppressor nor longer oppressed, but human in the process of achieving freedom. (p. 49)

Liberation from the segregation of the mind, heart, and body requires interrogation of oneself and one's societal position. For white teachers, this means confronting the constructed identity of whiteness and its implications. By embracing this introspection, they take an essential step toward transcending the oppressor-oppressed contradiction and toward building relationships of Caring Solidarity with students and communities of color. Such relationships, grounded in mutual respect and genuine understanding, become the foundation for humanization and collective freedom.

Grace as a Mindset Conduit to Action. Grace is not usually something written about in academic texts, but the concept is so crucial to the experience of solidarity that to ignore it would leave a gaping hole in the definition. Berry (2018) described grace as a "multidimensional phenomenon" (p. xvi), and the concept of grace is tied to sin, followed by forgiveness as a consequence of grace. As a matter of definition, grace is not earned but is given. The American concept of grace is primarily informed by the Protestant Church, which views grace as a central tenet of the faith.

In the late 1950s, Dr. Martin Luther King, Jr. (2017) explained that while the gift of grace is free, the need for grace is rooted in sin. King unapologetically names sins beyond what many white people would list, to include the progeny of white supremacist ideology and capitalism. The logic goes that a fallen humanity deserves death but can be redeemed through grace. The acceptance of grace is a central marker of the Protestant concept of Christianity:

And so, it boils down that we are sinners in need of God's redemptive power. We know truth, and yet we lie. We know how to be just, and yet we are unjust … We know the ways of peace, and yet we go to war. We have resources for great economic systems where there could be equitable distributions of wealth, and yet we monopolize and take it all for ourselves and forget about our brothers. And when we come to see ourselves, we discover that all of us are sinners. "All we like sheep have gone astray." (p. 384)

This need for grace because of the sin of white supremacy is deep. It has hampered the most powerful creed in human history: "All men are endowed by their creator with certain inalienable rights, among those are life, liberty, and the pursuit of happiness." It has made those words ring hollow from the moment they were penned by Thomas Jefferson, an enslaver, even as he argued to stop the slave trade through the first, unused draft of the Declaration of Independence. There has never been a time when white supremacy has not been the agreed-upon ideology of those in power.

To dismantle white supremacy, white people, and especially white teachers who want to succeed across the color line, will have to become the recipients of grace from their students and communities. This isn't easy in that many white people do not believe they need grace or forgiveness, as they themselves maintain that they have not done anything that needs forgiveness. They maintain that they never enslaved people, enforced segregation, or used racial slurs, so why would anyone need to forgive them?

To understand how to answer that question, we turn to a metaphor. If a man lives in a stolen house and lives off stolen money, he may not be a thief, but he still has a responsibility to the victims of that theft. White supremacy maintains that white people never have to apologize or admit wrong to their victims, as we have seen over the last decade from people in power. But those who wish to work in solidarity with communities of color must also work to dismantle the mental structures of white supremacy in addition to the societal ones. The mentality of white supremacy inhibits people from any work in solidarity. It pops up at times when it is neither welcomed nor expected. The mental frameworks, misinformation, prejudice, and miseducation are all difficult and time-consuming to unravel, but the work of solidarity demands a constant state of readiness to fight against whiteness embedded in every aspect of American life. To do so means that they also need the grace and forgiveness of those wounded by whiteness. Dr. King offered grace even amid his deep struggles against white supremacy:

> Western civilization, you've gone into the far country of imperialism and colonialism. You have trampled over more than one billion six hundred million of the people of the world. You have exploited them economically, you have dominated them politically, trampled over them, humiliated them, and segregated them … And there you are in this far country of oppression, trampling over your children. But western civilization, America,

you can come home and if you will come home, I will take you in. And I will bring the fatted calf, and I will cry out to all of the eternities, 'Hallelujah', for my nation has come home. (p. 390)

The good news for white teachers is that children have an enormous capacity for grace. Every day, they come to school full of hope and promise that the system will nurture them. If it does not today, they hope it will tomorrow. As Dr. King (2017) reminded his audience:

Grace has a very vital place in any life. It has a very vital place in understanding the whole predicament of [humanity] and the whole predicament of the universe, for you can never understand life until you understand the meaning of [grace]. (pp. 387–388)

Accepting grace from communities and the willingness to forgive oneself when mistakes or oversights cloud the work of building relationships of solidarity are also essential steps in building it (Harvey, 2007). This process will include missteps, mistakes, and downright mess-ups. The ability to keep trying when everything is crumbling is the true measure of commitment, endurance, and grace. It is the kind of grace that can lead to solidarity.

The Commitments—Commitment to Action

Once a white teacher has reconciled the shock of recognition, experienced love for students, moved into proximity with communities, interrogated their whiteness, and accepted grace from themselves and their communities, it is time to act. The actions that lead to relationships of Caring Solidarity are threefold: personal, structural, and societal.

Personal. A commitment to action must include an ongoing dedication to personal growth and learning. This journey begins with interrogating whiteness, a process that is neither passive nor abstract but profoundly transformative (Keating, 1995). When white teachers critically examine their racial identity, privilege, and positionality, they fundamentally alter their perception of the world. Prior to this interrogation, they navigate society with blinders on—seeing only a narrow, curated version of reality, one that has been structured to minimize their discomfort and mask systemic oppression. But during and after interrogation, the blinders fall away, revealing a wide and complex world where easy answers are not found.

Into this new world, white teachers plunge and act, regardless of understanding. They do not wait until they have a perfect understanding before moving forward; instead, they recognize that action and learning must happen simultaneously. The key difference post-interrogation is that their actions are now more informed, intentional, and reflective of the broader realities in which they teach. Without this critical self-examination, teachers risk perpetuating harm, even when acting with good intentions.

Freire's (2014) concept of praxis, the process of reflection and action, offers a necessary framework for how white educators should engage with their personal transformation. As Freire explained, "Knowledge emerges only through invention and re-invention, through the restless, impatient, continuing, hopeful inquiry human beings pursue in the world, with the world, and with each other" (p. 72). This underscores the necessity of an ongoing process—teachers must continually reflect on their positionality, learn from their students and communities, and take action in responsive and responsible ways. Personal action is not a one-time event but a continuous practice that reshapes both the individual teacher and the educational spaces they inhabit. Through this commitment, white educators move beyond allyship toward Caring Solidarity. They are not only aware of injustice but also actively work to dismantle it in their classrooms and communities. In this process, they do not seek to change students of color but rather to stand alongside them, learning from their experiences and working collaboratively toward a more just world. Ultimately, the teacher who commits to this journey does not simply *adapt to the world* as it is—they *reimagine it* and, through their actions, help to shape what it can become.

Structural. Teachers moving to Caring Solidarity must take their knowledge of their communities and themselves and stand against the anti-Black violence that inhabits so many schools where students of color attend. The systems of suspensions, hall sweeps, bull horns, police in the hallways, and generally oppressive environments are not part of a healthy school. Teachers can and do have control over the atmosphere of their buildings. As referred to in Chapter 2, the school-to-prison pipeline begins with the actions of individual teachers and administrators, and the white teacher moving toward Caring Solidarity will be the voice against the violence that is daily visited upon students. Taking that stand includes pushing against absurdity, like teachers carrying weapons in schools and zero-tolerance policies. It consists of a general demand to stop the creation of police states in schools where Black children come to learn.

It also involves creating spaces where students have a say in shaping the curriculum, ensuring it reflects their needs, interests, and lived experiences. This includes offering cultural studies courses designed to make all students feel seen, included, and valued. Schools should go beyond superficial celebrations like *culture day* to provide sessions and assemblies that foster critical dialogues about real-world issues that resonate with students' lives and empower them to effect change. For example, instead of defaulting to punitive measures like suspension, educators should ask why conflicts arise and explore restorative approaches that teach students how to reconcile, build relationships, and grow after disputes. This requires actively collecting and analyzing data in collaboration with students, then sharing the findings with teachers and the broader community to foster shared accountability and understanding. Build a school where everyone in the building, especially the students, knows, without a filament of doubt, that Black Lives Matter and that they matter to every person in that school (Dixson, 2018).

Societal. Any threat to white supremacy is perceived as a threat to the established social order—a social order rooted in the oppressive structures of colonialism, slavery, Jim Crow laws, mass incarceration, and the school-to-prison pipeline. These systems are not random but deliberately constructed to maintain inequities that benefit a few while marginalizing many. Confronting these entrenched systems requires courage, collective action, and a commitment to disrupting harmful norms. As civil rights icon John Lewis powerfully stated in a 2016 interview:

> We have been too quiet for too long. There comes a time when you have to say something, when you have to make a little noise, when you have to move your feet. This is the time. Now is the time to get in the way. The time to act is now. We will be silent no more. The time for silence is over. (Mettler, 2016)

This calls educators to take meaningful action within and beyond the school walls. Moving toward Caring Solidarity, grounded in recognition, love, proximity, interrogation, and grace, requires acknowledging that societal transformation cannot be confined to classroom efforts alone. It demands active participation in dismantling the systems of oppression that extend into every facet of society.

This work begins with recognition: understanding the historical and ongoing injustices that sustain racial inequities. It is guided by love: a commitment to seeing and affirming the humanity and dignity of all students. It is deepened by proximity: building authentic relationships with those most impacted by systemic injustices. It requires interrogation: questioning personal biases, institutional practices, and societal norms that uphold white supremacy. And it is sustained by grace: the humility to learn, make mistakes, and continue striving toward justice.

For white teachers to embody Caring Solidarity, they must embrace this call to action—not as an optional add-on but as a moral imperative. The fight for equity and justice is not limited to the classroom; it extends to every part of the community and society. As Lewis reminded us, the time to act is now, and the silence that has long enabled these systems must be broken.

In July 2016, Police Officer Jeronimo Yanez shot and killed Philando Castile, a kitchen supervisor at J. J. Hill Montessori School in St. Paul, Minnesota. Castile was in his car with his partner and child during a racially profiled traffic stop. Castile warned the officer that he had a legally purchased and licensed handgun. While sitting in his car, Castile was shot by Yanez with seven point-blank rounds, five of which entered his body and pierced his heart, while his girlfriend, Diamond Reynolds, broadcast the murder live on Facebook. The father of her child, bleeding and dying in her car, Reynolds, distraught, was the one arrested. The police dashboard camera recorded Reynolds' and Castile's four-year-old daughter attempting to comfort her and appealing to her mother, "Moma, please stop cussing and screaming 'cause I don't want you to get shooted" (Xiong & Stahl, 2017).

Later that month, at the annual meeting of the teachers' union, the American Federation of Teachers (AFT), teachers filed out of the building and marched through the capital city's streets and across the bridge to Minneapolis. "Today, we march to remember Philando Castile, our student, our co-worker, our union brother," Kimberly Colbert, secretary of the St. Paul Federation of Teachers, said in a statement (Delage, 2016). Recorded by bystanders and chronicled under the hashtag #Teachers4BlackLives, twenty-one teachers sat down in a circle, blocking a busy street in front of US Bank and Wells Fargo, Minnesota's largest banks, which finance private prisons and help cities pay off "police misconduct settlements" (Sawyer, 2016).

All twenty-one were arrested for blocking the Nicollet Mall in the center of the state's largest city.[1] This demonstrates action in Caring Solidarity with communities. None of these teachers were the same after being arrested for their acts of solidarity with the community. They had crossed into a new territory of solidarity. Freire (2014) explained,

> The revolution is made neither by the leaders for the people, nor by the people for the leaders, but by both acting together in unshakable solidarity. This solidarity is born only when the leaders witness to it by their humble, loving, and courageous encounter with the people. Not all men and women have sufficient courage for this encounter—but when they avoid encounters, they become inflexible and treat others as mere objects; instead of nurturing life, they kill life; instead of searching for life, they flee from it. And these are oppressor characteristics. (p. 129)

Caring solidarity requires that teachers demand more of themselves. Freire's revolution is in ourselves, our schools, and our communities. It will not be enough to revolutionize the classroom or even the school building if it stays there. Caring Solidarity is a commitment to students, communities, and then out into the world.

Discussion Questions from Chapter 6

1   How does Caring Solidarity address the structural challenges of racism and white supremacy in education? Discuss specific ways in which this framework might create systemic change in schools and classrooms.

2   What role do the mindset conduits of love and grace play in the journey toward Caring Solidarity? Reflect on how these conduits facilitate a deeper understanding and connection between teachers and their students of color.

3   The chapter emphasizes the importance of teachers interrogating their own whiteness. What practical steps can educators take to begin this process, and how might it impact their relationships with students and communities of color?

4   The idea of "shock of recognition" is a pivotal moment in the journey toward Caring Solidarity. How can teacher education programs prepare white teachers for this experience and support them in navigating its challenges?

5 Freire's concept of praxis—action and reflection—is integral to the commitment to action in the Caring Solidarity framework. How can teachers incorporate praxis into their everyday practices to create transformative classroom environments?

6 The chapter discusses proximity as a necessary step toward solidarity but acknowledges challenges like gentrification. How can teachers balance the need for proximity with an awareness of the potential harm caused by their presence in historically marginalized communities?

7 How does developing a positive white racial identity, as described by Helms, influence a teacher's ability to engage in relationships of Caring Solidarity? Reflect on how this development can impact their interactions with students, families, and communities of color.

Actionable Classroom Practices from Chapter 6

- **Engage in Proximity:**

  To build understanding and community with the places your school serves, you can use services and buy from businesses, attend cultural events, and frequent community spaces where your students and their families live.

- **Practice Active Recognition:**

  Consciously acknowledge each student's individuality and humanity by learning their names, interests, and cultural backgrounds without relying on stereotypes.

- **Use Shibboleths Respectfully:**

  Learn and use culturally relevant language or gestures your students identify with, ensuring you approach this practice with humility and respect. Listen to music they like. Read what they want to read.

- **Build Relationships Through Love:**

  Actively show care and commitment to your students by supporting their extracurricular activities, celebrating their achievements, and being present for them as individuals.

- **Cultivate Grace in Responses:**

  Respond to challenges or misunderstandings in the classroom with empathy and a willingness to interrogate your own actions and assumptions.

Note

1 Two of my former South High colleagues were arrested that day. They inspire me still.

7 Crossing the First Boundary
Entering Solidarity

If a white teacher has gone from the *shock of recognition* through love, moved into proximity, interrogates whiteness, and is moving to action through grace, they will likely be a good teacher across the color line. They may even be an award-winning teacher, and students may respond very well. Parents and the school board may be happy. A white teacher can spend their whole career outside of Caring Solidarity relationships with students and communities and still be a force for good in the world. But to be a force for change, dismantling the structures that have caused the oppression of Black students and communities will take more than the rewards that come from being good. The door the teacher must go through is the recognition, not just of the students, but of the need for solidarity. In some cases, this will mean rejecting conservative ideologies that have hampered solidarity, whether they come from religion, class, or the *common sense* of cultural or geographic locations.

American Conservatism as an ideology is the process of flattening facts and narratives to fit a simple frame of white male Christian supremacy. As a historical and ideological construct, it has simplified complex sociopolitical realities to reinforce a framework that centers and perpetuates the dominance of racialized patriarchy. This flattening of facts and narratives involves selectively emphasizing or omitting historical events, systemic inequities, and cultural contributions in ways that align with a Eurocentric and patriarchal worldview. By reducing diverse experiences and histories into a single, simplified narrative, this ideological process marginalizes alternative voices and perspectives, such as people of color, women, and non-Christian communities. This simplification seeks to maintain the sociopolitical status quo and legitimizes policies and cultural norms that reinforce structural inequalities, often under the pretense of preserving tradition or protecting freedoms. Through this lens, Conservatism functions as a tool to naturalize and sustain the systemic hierarchies that privilege white males while sidelining others. Because white supremacy demands that only the experiences of white people exist, Conservatives assume nothing on the other side of the color line is real. This is shown daily in Conservative media and in the ways that Black children are perceived as older than they are, more likely to be perceived as dangerous, and more likely to be the subject of deficit models about their homes and families, as explained in Chapters 2 and 3. It also explains why Conservatives continually downplay the role of racism and race in American society against all reason and historical literacy.

Conservatives assume that the only reason a white person would want to be in solidarity with Black people is that they are unable to find solidarity with anyone else, so they must be crazy, irrational, uninformed, or liars themselves. Because Conservative people do not believe that experiences outside of their own experiences are real, the common theme of discourse within Conservatism is that when people of color demand their rights, they are ungrateful, undeserving, crazy, stupid, or larcenous. Conservatism does not leave room for others to understand that justice and equality are the best way to live. They can only see their own power as the cornerstone of any relationship. When African American people march for #BlackLivesMatter, they are assumed by Conservatives to be paid actors because white Conservatives would not seriously consider that the lives of Black people are at risk, or if they are, that they are of value. That flattening process creates half-truths, untruths, mistruths, and outright lies, but all of them serve the purpose of propping up the order put in place to serve white males.

White teacher candidates and educators in multiracial schools are often ill-equipped to abandon their ideologies. However, those who aspire to build relationships of solidarity must recognize that embracing perspectives beyond their own white experiences provides a broader, more nuanced understanding of the world, their communities, and the schools they serve. Like a house of cards, once a few pillars of Conservative ideology fall, the whole contraption collapses and can be replaced with a more realistic and meaningful new reality. As teachers weigh their actions, privileges, and consequences, they must be ready to meet Conservatives' criticisms. They must decide that they need and want to be in solidarity with communities of color and reject the ideologies that would keep them from acting. White people who act in solidarity with communities of color are especially vilified, as will be discussed in Chapter 8.

However, if a teacher decides to step through that door and move toward Caring Solidarity, the experience has the potential to transform their identity and revolutionize their approach to teaching. Paulo Freire (2014) captured this transformative potential when he stated:

> At a certain point in their existential experience, under certain historical conditions, these leaders [teachers in this case] renounce the class to which they belong and join the oppressed in an act of true solidarity (or so one would hope). Whether or not this adherence results from a scientific analysis of reality, it represents (when authentic) an act of love and true commitment. (p. 163)

When applied to the concept of identifying the need for solidarity, Freire challenged white teachers to consciously and rationally align themselves in solidarity with marginalized or oppressed communities and to directly engage with their students' lived experiences and realities. By doing so, the teachers affirm their commitment to addressing the inequities their students face.

Extending this idea to schools, Freire's concept implies that students, as emerging leaders within educational spaces, require solidarity from their teachers. For white teachers, achieving solidarity is essential to their professional effectiveness and their own humanization—a humanization that whiteness and Conservatism constrict through their detachment from authentic relationships. Teachers need solidarity to complete the humanization that white supremacy strips away. Both need each other, and both benefit from the relationship.

Identifying Solidarity as a Need: Identity and the Door to Caring Solidarity

Becoming a teacher means adopting and creating a *teacher* identity and viewing it as central. Identity is not a fixed condition but rather an ongoing dialectical process occurring between the individual (internal states) and other people (external conditions) (Danielewicz, 2001). This dynamic of social identification is one routine that constitutes identity. Others have a role in making that identity: "It is not enough to assert an identity. That identity must also be validated by those with whom we have dealings" (Jenkins, as quoted in Danielewicz, 2001, p. 10).

As explained in Chapter 6, teacher identity is shaped by their capacity to build solidarity with students, their theoretical understanding of why they teach in a particular context, and their pedagogy, which reflects both their self-image as educators and their personal commitments (Danielewicz, 2001). The metaphor of the door allows for an image of understanding that solidarity with students and communities is fundamental to effective teaching across the color line. The decision to go through the door and live on the other side is an ethical one and will involve creating an identity as an educator of Black children.

Danielewicz (2001) and Britzman (2003) both argued that teaching is a process of becoming. "Education is about growth and transformation, not only of culture, but of persons too" (Danielewicz, 2001, p. 1). To effectively teach children across the color line requires a new way of thinking about students and the teacher's role in their lives. With all of these factors considered, it is reasonable to ask what motivates a white person to become a teacher who crosses these lines of race and class. Duncan-Andrade (2007) described the commitment of teachers he worked with:

> They said that they teach because they believe their students, specifically low-income children of color, are the group most likely to change the world. They explained this belief by saying that the children most disenfranchised from society are the ones with the least to lose, and thus are the most likely to be willing to take the risks necessary to change a society. (p. 625)

To Danielewicz, teachers are constantly in the process of identity formation. While teachers adopt an identity at the beginning of their teaching career as *teacher*, the definition of what teacher means continues to sharpen and develop over time. Great teachers are aware of this process and are open to it. They embrace the learning and growth that occur throughout their teaching lifetime. Danielewicz explained, "Becoming a teacher means an individual must adopt an identity as such," and the process is "so complicated and deep, [because it] involves the self" (p. 9).

The identity of a white teacher in a multiracial classroom is all of this and more. According to Duncan-Andrade (2007), there are five pillars of successful teaching across the color line:

1 Critically conscious purpose, where teachers define their motives for teaching based on the needs of the community.
2 Duty, where teachers have made a commitment to living in and serving the community and their students.
3 Preparation, where teachers are hard at work making curriculum relevant and rigorous for students and constantly reflecting on their practice.
4 "Socratic sensibility," the practice of co-learning with students and never fearing to ask, "Why?" Teachers with this sensibility strike "a delicate balance between confidence in their ability as teachers and frequent self-critique" (p. 632).
5 Trust, the result of teachers sometimes standing in solidarity with students in opposition to the institutions of the school and even the community at large.

The motivation should be that the teacher sees the situation of their students in the school and society, and decides that they will throw their lot in with their new communities. Identifying solidarity as a need is often a way to resolve conflict within the teacher. Teachers who are searching for solutions as to why their classes are not working as they want them to, why communities are not embracing them the way that they feel they need, or just a general sense that something in their identity as a teacher is not lining up with what they see at school and in the community. Honneth (1995) explained:

> Since, within the framework of an ethically established relationship of mutual recognition, subjects are always learning something more about their particular identity, and since, in each case, it is a new dimension of their selves that they see confirmed thereby, they must once again leave, by means of conflict, the stage of ethical life they have reached, in order to achieve the recognition of a more demanding form of their individuality. (p. 17)

That "more demanding form" of identity is one where solidarity is sought in and out of the classroom. Once that threshold has been crossed, the teacher will be asked to do more than many are comfortable or able to do. The teacher who recognizes the need for solidarity will see the world differently, and the world will perceive them differently as well.

Empathy: The First Level of Solidarity

As the model indicates, there is a region of empathy after passing through the door to move toward Caring Solidarity. Nieto (2006) explained that empathy and solidarity are not "simply sentimental emotions." She explained, "For teachers who think deeply about their work, solidarity and empathy mean having genuine respect for their students' identities—including their language and culture—as well as high expectations and great admiration for them" (p. 466). Empathy is a form of solidarity, but it is also the limit of what many people can conjure when thinking about or entering into solidarity (Warren, 2013). Empathy is an intense feeling of mutuality with a person who suffers. It can be temporary and contextual. It can involve helping, raising money, feeding or housing, or expressing support in a forum that matters to the victims and the empathizer. Empathy is situational and meaningful, and it is a crucial step toward Caring Solidarity relationships.

Crossing that region of empathy takes time and is an individual experience. Empathy is a deeper emotional response to conditions than is sympathy. Sympathy is when one person sees a tragedy and feels sorry for another person. They are vibrating on the same wavelength, emotionally. That person feels bad, and the sympathetic person feels sorry for them, but there is never an expectation that the sympathetic person will do anything personally to relieve that suffering. There are mechanisms for people to act in sympathy. For example, relief organizations depend upon sympathy to help victims of natural and human-made disasters. People can be sympathetic to many things at once. They can be sympathetic to migrants coming to the United States in search of a better life and to the victims of an earthquake far away. No person can do everything about every problem, so sympathy is a good emotion that allows people to feel the suffering of others they will never know (Masoom, 2017). It is not inconsistent nor shallow to be sympathetic to many things at once that may be distant from a person's experience. Empathy, on the other hand, is much more active. Katsarou et al. (2010) explained:

> Teachers need to develop empathy and see the strengths and assets of the students and communities in which they teach. Their classrooms must be in

and of the community, blurring the boundaries between who teaches and who learns and the borders between schools and neighborhoods. It is critical that they are able to recognize the structural forces that impact their students' lives and have the sense that they are in a position to act upon them. (p. 152)

Empathy involves doing something to relieve the suffering of those in need. It is much closer and more personal. For example, if a child is hurt in a country thousands of miles away, an ethical, caring person would feel sympathy and hope that someone could help that child. If a child is hurt on the street in view of others, the ethical, caring thing to do would be to get that child the necessary care and healing.

To simply look and feel sympathy in that second scenario, then walk away, would not be the act of a caring person but rather that of an unethical monster. So, empathy has as much to do with the ability to do something as with the desire to do so. Empathy can also be a reason for travel. A person may go where there is pain and help. That is also a form of empathy, but action and proximity to the issue are important distinctions between sympathy and empathy. A critical distinction between sympathy and empathy is the desire to act or at least think about how to act.

While empathy is a *form* of solidarity, it is often confused with full solidarity. Warren (2018) described teachers who practice empathy:

Empathy is the piece of the student-teacher interaction puzzle that connects what a teacher knows or thinks about students and families to what [they] actually [*do*] when negotiating appropriate responses to students' needs, or when the teacher is arranging learning experiences for students. (p. 171)

Warren explained that an effective way to describe and create empathy in teachers is to use the concept of perspective-taking (Warren, 2018). Perspective-taking is an exercise that allows a person to describe the frames through which they view a particular phenomenon. Are they looking at it as *imagine self* (IS) or as *imagine other* (IO)?

Imagine self (IS) is when an observer responds to a target's situation or condition based on personal experience/preference, or a vision/ construction of the observer's own self in the target's shoes. On the contrary, *imagine other* (IO) is when an observer responds to a target's situation based on knowledge of the target's personal experience/ preference in the moment, if the target were in a position to respond to their own circumstance … This dimension of perspective-taking, thus, leads the observer to respond in a way the target would respond to her or his circumstance if this individual had the power or wherewithal to respond in [their] own favor. (p. 174)

As Warren described, the person using the IO perspective looks at situations as the person *impacted* or the *target*. This encourages a white teacher to see the curriculum, the school structures, and even the school building through the lens of another person, specifically the teacher's African American students. Truthfully, this change in perspective is also necessary for building empathy and a crucial step to creating solidarity with students and communities. As Warren explained:

The IO form of perspective taking acknowledges the range of external social and cultural variables that may be determining the student's academic performance. The teacher engaged in the IO form of perspective taking more often first looks at [their] own failures in the initial response to the academic interaction with the student, and the role of the institution for contributing to the student's academic vulnerability. (p. 174)

It is vital to avoid a false empathy. False empathy comes when someone assumes that these imagined perspectives are the actual perspectives of others. Truthfully, we can never completely understand other people, even those with whom we are most intimate. Also, the power structures of white privilege require constant interrogation as one travels the road toward Caring Solidarity. DiAngelo (2018) framed the issue of identity and of false empathy:

I repeat: stopping our racist patterns must be more important than working to convince others that we don't have them. We do have them, and people of color already know we have them; our efforts to prove otherwise are not convincing. An honest accounting of these patterns is no small task given the power of white fragility and white solidarity, but it is necessary. (p. 129)

There are always gaps, and learning will always be needed, but gaining others' perspectives allows teachers to empathize with students.

False empathy comes from teachers who hold deficit models of their students of color. The teacher who looks at their students as a bundle of *if onlys* (if only the parents … or if only the community wasn't so … or if only they had … or hadn't …) then there is no ability to build relationships of solidarity. As Katsarou et al. (2010) found with their teacher candidates:

> Seeing their students only as a laundry-list of problems, these educators are unable to look past students' more challenging behavior, making meaningful and reciprocal relationships impossible. Unable to connect to their students, their efforts at classroom management and instruction fail, and they, in turn, blame their students for what has ultimately stemmed from their negative and stereotyped views of their students. Until this pattern is addressed, teaching for social justice is an impossible hope for such candidates. (p. 140)

There are teachers who will assume that they are in solidarity because they are empathetic to students' needs and will even provide for them at times, but false empathy comes from a place of privilege and an unwillingness to see the world differently.

This often comes into play when teachers lower expectations because of perceived differences, such as race or culture. Sometimes, teachers assume that because students are Black, or from a specific *neighborhood,* or have a language difference, they are not able to be challenged. These low expectations are couched in the language of caring but are actually *false caring* and *false empathy.*

Many white teachers get lost in empathy. Even if a teacher is not in false empathy but genuine empathy, it can be overwhelming to constantly move from one crisis to another, as some teachers do. It is strenuous work to be empathic and to show empathy with students who are under threat and in systems that literally devalue their lives. The psychic energy and emotional labor of empathizing can even cause teachers to leave the profession (Herman et al., 2017).

Entering into empathy should trouble one's understanding of the world, as one empathetic act uncovers the need for more empathy in places where people do not know it is needed. Utt and Tochluk (2016) explained that when white teacher candidates begin the journey of uncovering whiteness and move into empathy with people of color, they can experience some problematic behaviors and can become culturally unmoored:

When white teachers cannot hold this tension of recognizing one's connection to whiteness and white culture while working to regain an ethnic or supportive cultural grounding, they enact a number of troubling behaviors:

1 Distancing from white culture: Altering dress, manner, or behavior in ways that indicate a lack of self-acceptance and a wish to be something other than white.

2 Distancing from white people: Decreasing ability to effectively encourage and support other white faculty to join efforts for racial justice.

3 Over-identifying with people of color: Appreciating the suggestion that one is not really white and distancing from white identity and the responsibility to interrogate how white privilege affects one's attitudes and behavior.

4 Over-identifying with European roots: Disavowing one's relationship to being white, leading to statements claiming that one is not part of white culture. There is, thus, less recognition regarding how white culture, whiteness, and privilege manifest in one's behavior. (p. 11)

Each of these behaviors results not from genuine empathy or solidarity but *false empathy*, as Delgado (1996) described. Delgado explored this concept through a counternarrative conversation discussing the concepts of justice and empathy (Solorzano & Yosso, 2002). Delgado did a thought experiment about building a perfect computer to mete out justice. He then surmised that this perfect machine and would be unacceptable to society because it would not delineate perpetrators by race. He explained that *false empathy* is the belief that you would like a perfect computer, but in the end, if it gave true justice to everyone, white people would assume that it was unfair because it would be equal. In this experiment, Delgado illustrated the predicament of false empathy. People are willing to engage in empathy as long as it does not cost them, even if it is measured and distributed dispassionately and equally. He contended that white people see the injustice of unequal justice AS justice and justice handed out equally as injustice, because of false empathy.

Toxic Empathy

Toxic empathy refers to a state where an individual's empathetic response to others becomes excessive or unregulated, causing harm to their well-being or relationships. Unlike healthy empathy, which fosters understanding and connection, toxic empathy leads to emotional overwhelm, blurred boundaries, and unhealthy patterns of interaction. For example, over-identifying with another's emotions can cause a person to absorb others' pain, making it difficult to differentiate their feelings from those they are empathizing with (Baron-Cohen, 2022). While empathy is crucial for fostering compassion and relationships, its unchecked application can result in emotional distress, burnout, and even codependency (McLaren, 2013).

One key characteristic of toxic empathy is *compassion fatigue*, where continuously absorbing others' emotions depletes an individual's emotional resources. This phenomenon is commonly observed among caregivers, educators, and healthcare professionals exposed to others' struggles over prolonged periods. Figley (2015) explained that constant exposure to emotional pain without proper boundaries can lead to secondary traumatic stress, a hallmark of compassion fatigue. When an individual cannot separate their emotional experience from someone else's, they may neglect their own needs, sacrificing self-care in the name of helping others (Singer & Klimecki, 2014). This overextension can create a cycle where the empathizer becomes overwhelmed and unable to provide adequate support.

Toxic empathy can also enable harmful behaviors in others. Individuals may support destructive actions by prioritizing someone else's feelings or avoiding conflict, inadvertently reinforcing unhealthy dynamics (Brown, 2023). For example, a person might avoid addressing a friend's harmful behavior out of fear of causing emotional discomfort. This tendency to *over-help* can stifle growth and accountability for both parties. McLaren (2013) highlighted the importance of maintaining boundaries, suggesting that empathy is not about solving others' problems or taking on their emotional burdens but rather about being present and supportive in ways that foster mutual growth.

To mitigate toxic empathy, it is crucial to cultivate healthy empathetic practices. These practices involve setting clear boundaries, regulating emotional responses, and balancing empathy with self-care (Singer & Klimecki, 2014). By recognizing the signs of toxic empathy, such as emotional overwhelm and neglect of personal needs, teachers can take steps to protect their own well-being while still effectively supporting their students.

The Differences Between Empathy, Toxic or Otherwise, and Caring Solidarity

The key differences between *toxic empathy* and *Caring Solidarity* lie in their focus, intent, and outcomes in relationships. Toxic empathy involves over-identifying with another's emotions to the point of personal harm or enabling unproductive behaviors. The empathizer absorbs the other person's struggles as their own, prioritizing emotional support without boundaries or accountability (Baron-Cohen, 2022). In contrast, Caring Solidarity emphasizes relational balance, responsibility, and empowerment. Rooted in mutual respect, it fosters personal growth and transformation for both the individual offering support and the one receiving it.

In toxic empathy, boundaries are often weak or nonexistent, leading to emotional overwhelm and burnout for the empathizer. Constantly absorbing others' emotions without self-regulation can harm both parties (Singer & Klimecki, 2014). On the other hand, Caring Solidarity maintains healthy boundaries that sustain support without martyrdom. Emotional regulation is central, ensuring the empathizer engages deeply while preserving their well-being. This balance creates a foundation for support that is both intentional and sustainable.

Toxic empathy often avoids confronting harmful behaviors or patterns for fear of causing emotional discomfort, inadvertently enabling those behaviors (Brown, 2023). Responsibility is an essential element in Caring Solidarity. It includes a willingness to address difficult issues as an act of care, promoting the other person's growth and agency. This approach encourages individuals to take responsibility for their own transformation rather than relying solely on emotional support.

Caring Solidarity incorporates a *systemic awareness* that toxic empathy lacks. While empathy tends to focus solely on the emotions and needs of the individual, Caring Solidarity is attuned to broader systemic and structural factors that influence their experience. By integrating advocacy and action into relational support, Caring Solidarity not only nurtures individuals but also challenges systemic injustices, promoting equity and meaningful change.

While empathy is undoubtedly a crucial attribute of good teaching and moral living, the expectation that one can maintain shallow empathy for an entire career is unreasonable. More often, empathy can be sustained for a while, sometimes even years. But eventually, it fades, sending white teachers back through the door, away from solidarity because of *those kids*. At that point, the long undoing of all the work that led them there is seldom evident to the person it is happening to. There is exhaustion, hopelessness, and defeat.

However, if the white teacher continues in their journey and moves beyond empathy to the most challenging obstacle, solidarity, then there is a greater purpose that leads to a more sustainable way to teach. It involves deep self-analysis and shedding solidarity with whiteness. Through that barrier lies a new way to be with students. It is a new way to be in communities. Caring Solidarity brings white teachers to their students and families, but it is not automatic, safe, or easy. It requires a shift in thinking, a shift in the soul.

Discussion Questions from Chapter 7

1   How does the chapter differentiate between empathy and solidarity? Reflect on a time when you've acted empathetically. Could this have been transformed into an act of solidarity? What additional steps would have been required?

2   The chapter discusses the process of forming a teacher identity, emphasizing bonds with students and communities. What role does solidarity play in shaping a teacher's identity? How might a teacher's willingness to engage in solidarity impact their relationships with students and their effectiveness in the classroom?

3   How does American Conservatism, as described in the chapter, flatten narratives and maintain systems of white supremacy? In what ways might this influence how white teachers view their students, curriculum, and communities?

4   The chapter identifies barriers white teachers face when crossing into solidarity, such as false empathy and ingrained Conservative ideologies. Why might these barriers be particularly challenging for educators? How can teacher preparation programs address these obstacles?

5   Caring Solidarity requires addressing power dynamics and systemic inequities in schools. Based on the chapter, how can white teachers engage with these systemic issues without perpetuating paternalistic attitudes or false empathy?

6   How can teachers prepare for the emotional and professional challenges of maintaining Caring Solidarity? What strategies might support their growth and resilience in this process?

Actionable Classroom Practices from Chapter 7

- **Create a Community Expert Series:**

  Invite members of the local community—especially people of color and those from marginalized groups—to share their expertise, histories, and experiences with the class, fostering connections between the classroom and the surrounding community.

- **Establish a Collaborative Classroom Governance Model:**

  Involve students in creating classroom rules and norms that prioritize equity, respect, and inclusion. Let students lead discussions on what a fair and just learning environment looks like and hold regular reflections on these practices.

- **Implement Restorative Dialogue Practices:**

  Instead of traditional punitive measures, use restorative conversations to address conflicts (Valenzuela, 2023). Create space for students to share their feelings and collaborate on solutions, emphasizing accountability and community healing.

  https://www.edutopia.org/article/using-restorative-conversations-mend-relationships-schools/

- **Integrate Activist and Change-Maker Models:**

  Teach students about historical and contemporary figures who exemplify solidarity and activism. Discuss their strategies and the systems they worked to dismantle oppressive structures and challenge students to identify ways they can emulate this work in their own contexts.

  https://www.edutopia.org/article/using-restorative-conversations-mend-relationships-schools/

8 Transference of Solidarity and Entering New Territories

Looking at the model, the dark, black line in the middle reads "*Transference of Solidarity.*" The line is thick with a narrow opening because transferring solidarity is an obstacle few are willing to overcome, and even fewer are equipped. This is the most controversial of the ideas outlined in the model. Transference of solidarity is the contention that committed white teachers, who have done the work from recognition to empathy, can transfer solidarity from whiteness to their Black students and communities, ending their solidarity with the privilege and white normativity that whiteness exhibits.

Because of our racialized society, white people will always be perceived as white and will always hold their privilege, no matter their place, work, or intentions. However, a positive white racial identity can produce a person who is able to use the privilege and the power structures that perpetuate white success and progress, transferring them toward communities and students of color. Transference of solidarity requires a positive racial identity to avoid false empathy or a fake identity where a person denies who they are and puts on solidarity like a cloak. True transference comes from a state of understanding and self-awareness, realistically assessing the need for solidarity to successfully live and work across the color line.

Whiteness Is Property

Whiteness is a construct created by white people to decide who is *in* and who is *out*. Being in the *in-crowd* has many advantages. Therefore, the idea of leaving that safe and privileged position is a hard one for white people even to imagine. Lipsitz (2006) explained that white people have an *investment* in whiteness. He described whiteness as perceived as a highly prized *normal,* and history has shown that white people are more invested in whiteness than they are in justice or democracy (Anderson, 2017).

Scholars contend that whiteness is property, a tangible means of exchange (Harris, 1993). *Cheryl I. Harris* is a prominent legal scholar and professor at UCLA, known for her groundbreaking work in Critical Race Theory (CRT). In her essay, *Whiteness as Property* (1993), Harris told the story of her grandmother, who identified as Black, left Mississippi in the 1930s, and boldly took a position at a major retailer in Chicago. There, she passed as a white woman and Harris explored the consequences of the life her grandmother led:

> Every day, my grandmother rose from her bed in her house in a Black enclave on the south side of Chicago, sent her children off to a Black school, boarded a bus full of Black passengers, and rode to work. No one at her job ever asked if she was Black; the question was unthinkable. By virtue of the employment practices of the "fine establishment" in which she worked, she could not have been. Catering to the upper-middle class, understated tastes required that Blacks not be allowed. (p. 1711)

Her grandmother had to suppress herself and accept the racism that was not directed at her because of assumed affiliation, but was part of the solidarity that comes from membership in the *white alliance.* While the psychological costs were high, Harris explained the benefits that came to a person who could move across the color line.

> Becoming white meant gaining access to a whole set of public and private privileges that materially and permanently guaranteed basic subsistence needs and, therefore, survival. Becoming white increased the possibility of controlling critical aspects of one's life rather than being the object of others' domination. (p. 1713)

These benefits of solidarity with whiteness are intentionally made invisible to white people who live in segregated suburban enclaves but are often expressly taught in places where Black and white people live in close proximity. Rothstein (2013; 2017) reminded America that in hyper-segregated cities like Chicago, these lines are clear and intentional, but even in smaller cities like San Antonio, Minneapolis, Austin, or Cincinnati, *good* and *bad* neighborhoods are delineated along racial lines, making the color line an actual geographic boundary.

Harris examined how that line has become normalized for white people. She observed, "Whites have come to expect and rely on these benefits, and over time, these expectations have been affirmed, legitimated, and protected by the law" (p. 1713). The *white hegemonic alliance* has enabled white people to avoid seeing the world as it is, as white people have made it (Allen, 2009). However, for white teachers to be in Caring Solidarity with students and communities who do not identify, or are not identified, as white, there must be an alternative.

The White Alliance and Solidarity with Whiteness

The transition from solidarity with whiteness to solidarity with Black students and communities is likely to unsettle colleagues, families, and friends. Many will attempt to correct those who distance themselves from behaviors aligned with whiteness and instead align with individuals whom their social circles may deem unworthy of attention, let alone resources. These efforts often manifest as attacks on the concept of solidarity itself, questioning its motives and working to reinforce the structures a teacher seeks to challenge. To explore how to break solidarity with whiteness and redirect it toward students of color, this chapter first revisits the foundational concept of whiteness.

As discussed throughout this book, whiteness is not a neutral descriptor; it is a construct rooted in power and privilege, situated at the intersection of white normativity and white dominance. The question of how white people can live morally within a world designed for their comfort is particularly pressing for white teachers working across the color line. European colonialism has shaped a global reality in which whiteness remains a desired and privileged trait, perpetuating inequities that educators must confront to foster genuine solidarity with their students. Samuel P. Huntington, a scholar and director of Harvard's Center for International Affairs, captured a haunting reality in his 1996 book, *The Clash of Civilizations and the Remaking of World Order*. He addressed the truths that white people push aside to maintain their imaginary worlds. He wrote:

> The West won the world not by the superiority of its ideas or values or religion (to which few members of other civilizations were converted) but

rather by its superiority in applying organized violence. Westerners often forget this fact; non-Westerners never do. (p. 51)

This quote encapsulates Huntington's examination of how power dynamics shaped the global order. It highlights the tension between how power is acquired and how it is justified. It underscores the stark difference in perception between Western and non-Western societies regarding the sources of Western dominance.

When discussing whiteness as a global concept, Huntington's analysis moves beyond debates about *white privilege*. It situates the position of white people in America within its rightful context: as colonizers on stolen land. While Huntington primarily refers to relations between Western nations and their former colonies in Asia and Africa, the lesson resonates deeply with the roots of racial tension in the United States. The founders, electorate, oligarchs, and general population have never fully confronted the realities of slavery, genocide, segregation, and imperialism—the bedrock upon which the *home of the free* was built.

After the shooting on *August 3, 2019*, at an El Paso, Texas, Walmart, Princeton professor Eddie Glaude expressed his outrage in an emotional and poignant statement on MSNBC cable news that shook the whole panel of white commentators. A gunman had opened fire, killing *twenty-three people* and injuring *twenty-two others* in an act of domestic terror. The perpetrator, a 21-year-old white male, drove from Allen, Texas, to El Paso and posted a manifesto online expressing anti-immigrant and racist views, specifically targeting Latino people. The attack is one of the deadliest mass shootings in modern US history and highlighted the ongoing issues of white supremacist ideology, gun violence, and hate crimes in the country (Scott, 2019). Dr. Claude explained:

America is not unique in its sins as a country. We are not unique in our evils, to be honest with you. I think where we may be singular, however, is in our refusal to acknowledge those sins. The legends and myths we tell about our inherent goodness serve to hide, cover, and conceal the truth, allowing us to maintain a willful ignorance that protects our innocence. When the Tea Party was happening, people—pundits especially—kept saying, "Oh, it's just about economic populism; it's not about race." But people knew. Social scientists were already writing that what was driving the Tea Party were anxieties about demographic shifts. The country was changing. They were seeing racially ambiguous babies on Cheerios commercials. The country wasn't quite feeling like it was a white nation anymore. People were screaming from the top of their lungs, "This is not just simply economic populism; this is the ugly underbelly of the country."

Emotionally, he had had enough of the ridiculous arguments over these horrors' causes.

Here's the thing—and I'll take the hit for saying this: there are communities that have had to bear the brunt of America confronting—white Americans, confronting the danger of their innocence. It happens every generation. Somehow, we keep going through this cycle of asking, "Oh my God, is this who we are?"

He continued,

It's easy for us to place it all on Donald Trump's shoulders. It's easy to place Pittsburgh, Charlottesville, and El Paso on his shoulders. But this is us. If we're going to get past this, we can't blame it on him. He is a manifestation of the ugliness within us … Either we are going to change, or we are going to go through this cycle again and again. Babies will grow up without mothers and fathers, uncles and aunts, friends—all while we're still trying to convince white folk to leave behind a history that will maybe, just maybe, they'll embrace a history that could finally set them free from being white.

The white American's need to be superior—always correct, the prettiest, the smartest, the richest, and everything else tied to the identity of whiteness in America—is literally killing both Americans and America itself. The myths we tell ourselves of freedom, justice, and equality disintegrate when confronted with the cold reality of history and data. Yet, we persist in the illusion that we can move forward and that things will improve without the *shock of recognition* that we, white people, are the invaders—and that *we* have the power to break this cycle of violence. Without this reckoning, we remain trapped in a destructive pattern, perpetuating harm to ourselves and the ideals we claim to uphold.

Frantz Fanon, author of *The Wretched of the Earth* (1961/2004), argued that the goal of colonization goes beyond conquering land or bodies; it seeks to conquer the mind. Colonialism convinces the colonized that the colonizer's culture is superior—the pinnacle of human achievement and perfection. This imposed desire for assimilation has had devastating effects on civilizations, corrupting not only the colonized but also deforming the humanity of the colonizer. In striving to assert superiority, the colonizer adopts a false persona, elevating themselves above others. This false consciousness is perpetuated across generations, poisoning cultures and eroding both humanity and the possibility of a positive identity. Most white people are casually able to live with the construct of whiteness and do all that they can to avoid thinking about the fact that their success stems directly from colonization, genocide, and racist systems. They go to work, enjoy the fruits of their labor, and do not question why their life is the way it is. This whiteness is pervasive across cultures, geography, and nations. Because of its power of normalcy, it is often hard for white people to see it.

Like the fish that do not know what water is, white people assume that their lives are the ones they are supposed to live, and to an extent, they are correct. It is the life each person throughout the world should live. It is one where people are valued, wealth is shared, police are polite, youthful mistakes are forgiven, and excellence is elevated. The assumption of goodness is like a shield against any action, giving cover when people do terrible things. White people who do Nazi salutes, or dress in racist costumes or blackface, are assumed to be good people who made a mistake or were ignorant of the historical context of their actions. Or, more likely, they deny it even happened at all, and they will claim that the person condemning the action is biased or racist and is targeting them.

It is also a world where a person in a position of authority is assumed to be there because of personal achievement. Unfortunately, that is not the world that most people of color experience. Instead, from outside of whiteness, the hoarding of riches and privilege is an affront to the promises of democracy that are broadcast from whiteness' walled fortress. These two worlds on one planet play out in extremes in schools and in higher education. Professors of color, women, and people from marginalized groups are routinely dismissed by white students and members of legislative bodies as DEI hires.

DEI, which stands for Diversity, Equity, and Inclusion, was a designation of commitment to equitable practices in academia and industry. However, white supremacists of all stripes have taken it to mean that someone is not qualified for their position. This dismissal of the credentials comes at a time when white people are seeing more and more achievements of people of color. Black millionaires in industry and entertainment are an affront to those white people who are mired in poverty. A Black president was an affront to their construct of who deserved to be their leader. Black presidents of universities have been railroaded out of their positions for being insufficiently deferential to white supremacists in the US Senate (Alfonseca, 2024). Ultimately, all of this stems from the existential fears of white people who neglected their education or their skills. Rather than blame the billionaires who hoard money and power, genuinely taking opportunities from ordinary people, they blame highly educated and skilled people of color, who they believe are inherently lesser, as having stolen their prosperity from them. Meanwhile, the real thieves live lavishly on the backs of these poor people, distracting them with stories of how the Black and Brown people have wronged them.

Allen (2009) explained that whiteness and its continued power derive from a unity of purpose that white people are initiated into early. He referred to it as the *white hegemonic alliance*. He argued that class differences between white groups do exist, but they do not substantially affect the behaviors white people exhibit when it comes to power relations, economics, and culture. For instance, poor white people overwhelmingly vote for wealthy white men to hold offices with little promise that these men will do anything to improve their lives. White women vote for white men and women who repeatedly promise to limit women's rights, hurt them economically, and keep their children from health care and education. Wealthy white people have been able to convince poor white people that it is in their best interests to keep the wealthy in power.

The *white hegemonic alliance* makes room for many different expressions of whiteness. Whiteness allows for wealth, poverty, addiction, violence, indolence, and orientations of many kinds under the big tent of whiteness, but these extensions are not available to people of color. Allen's concept of the *white hegemonic alliance* allows for a form of solidarity that asks little of the in-group and is similar to the second version of Bayertz's solidarity, as explained in Chapter 5. This type of unquestioned solidarity does not rely on any commitment; it depends on the opposite. It is a solidarity of the lazy. This type of solidarity comes from the lack of questioning, the lack of reflection, or interrogation. It refuses to look at history and refuses to acknowledge the legacy of colonialism. The solidarity with whiteness comes with the price of loyalty without conviction, without understanding, and without consciousness. It is the default position of white people across the world and is the type of solidarity that allows people to turn away from atrocity, deny mass murder, and ignore science if it does not fit into the narrative of white goodness, white innocence, and white supremacy.

The alliance is pervasive in how all areas of society, and, by extension, schools are operated. The curriculum, the schooling structures, and the placement of programs all reflect the needs and desires of white people, and white people's desires are privileged over the needs and wants of communities of color. When those communities demand better, they are accused of playing the *race card* and are rebuked as *divisive*, but when white communities seek to segregate themselves, even literally dividing towns by race, they are viewed by other whites as bravely looking out for their children (Harris, 2019).

It is also a solidarity that is based on fear. Europeans are facing a demographic collapse because of their aging population and low birth rate, combined with a high death rate due to COVID-19. These forces have created a situation where there will not be enough Europeans to sustain nationhood in many European Union (EU) countries by 2100 (Bello, 2023). However, the solution is simple. To increase immigration and build a multicultural and multiracial Europe. However, the thought leaders of Europe do not entertain that solution, and they continue their handwringing while the solution stares them in the face. The same is true in the United States, where white people will be replaced as the majority by 2045 (Frey, 2022). This forces the question of who will run the country in the next twenty years. The answers are frightening to white people and their alliance. Across the globe, white-majority countries are choosing to destroy their democracies rather than share with people whom they look down upon. Illiberal regimes are rising in response to demographic changes and increased immigration. And, of course, Trump was elected twice on a promise of extending white rule. In the end, while pundits who are afraid to break with the white alliance talked about the prices of groceries as a cause of the Trump victory, the reality is much darker.

Fear of losing white, male majority status caused white Americans to choose authoritarianism over democracy in the vain hope of extending their rule. The question that haunts me is this: how far will white people go to preserve their perceived dominance? Will they abandon democracy entirely, trading it for authoritarian rule to maintain control? Trump's promised "mass deportations" are serving as a vehicle for ethnic cleansing, reshaping the country through force and fear. Will it continue to its ultimate, logical, and horrifying conclusion? When I began writing this book in 2013, such questions would have seemed absurd—hyperbolic and unthinkable. Yet, as the years have unfolded, these possibilities no longer feel so far-fetched, as masked ICE agents invade communities, schools, and detain children across the country in a cruel attempt to spread fear and force migrant parents into the open. The resurgence of white nationalism, the erosion of democratic norms, and the global rise of authoritarian leaders paint a chilling picture. To dismiss these scenarios now is to blind ourselves to the patterns of history and the warning signs all around us. The rhetoric and policies we see today are echoes of past atrocities, and those who believe *it can't happen here* forget that history's most horrifying chapters often began with small steps justified as necessary or inevitable. The question is not only whether white people will go to these lengths but whether those who see the danger will act enough to prevent the worst of it.

Can White People Be Traitors to Whiteness?

Ignatiev and Garvey (1996) called for an end to the white race to answer this kind of unenlightened solidarity. Not the humans now considered white, but the concept of whiteness as a normative power. This is a different concept of whiteness than outlined by McIntosh (2001), who described it as a *knapsack* of passes and passports that allowed white people to walk freely in the world constructed by and for them. Ignatiev and Garvey described whiteness as a club that, while not secret, allowed members to be waved through gates that are closed to others.

However, membership in the club only works if all members are willing to follow the rules that keep the club exclusive and privileged. "It is based on one huge assumption: that all those who look white are, whatever their complaints or reservations, fundamentally loyal to it" (Ignatiev & Garvey, 1996, p. 36).

Ignatiev and Garvey's answer to the solidarity of whiteness was to break the rules that hold it together and become what they termed a *race traitor*, a traitor to whiteness itself:

The way to abolish the white race is to disrupt that conformity. If enough people who look white violate the rules of whiteness, their existence cannot be ignored. If it becomes impossible for the upholders of white rules to speak in the name of all who look white, the white race will cease to exist. The abolitionists are traitors to the white race; by acting boldly, they jeopardize their membership in the white club and their ability to draw upon its privileges. (p. 36)

A race traitor is a person who breaks with the solidarity imposed upon white people by society by refusing to participate in the system. Race traitors seek an end to whiteness, but what is the replacement? Whiteness and white supremacy, as this book has described, are the organizing principles of American society. The economy, politics, media, and social conventions all serve the same goal of maintaining, extending, and solidifying the illusion of white supremacy. Dropping out is undoubtedly an option, but dropping into something else is needed.

Casey (2016) elaborated, "For me, the essential flaw in the *race traitors* theory is this: whiteness is not something individual white people are capable of manipulating" (p. 79). He went on to explain:

> Regardless of belief or intention, white people are themselves caught up in the cultural logic, discourses of power, signs, and frames of domination present in the very phenotypic edifice of whiteness. Each of these things makes individual actions to "rid one's self of whiteness" more than impossible because whiteness does not exist on the individual body but on the collective bodies of white people, a shifting and complex cultural as well as racial group. (p. 80)

While certainly, a race-traitor-inspired disruptive strategy could work to break the hegemonic power of whiteness if a critical mass of white people participated, it is not a realistic answer to today's issues, and it does not answer the question of how to teach across the color line successfully. It assumes that a lot of white people are willing to throw off all that whiteness gives them, and given the current moment, that is extremely unlikely.

Transference of Solidarity

Because of the inability to simply throw off solidarity with whiteness without a replacement, the race traitor concept, as attractive as it is, is not a viable solution for those white teachers who already work and live across the color line. As social animals, we must be in solidarity with other people. The passive, default solidarity described by Bayertz, the emotional solidarity of empathy, and the situational solidarity of allies are all inadequate to address the current state of schooling.

Since 2015, Nazis have been marching on college campuses and American cities, children have been in cages at the border, and children are being gunned down in schools. The killing of Black people by police continues unabated despite the convictions of police officers who murder, despite the protests and the demands for change. According to Mappingpoliceviolence. org (2024), 1260 Americans were killed by police officers in 2024. Of those people, 28 percent were Black. This state-sponsored murder, without trial, juries, or process, is defended in the halls of power while the carnage goes on. Republican Lawmakers wear AR-15 pins on their lapels to show their solidarity with white supremacy and their determination to make sure that white ownership of weapons is prioritized in legislation (Clayton, 2023).

Accordingly, in 2024, the United States experienced thirty-nine school shootings resulting in injuries or deaths, marking the second-highest annual total since *Education Week* began tracking such incidents in 2018 (Lieberman & Kim, 2024). Data indicate that firearms have surpassed motor vehicle accidents as the leading cause of death among children and young adults in the United States. According to a study in *Scientific American* (Lewis, 2022),

> The switchover, which happened in 2017, stems from both a reduction in vehicle-related deaths and a grim uptick in gun-related fatalities. From 2000 to 2020, the number of firearm-related deaths in the one-to-24-year-old age group increased from 7.3 per 100,000 people to 10.28 per 100,000, age-adjusted data from the Centers for Disease Control and Prevention reveal. During the same period, motor-vehicle-related deaths declined from 13.62 to 8.31 per 100,000. (Lewis, 2022)

All of these and many more are the consequences when colonialism and whiteness are allowed to run their natural courses. This is the world white people have created. It is time to do more than symbolic moves. The other, less transformative versions of solidarity are also unsustainable over a career or lifetime. However, the transfer of solidarity can only occur when a white person has a positive white racial identity, not based on guilt, fear, or superiority, but grounded in realism and integrity, with moral empathy (Harvey, 2007). This is not a light concept or one that should be approached lightly. Returning to Honneth (1995), he explained that a new identity is needed to fully come to a new recognition. This new identity comes from an understanding that the old one is insufficient to bring about relationships of solidarity:

A subject's personal identity presupposes, in principle, certain types of recognition from other subjects. For the superiority of interpersonal relationships over instrumental acts was apparently to consist in the fact that relationships give both interlocutors the opportunity to experience themselves, in encountering their partner to communication, to be the kind of person that they, from their perspective, recognize the other as being. (Honneth, 1995, p. 37)

It is time to throw off whiteness and adopt a new identity that stands against the made-world and strike out to create a new one.

For the most patient, committed, and resilient white teachers who have recognized their students, interrogated their whiteness, and moved toward empathy, they will be able to build a pathway to Caring Solidarity. Those who do it will be perceived as radical, crazy, or ill-informed. Friends and family will work to pull them back into the alliance. They will lose friendships and possibly alienate coworkers who choose to stay in solidarity with whiteness and impose a white supremacist frame on their teaching of Black students. But those charges have always been levied against people who challenge white supremacy. This is the level of solidarity that is needed. That is the level of solidarity that will change the world that students and their teachers live in.

Transference of Solidarity Versus False Empathy

Some would say that white people can't shed their solidarity with whiteness. In his counternarrative, Delgado (1996) expressed that white people are unable to be in full solidarity with Black people because they lack "double consciousness," as W. E. B. Du Bois described in his narrative, *The Souls of Black Folk* (1903/1994).

Double consciousness, as described by Du Bois, is a sense of otherness, of not belonging in America. It is how one feels in a foreign country, even if one speaks the language and is familiar with the landscape. It is never truly home. A person with double consciousness feels conscious of others looking, judging, and creating a narrative of them without their permission or consent. Add to this the realities of harsh segregation and the constant threat of deadly violence, and it becomes clear that no sense of home can be forged in an America so deeply rooted in the subjugation of people not identified as white. Du Bois (1903/1994) explained:

It is a peculiar sensation, this double-consciousness, this sense of always looking at one's self through the eyes of others, of measuring one's soul by the tape of a world that looks on in amused contempt and pity. One ever feels his two-ness,—an American, a Negro; two souls, two thoughts, two unreconciled strivings; two warring ideals in one dark body, whose dogged strength alone keeps it from being torn asunder. (p. 2)

Delgado (1996) contended that because America is *home* to white Americans by design, they do not have that double consciousness and, therefore, cannot be in solidarity with Black people who do.

Delgado continued, "[They walk] on the surface, [use] the wrong metaphors and comparisons. It's a little bit like false piety, like those folks who go to church on Sunday but don't allow themselves to be seized by real religion" (p. 72). He draws a parallel between white people who view themselves as allies to Black people yet act in ways that contradict this solidarity with those who attend church but seize every opportunity to sin with impunity. Even if a person with false empathy is able to do good work, it will be incomplete because they do not have the knowledge or the desire to know what is truly needed. Based on their own frames, they assume what is needed, which is usually incorrect. Solorzano (1997) explained that these kinds of false empathies are used to justify:

(1) having low educational and occupational expectations for Students of Color; (2) placing Students of Color in separate schools and, in some cases, separate classrooms within schools; (3) remediating the curriculum and pedagogy for Students of Color; (4) maintaining segregated communities and facilities for People of Color; and (5) expecting Students of Color to one day occupy certain types and levels of occupations. In fact, when we think of welfare, crime, drugs, immigrants, and educational problems, we racialize these issues by painting stereotypic portraits of People of Color. (p. 10)

The list above is commonplace in American schools. Some schools are demographically diverse in the aggregate but segregated within their walls. Solidarity rejects the surface-level engagement of those who claim to support students of color while perpetuating practices that harm and marginalize them. It demands that educators dismantle the biases, structures, and systems that segregate schools.

Solorzano is correct in that white people seldom feel the double consciousness that Black people do; however, in transferring solidarity, there is a possibility that they will, especially if America descends toward a newly segregated state. To see flags and statues of racists go up and redesigned in the twenty-first century should make white people of good conscience feel like outsiders. They should feel like the country is no longer for them. Their solidarity with others based on ethical, religious, or moral views will create a distance between them and other white people who casually say and do racist things. While it will not be a complete double consciousness, it will be a type of *otherness* that will be healthier than their white counterparts. Solidarity requires stepping into a space of vulnerability and humility, recognizing that one's perspective is shaped by privilege and limited by the absence of double consciousness. While white educators cannot fully experience the lived realities of their Black and Brown students, they can work to affirm those realities. This involves rejecting solidarity with whiteness and instead standing in authentic partnership with students and communities who have been excluded and devalued.

Solidarity is not a destination, but a journey that challenges educators to continually examine their positionality, learn from their mistakes, and build relationships grounded in trust and mutual respect. It calls for the kind of courage that Du Bois (1903/1994) alluded to in his description of *two-ness*—the courage to confront the truths of history, the structures of inequality, and the personal discomfort that comes with dismantling them. Only through this long and deliberate process can white educators begin to move toward Caring Solidarity with students and communities.

Discussion Questions for Chapter 8

1 What does "transference of solidarity" mean in the context of white teachers working across the color line? How does this differ from other forms of solidarity, such as empathy or allyship?

2 Cheryl Harris described whiteness as a form of property. How does this concept influence how white people navigate power and privilege in educational and societal structures? In what ways can educators challenge and dismantle this construct within schools?

3 The chapter discusses the idea of "race traitors" breaking solidarity with whiteness. How realistic or feasible do you think this concept is

for white educators working in diverse school environments? What challenges might they face, and how can they overcome them?

4 The text argues that transference of solidarity requires a positive white racial identity rooted in realism and moral empathy. How can white educators cultivate such an identity, and what role does self-awareness play in this process?

5 Delgado argued that white educators cannot fully achieve solidarity with Black students because they lack the "double consciousness" described by Du Bois. How can educators navigate this limitation to foster solidarity?

6 Authors like Huntington and Glaude highlight how historical myths and systemic inequalities perpetuate white supremacy. How can educators integrate this critical understanding into their teaching practices while fostering solidarity with their students?

7 What are some of the risks and sacrifices white educators might face when breaking solidarity with whiteness? How can they prepare themselves to navigate these challenges while maintaining their commitment to equity and justice?

Actionable Classroom Practices from Chapter 8

- **Replace One Text with an Inclusive Alternative**

  Select one book, article, or historical text currently used in your curriculum and replace it with a piece by a Black or Indigenous author that directly challenges dominant narratives. For example, swap *Of Mice and Men* with *A Lesson Before Dying* by Ernest J. Gaines or include an essay by Audre Lorde.

- **Create a Classroom Agreement on Equity**

  Collaborate with students to draft a classroom agreement that explicitly includes commitments to equity, respect, and the value of diverse perspectives. Display the agreement prominently and refer to it during conflicts or sensitive discussions.

- **Invite Community Leaders**

  Reach out to local activists, historians, or artists from communities of color and invite them to speak to your students about their lived experiences and insights into racial justice.

- **Start a Mini Research Project on Structural Inequities**

  Ask students to investigate one local or national policy (e.g., housing segregation, school funding disparities) and present their findings to the class. Provide scaffolding to guide their research and encourage critical analysis.

- **Implement a Restorative Justice Activity**

  For instance, if a conflict arises between students, facilitate a conversation where they express their perspectives and collaboratively decide on steps to repair harm.

- **Challenge Deficit Language in Staff Meetings**

  The next time you hear colleagues describe students or families from a deficit perspective (e.g., "These parents just don't care"), counter it with asset-based language: "How can we better engage families who are balancing multiple responsibilities?"

- **Post Resources in the Classroom**

  Create a visible resource wall with posters, book recommendations, or QR codes linking to websites like the Zinn Education Project, Teaching Tolerance, or locally relevant anti-racist organizations. Update it regularly to keep it relevant and engaging.

9 Caring Solidarity as an Advocate and Accomplice

Advocacy in the Caring Solidarity model represents the heart of transformative teaching. This chapter delves into the indispensable role of teachers when they move beyond traditional classroom responsibilities to actively advocate for their students and communities. Advocacy, in this sense, is not limited to curriculum or pedagogy but stands against systemic injustices embedded within school and societal structures. It requires teachers to act as more than allies, but accomplices, challenging harmful norms and policies while fostering environments where all students can thrive. Advocacy calls for teachers to engage in daily, moment-to-moment decisions that prioritize students' well-being over the rigid demands of institutional structures rooted in white supremacy. It demands courage, persistence, and an unwavering commitment to equity and justice.

At the heart of advocacy is a clear understanding of systemic inequities and the courage to confront them. Teachers in solidarity acknowledge the labyrinth of barriers that disproportionately impact Black and Brown students, from the school-to-prison pipeline to inequitable discipline practices. They challenge harmful policies, such as the presence of police in schools and the use of suspensions, which disproportionately target students of color and perpetuate cycles of marginalization. Advocacy also involves standing against these structures by fostering humane and logical classroom practices that prioritize relationships and learning over compliance and control. Teachers who embrace this level of solidarity actively disrupt the mechanisms that feed systemic oppression, replacing them with practices that empower and uplift.

Moreover, advocacy in Caring Solidarity is not solely about resistance but about building possibilities. This chapter explores how teachers can prepare students for adulthood by providing tools to navigate, challenge, and ultimately transform the systems around them. Through culturally sustaining pedagogies and curricula that center the experiences and voices of marginalized communities, teachers can create classrooms where students are empowered to explore their identities, develop critical consciousness, and create a more just world. Advocacy is more than a reaction to oppression; it is a proactive commitment to liberation, transforming the classroom into a space where equity is taught and practiced.

Caring Solidarity as an Advocate

The first of the two inside levels inside Caring Solidarity is solidarity expressed through advocacy for students and communities. This level is where the best teachers often stay. Daily, they meet students where they are. They create lessons and experiences for students that empower, build, and restore. Advocacy can take many forms and is a moment-to-moment decision-making paradigm that puts students' needs ahead of the school's structures.

Advocates are realistic about the structures of their school as rooted in white supremacy and are annoyingly, vocally, ready to call out structures and roadblocks to their students of color. As Harvey (2007) explained, white advocates, in solidarity with their students, move together toward shared goals.

> First, solidarity involves at least two individuals or two groups: one is in solidarity with another. Second, we are in solidarity with those suffering from immorality or injustice, not from some natural disaster. Third, action may be involved, but there seems at least to be agreement that action alone is not enough. (Harvey, 2007, p. 22)

Structures

As explained in Chapter 3, few schools are places of solidarity and caring for Black students. Instead, they are a labyrinth of potential pitfalls that will sweep students into the school-to-prison pipeline. Still, teachers who are in solidarity with students will do all they can to advocate for them and disrupt that pipeline. Often, that means standing up to other adults, even the police. Beyond that, teachers in solidarity keep their students close and resolve conflicts so that they do not get out of their jurisdiction. Once an administrator, or worse, the police, is involved, the results could be deadly. But even if the student survives the encounter, they will never be better off for having been removed from the learning environment.

For the teacher in solidarity, this means having a humane, logical classroom learning management system where students want to be in the classroom. Students know which teachers are in solidarity with them, even if they do not always act as though they do. The teacher's reaction to a challenge is the dividing line between teachers in solidarity and those who are not. The school-to-prison pipeline is maintained by the individual decisions of teachers and administrators, so teachers in solidarity will do what they can to disrupt the pipeline through demands on the school structures. Structurally, several steps can be taken to disrupt the school-to-prison pipeline, and these two can be implemented immediately.

First, Remove Police from Schools. Teachers in solidarity will advocate and demand that armed police officers be removed from schools and that trained education-oriented administrative aides and counselors be put in their place. These aides should not be armed but should be trained in humane restraint, conflict resolution, de-escalation, and mental health crisis management. No matter how good the police officer is in the school, they will always be the person who ultimately decides *on their own* when deadly force is to be used. Since it should never be used on children, there is literally no place for police officers as a regular part of the school environment.

To be absolutely clear, if there is no need for deadly force, there is no need for armed police officers. To repeat, if there is no need to kill a person, there is no need for a police officer, because even non-deadly weapons are damaging beyond any need. Teachers in solidarity understand that the reasons for keeping police officers in schools are based on white supremacy and anti-Blackness. The fact that police are in schools is a failure of leadership, pedagogy, and curriculum to empower Black and Brown students. It is a failure to understand the racial history of the United States and the function of police as forces of slavery, segregation, and anti-Blackness.

Those who would equivocate on keeping police in schools are making sure that they always have the option to use deadly force against students. Taking this option away from schools will result in one of two things. Unfortunately, it could mean a decline in discipline standards as teachers who already did not understand how to relate across the color line are no longer able to use the threat of deadly force as an option to keep Black students in line. No matter how quiet the hallways are, these schools are not places of solidarity, caring, or education; they are warehouses for youth until they leave, some with diplomas, most without. The better option is for schools to find ways to be in solidarity with students of color and to root themselves deeply in communities, using culturally relevant curriculum and humane discipline that teach students to use their positions to call out injustice, and their minds to find new ways to bend the world. These schools will do fine without police because their discipline model will be based on empowering students rather than suppressing them.

Teachers decide what kind of school they are in, and the question is simple. "If police were removed from the school, could the school continue to run, and could teachers continue to teach?" If the answer is "no," then the school is not a place of Caring Solidarity and, instead, just one more pipeline from the school to the jail. If the answer is, "Yes, but we have work to do," that place can be in solidarity with students. It is a simple yet effective mental test that each teacher and administrator should do.

At a conference on educational law during the pandemic, I was asked to speak with the Texas group, which included 30 or so Texas school superintendents and an equal number of school attorneys. After discussing the concept of Caring Solidarity, I was asked how to implement it in schools. After I told them to remove the police from their schools, there was an uncomfortable shift in the conversation, where the main speaker said that it was impossible because of state mandates. It was obvious that they were unwilling to make such a shift. It is not unusual that a former slave and current segregation state would want to keep their students of color in control through the threat of deadly force. Still, you cannot state that educating these students is your priority, nor that you are in solidarity with these students and their communities, if your top priority is merely controlling them so you can continue to make a living off their existence.

Second, Stop Suspensions—In or Out of Schools. Suspension is another function of anti-Blackness and is not a part of schools seeking to work in Caring Solidarity with students. Suspension is an easy out for schools that demand consequences. The people in charge of buildings (these are not actual schools) are under the delusion that depriving students of their authority and presence for the day is a punishment. For schools and teachers who are part of the school-to-prison pipeline, the suspension is the opening that rinses students away from them to the jailhouse. The other purpose of suspension is to inconvenience parents in an attempt to motivate them to get their child to comply with administrators' and teachers' orders. Sometimes, it works. However, it does not demonstrate or build solidarity to forcibly demand compliance.

In-school suspension is hardly better, since the detention room is not a place for interactive learning. It reinforces the narrative that school is punishment and that, while the classroom may be dehumanizing and uninviting, some options are worse (Bartolome, 1994). Overall, detentions and suspensions, both in and out of school, are counterproductive if the goal is to raise students up and empower them to become engaged citizens. I want to emphasize that engaged citizens are not compliant, and compliant students are not engaged. Compliance is the goal of colonialism and white supremacy. The goal should not be creating quiet, disengaged adults but bright, alive, and thinking individuals who understand democracy and can create a more equal, more just, and *more perfect union*. Pushing students out of the classroom and the school until they comply does not create a person who can become a citizen of a democracy. It is more likely that, even if the student is able to elude the prison part of the pipeline, they will see school as a type of prison, the exact opposite of the purpose of the schools.

Colonialism does not wish to eliminate the colonized. It seeks compliance using punishment, shame, intimidation, and fear. These same weapons are used in schools to suppress Black students into compliance. Ultimately, that is not a sustainable model, and it degrades the souls of students and adults alike. All the people in these schools who participate in this violence, either as victims or perpetrators, are soul-sick. The answer is to stop hurting and begin healing.

Pedagogy

As leaders in pedagogy, advocates who have done the kind of internal work needed for Caring Solidarity will advocate for students to use their authentic voices in the classroom. There are many ways to do this, but some elements will be evident in classrooms.

Students ARE and Feel Valued. In a classroom where the teacher is a Caring Solidarity advocate, the students will feel valued by the teacher. Several frameworks will allow students to be valued and to feel valued. Asset-based pedagogies like Culturally Sustaining Pedagogy (Paris & Alim, 2017) and Hip-Hop pedagogy (Stovall, 2006) are ways to teach students that also let them know they matter to the teacher. Through pedagogy that daily reminds students that they are at the center of the classroom, teachers build relationships of solidarity.

When it comes to learning management, a teacher who is an advocate will not engage in *classroom management* in the traditional way. Instead, the teacher will focus on managing the learning and classroom environment. Where there are students who are disinvested in learning from previous encounters, the pedagogy of the advocate works to gain the student's trust in the classroom through engagement with the student. Teachers will participate with students in a social contract rather than a set of rules. The social contract will invite students to invest in the classroom environment and to care for and about one another. As bell hooks (1994) explained:

> To educate as the practice of freedom is a way of teaching that anyone can learn. That learning process comes easiest to those of us who teach who also believe that there is an aspect of our vocation that is sacred; who believe that our work is not merely to share information but to share in the intellectual and spiritual growth of our students. To teach in a manner that respects and cares for the souls of our students is essential if we are to provide the necessary conditions where learning can most deeply and intimately begin. (p. 13)

Many authors have worked tirelessly to provide teachers with ways to humanize pedagogy that it would take another book to explain them all, however, a few authors have profoundly influenced the creation of this model, and so I recommend these as a start in no particular order, Gloria Ladson-Billings, Paulo Freire, Bettina Love, Sonja Nieto, Lisa Delpit, Herbert Kohl, Django Paris, Sami Alim, and Geneva Gay. Each of these authors approaches pedagogy differently, but all focus on humanizing the classroom and making it a place of possibility (Bartolome, 1994). This is certainly not *the list*, but it is *a list,* and a person who gets through these authors' works will be pointed to a host of others with the same commitments.

Students Are Being Prepared for (Actual) Adulthood. Teachers and administrators, in their language about being student-centered, sometimes forget that the goal of education is not to produce kids, but adults. This is evident in the types of skills that teachers focus on. Frustratingly, schools focus on behaviors that are not necessary for anyone working outside of school. Having a pencil and *being ready to learn* is an urgency to some teachers. They even keep charts and graphs of students' school skills, which are literally skills only needed in school.

Yet, pencils are seldom used outside of schools. Pens rule the workplace, and there are a lot of them. Bankers do not need to bring their own pens to the office. Lawyers do not stop lawyering for the day if they do not have a pen. Imagine a world where school skills ruled in the business world. No work would get done until everyone stopped talking. No one would get lunch unless everyone stood perfectly still in a line. Requiring students to line up for lunch and move through hallways in single file is a function of anti-Blackness that reinforces behaviors associated with control and surveillance rather than those cultivated in spaces of power. Traveling with influential people is an affair where gaggles of people talk and discuss all at once while engaged in meaningful work. They are not lined up and silent.

Teachers complain that testing takes too much time. Add thirty minutes of instruction time by not waiting for every child to stand up straight, look forward, and walk in lockstep. Elementary students spend too much of their school day waiting to go from one place to another, and this practice is creeping into secondary schools as a sign of respectability politics, where Black students are paraded to show off their humanity. There is one industry where these skills do matter: prisons. These practices are much too close to the ways that prisoners are paraded up and down halls. It makes one wonder what teachers think of their students when lines and supplies are their overriding priority.

The worst part of these practices is how they are racialized. Studies show that Black children as young as four years old are continually judged by teachers as having behavior *problems* (Bryan, 2017). Black students through the twelfth grade, as explained in Chapter 3, are continually overcorrected and over-punished for minor infractions. This overcorrection has a devastating effect on Black students but also may have an impact on white students, reinforcing stereotypes given to them by adults that Black people are dangerous and need to be controlled.

As Bryan (2017) explained, "white children not only witness the pedagogical practices of their white teachers, but they also witness the ways teachers disproportionately target Black boys for school discipline" (p. 338). Disproportionate punishment diminishes Black students' self-esteem and contributes to their disinvestment in school. At the same time, it teaches white students to accept racial hierarchies as normal, reinforcing white supremacy and undermining the positive effects of integration, which depend on students of different races having meaningful opportunities to learn and interact together. Teachers in Caring Solidarity prepare their students for adulthood by teaching them skills that matter. They teach them to work together and divide tasks. They help them learn responsibility, not through punishment but by giving students age-appropriate responsibilities to build self-esteem.

Students Learn Consciousness. Teachers in solidarity help students explore who they are. Teachers tap into their students' selves, and students explore unmapped areas of themselves. Students of color will benefit from this, but it also extends to white students. Gaining a positive white racial identity leads to a resolved consciousness for white people. Uncovering white supremacy allows all students to see who they really are outside of the prison of whiteness. It is like a person waking from sleep. Consciousness is freeing.

White supremacy is an uncomfortable, unethical, and destabilizing mental condition. It makes white people miss the obvious beauty in others, destroys the possibilities for friendship and love, and creates a hole in one's consciousness as they avoid uncomfortable truths about history, society, families, and themselves. Teachers in solidarity with their Black students are able to help all their students build new frames that resolve that consciousness.

Curriculum

The curriculum, particularly the history curriculum, delivered on a daily basis to students of color, is a violent act. Students of all races learn that whiteness is goodness and innocence, that the rich have nothing but our best interests at heart, and that the downtrodden, when there are any, are simply able to peacefully appeal to white people for relief. That request for relief, if constructed from the basic goodness of white people with a dab of *All men are created equal,* will be granted. Sometimes that support is offered grudgingly, yet the generosity of most white people—who are kinder and more enlightened than those in the history books who stood on the necks of peaceful protesters fighting for their rights—is rarely questioned. Students learn that only peaceful protests are productive, while organized unions of people are unproductive. The narrative is that a logical argument will always be well received, but anger will be met with indifference or, at worst, unavoidable, but never excessive, violence. All children are taught the basic building blocks of white supremacy, beginning with their first words. Great teachers who are in solidarity help their students unlearn those lessons.

Fundamentally, the portrayal in the American curriculum is that by default, all civilization is white and that all peoples who are not identified as white are better off for their contact with white people. Whether it is Columbus, Thanksgiving, the Colonial period, or the Constitution, the story is whiteness, white innocence, and white goodness.

Even slavery is often taught as a salvation story, at least in the Northern version; People wrongly stolen from Africa became Americans and convinced the white people of the United States to give them their freedom. Some books even equate enslaved people with other immigrants (Isensee, 2015).

The story continues that it took a war to convince some white people that Black people should not be enslaved, but in the end, goodness won over evil and hatred. Then, some of those similar white people who had fought on the wrong side of the Civil War also suppressed some Black people. Dr. King made a passionate and reasonable plea on television, convincing white people to save them, and now things are fine. As ridiculous as this may seem to most educated people, the average American will repeat this basic narrative if asked, and many do, even prominent lawmakers (Lam, 2019; Wu, 2019). As historian Walter Johnson (2019) wrote,

> At the bottom of it all, I would like for children to be taught that the modern United States was built on Indian land by African labor. No mills without plantations; no railroads without reservations. After all the quantification and qualification, those two basic historical facts remain at the foundation: extermination and enslavement. That might seem harsh, but history is harsh—though not so harsh, perhaps, that we should abandon hope of changing it. (online)

This simple and direct narrative is the opposite of the one that students are usually fed and is one that will begin to topple the flimsy logic of white supremacy. From here, the curriculum can be revised and restored. From here, we can finally have that *new birth of freedom* that King described on that day at the Lincoln Memorial. We cannot have that rebirth until white supremacy is cracked and its yolk spilled out for all to see. We cannot *be* who we say we are until we *deal with* who we really are.

While social studies is the most important and egregious of the disciplines in shaping the narrative students get from the curriculum, it is by no means alone (King, 1991). The books teachers have students read, and the ones they do not, the stories they use in examples, and the ones they leave out in biology, chemistry, math, and literature classes, all teach white supremacy in overt and covert ways. The teachers who are advocates in solidarity with students will abandon the canon of white authors, not just to add in others and *round out* the curriculum. They will seek to replace the old and see literature with new eyes.

They will work to value their Black students and challenge their white students to see the world through perspectives that are, truthfully, more real than the ones we have now. For example, does *Frankenstein* teach valuable lessons? Absolutely. Does *Native Son* teach more valuable lessons? "Absolutely," says the teacher in solidarity. As of 2025, there were over four hundred movies about Frankenstein. 2019 marked the eightieth anniversary of Richard Wright's brilliant novel and saw the first film adaptation since 1986, following an earlier version in 1951. Yes, Frankenstein is a good book with lots to teach, but Wright's novel is much more important, especially now.

A curriculum that shows students their school is committed to Black lives empowers them to change the world. It imbues students with the capital that they will be able to use once they leave to make that change. Yosso (2005) listed six forms of capital that should be instilled in a curriculum that values Black lives and demonstrates Caring Solidarity with Brown and Black students and communities. While these overlap, she explained that these types of capital offer specific goals that a curriculum and pedagogy would impart to a certain extent.

1 **Aspirational Capital:** The kind of resiliency that allows children to dream of a brighter and bolder future than their present circumstances. It is the kind of capital that adults who are not in solidarity will stamp out of students by telling them to *be realistic*. Realism is what got us here; aspiration will help us move forward.

2 **Linguistic Capital:** Black and Brown students are often multilingual with their friends and families. Schools frequently try to stamp out multilingualism rather than value students and communities for their funds of knowledge. Students who arrive speaking Spanish are taught to devalue their home language and, by extension, their culture by schools and teachers who feign care while crushing students' identities. Teachers in solidarity with students who demonstrate multilingualism, celebrate it, and guide students into code-switching skills to help them navigate the world and bend it to them, not the other way around.

3   **Familial Capital** refers to the type of capital that comes from being connected to families and communities, "a sense of community history, memory, and cultural intuition" (Yosso, 2005, p. 79). Families are an asset, yet so many deficit models of students by teachers and administrators see families as an impediment to a student's progress. Teachers often say, *I only have them for a few hours a day*, referring to families they perceive as undermining their positive efforts during school hours.

    Teachers who are not in solidarity with families and communities will blame them for not *being engaged* with the school and for not participating, but have a difficult time acknowledging the barriers to participation thrown up by schools, such as times when things are offered or the inability to feed siblings before attending school events and meetings. Students' families are a source of strength, but sometimes they face challenges. Schools in solidarity with communities will help families address those challenges and join in solidarity with families to advocate for their community to overcome those challenges, like jobs, services, food deserts, and housing.

4   **Social Capital:** This is the capital of *who you know*. It is the capital that allows students to collect letters of recommendation to college, gain summer and after-school employment, and connections with local elected officials and businesspeople for internships. Teachers in solidarity with their communities will connect students to people who can help them take advantage of opportunities.

    Teachers can invite local politicians into the classroom. Administrators can cultivate relationships with local community leaders. All of this is done through relationships and investment in the community. It sees the people of the community as a strength and as resources to help students fulfill their potential.

5   **Navigational Capital** refers to "skills of maneuvering through social institutions." Historically, this infers the ability to maneuver through institutions not created with communities of color in mind. For example, strategies to navigate through racially hostile university campuses draw on the concept of academic invulnerability, or students' ability to "sustain high levels of achievement, despite the presence of stressful events and conditions that place them at risk of doing poorly at school and, ultimately, dropping out of school" (Yasso, 2005, p. 80).

    Teachers and schools should offer students classes in navigating college, filling out forms, budgeting money, and time management to equip them with the skills they need to navigate the world outside of school.

6 **Resistant Capital** refers to the knowledge and skills necessary to build movements, resist oppression, and create a new world. This capital is the type of work that advocates and accomplices must do in caring solidarity. To accomplish this, teachers must unveil the hidden curriculum of white supremacy, teach students the skills to organize and work together, and create meaningful opportunities for data gathering and the implementation of real-world problem-solving.

   This is not a curriculum or pedagogy outside of the mainstream. This is the core curriculum for children of the elite that empowers them to make decisions, run complex organizations, and create change. Yet, schools constantly work to crush those same impulses in students of color. A teacher in Caring Solidarity will build a curriculum that does not simply pass on the white supremacist frame but empowers students to see it, analyze it, and ultimately dismantle it (Love, 2019c; Yosso, 2005).

When schools continually devalue students, marginalize them, demonstrate that they are uninteresting, unimportant, and that their lives, culture, contributions, stories, and very selves are so disturbing as to be unmentionable, how can they be expected to buy into school as the pathway to success? Because of the way schools are run, is it logical for Black students to go through the first ten years of education believing that, in the end, they will be successful?

Teachers in solidarity with their students challenge them with a curriculum that makes them stronger, better able to fight the system, and more likely to win. Teachers in solidarity with students equip them to fight whiteness and white supremacy. They have transferred their solidarity to their students. They have joined the fight.

Caring Solidarity as an Accomplice

As the diagram moves to the center, the circles shrink and the openings narrow. This symbolizes both the difficulty of moving to that metaphorical space and also the relatively few who will occupy it. White teachers who work and live across the color line are increasingly needed to join the activists in the space of Caring Solidarity Accomplices (Indigenous Action Media, 2014; Hackman, 2015; Love, 2019c; Osler, 2016; Powell & Kelly, 2017).

As this book has explained, the issue of the school-to-prison pipeline is the moral outrage of our time, and a sole focus on that would be appropriate. However, it is certainly not the only disgrace even if we narrow our focus to education. As a function of white supremacy and white normality, schools are becoming increasingly segregated. According to the nonprofit, nonpartisan organization Edbuild (2019), which uses data to expose America's segregation in terms of dollars:

> Nationally, predominantly white school districts get $23 billion more than their nonwhite peers despite serving a similar number of children. White school districts average revenue receipts of almost $14,000 per student, but nonwhite districts receive only $11,682. That's a divide of over $2,200, on average, per student. (p. 4)

This funding gap is only part of the segregation story, but suffice it to say, it is a major contributing factor to students' ability to succeed in school and after graduation. Books in segregated, predominantly Black schools are old, activities are scarce, and resources for enrichment are even scarcer. In 2018 and 2019, teachers across the country went on strike. They stood up to their state governments, demanding better pay and benefits for themselves and more resources for their students.

A 2024 report by researchers at Stanford and University of Southern California revealed that seventy years after the *Brown v. Board of Education* decision, racial and economic segregation in large US school districts had increased significantly over the previous three decades. The study indicated that this rise was primarily due to policy decisions, such as the expansion of charter schools, rather than demographic changes. Notably, segregation between white and Black students surged by 64 percent since 1988, and economic segregation climbed by approximately 50 percent since 1991 (Spector, 2024; The Education Opportunity Project at Stanford University, 2024).

To be clear, teachers who have to work three jobs to feed themselves and a cat, let alone a family, in places like Oklahoma or West Virginia, are less likely to be able to spend the time to do interrogation and community building that Caring Solidarity requires. When teachers can never focus on their students because they are too busy trying to keep their car and house in their possession, the level of education and solidarity decreases precipitately. In 2018, Teachers in Colorado, Oklahoma, West Virginia, Arizona, and Kentucky stood up and walked out of their classrooms straight to the capital. They were fighting for their lives, schools, students, and communities against Republican Governors who were more interested in tax cuts for the wealthy than providing an excellent education for students and investing in their state's economic and social wealth. In West Virginia, for example, teachers broke the law by striking against every single county in the state. The unity was staggering, especially in a state with as much poverty as West Virginia. Teachers defied critics, legislators, police, and the media, singing a full-throated rendition of "We're not going to take it" at the capital (Park et al., 2018).

Each state's situation is different, and each teacher group won and lost within its own demand list. Still, overall, teachers put their leaders on notice that the time when teachers are easily pushed down and down while legislators demean and threaten them is over (Flaherty, 2019). However, as we have found since, the people who seek to wage war against teachers and schools never let up. Gains made in some states have already been rolled back, and teachers are leaving the profession in droves due to disrespect from administrators and lawmakers.

In a 2024 Forbes article titled "*No More Teachers: The Epic Crisis Facing Education in 2024*," Perna (2024) highlighted the escalating teacher shortage in the United States, exacerbated by inadequate compensation, increased workload, and declining respect for the profession. He emphasized that the COVID-19 pandemic intensified these challenges, leading to higher stress levels and burnout among educators. He advocated for systemic changes to address this critical issue, including better support for teachers, competitive salaries, and a renewed societal appreciation for the teaching profession.

But teachers are fed up. In the past, they had abdicated their responsibilities to be engaged and allowed white male legislators to crush unions, demonize primarily female teachers, and bury them with mountains of tests and *accountability* measures, but they are finally fighting back. They are running for state and national legislative seats. They are protesting and demanding change from their state and federal representatives; however, more need to join the halls of power for any long-term, sustainable change to occur.

While these striking teachers were not explicitly talking about race, this spirit of activism is a fire that teachers who seek to be Caring Solidarity accomplices will catch and spread. To be an accomplice in solidarity includes all that has been discussed thus far, and is also willing to take the next step. White accomplices put their bodies, their money, their jobs, and their whiteness on the line, not to request but to make demands of other white people (Harden & Harden-Moore, 2019; Love, 2019c; Nieto, 2006).

Powell and Kelly (2017) argued that "the core idea that separates white allies from white accomplices is risk" (p. 43). To be in Caring Solidarity with communities, the teacher who seeks to be an accomplice will be more than an ally in the classroom and an advocate in the school and community. They must use their privilege to shield those who are most at risk of losing their lives, their freedom, and their humanity in confrontations with police and others who would force compliance.

This means that teachers show up when Nazis parade in their streets, and it means that they show up in the streets to demand prosecutions for police violence and murder. Accomplices shield demonstrators from tear gas; they put their arms into the wheel wells of vehicles of ICE agents stealing the parents of students. They physically block the doors when ICE comes to schools to grab students to capture their parents. Accomplices are people who care enough to be led by Black people, directed by Black people, and stay when the canisters fly.

Besides their bodies, accomplices use their resources to support full equality for Black people. Powell and Kelly (2017) stated:

An important distinction between an ally and an accomplice is the intentional manipulation of resources to support racial justice … Accomplices notice and share what resources might be available as an academic [or educator] that are not available to communities who are actively working to challenge unjust and white supremacist systems. This may be access to grant bodies, office supplies, printing, meeting space, library and research resources, and otherwise. This may also include leveraging "service learning" opportunities for students to be a part of canvassing for ongoing social movements. (p. 60)

The only way to heal the hole that white supremacy creates in individuals and communities is to fill it with active love, the kind that is discussed in Chapter 6. That love will allow white people who have transferred their solidarity to be directly involved in the battles for justice and basic humanity.

Teachers who are in Caring Solidarity with communities will be there, working to stop this violence against communities and also prevent future incidents. The Movement for Black Lives (2016) released their platform that included ending the war on Black people, reparations, investment in education, and divestment from prisons and other methods of oppressing Black people, economic justice, community control, and political power (Movement for Black Lives, 2016; Newkirk, 2016).

These parts of the mission statement are often left out in schools that claim to teach in a culturally relevant manner. However, to be culturally relevant, schools must take direction from the people in that culture. Too many people think that cultural relevance means only to uplift the icons of the past. Past gains by prominent icons carry important lessons, but the current generation of leaders is here and accessible now. Being in solidarity means being part of the generation fighting for equality.

Beyond direct action at protests and other ways to get in the way of white supremacy. White teachers should get in the way at official functions. Leveraging white privilege in the service of people who do not have it is absolutely necessary if white supremacist structures are to be dismantled. School board meetings are often a place where Black parents are patronized, drowned out, or dismissed, even though these are supposed to be places where the people are there to hold the powerful accountable.

Yull and Wilson (2018) described a school board meeting where the Black researcher (Yull) was accused of "race-baiting" and "wanting a race war" while the white researcher (Wilson) used racially conscious language to describe the district's participation in the school-to-prison pipeline with no condemnation.

> Wilson had the privilege to speak freely about the racialized dimensions of the district's disciplinary practices and remain invisible and immune to these critiques. At one school board meeting … Wilson introduced herself as a University professor and directly named the "school-to-prison pipeline" as "one of the most important problems facing our schools today." Within the [district] context, even the mention of "race" is automatically assumed to be racist, and yet Wilson escaped scrutiny for using such language publicly. Clearly, anti-Blackness creates a situation where the race of the speaker determines the consequences they face. (p. 12)

White accomplices put themselves at risk, but to be clear, they do not face the same, or some would argue, even similar consequences that Black people do at the hands of police or the justice system.

This example shows how to use the power of whiteness against the system. While there is certainly no guarantee that it will always be the case, white people can count on a certain degree of decorum in how they are treated when participating in actions. Thus, there is no reason not to be bold. There is no reason not to be strident, uncompromising, angry, and all the other words that misogyny and white supremacy will throw at those who stand for justice.

What To Do

Moving from ally or advocate to accomplice means finding opportunities to get in the way of white supremacy. Educator and writer Jonathan Osler described ways that white people can become an impediment to whiteness and work to dismantle structures of white supremacy.

An accomplice does more than empathize: it's more than just listening to others talk about the struggle. It is about solidifying a course of action that helps you commit to undoing it.

- It is about vocally calling out the family members and, unfortunately, educators, you know, who vote for white supremacist politicians.
- It is about holding people accountable for their racist and anti-Black and Anti-Brown antics.
- It is about holding folks in privileged positions accountable for their passivity on anti-queer rhetoric.
- It is calling out toxic masculinity and misogyny when it comes up in conversation.
- It is about researching topics you don't understand but want to help support. (Dr. John Paul Blog, Osler, 2016)

Osler (2016) also described the work of accomplices. Here are the categories with interpretation for white teachers:

Protesting. Being conscious of how a white person takes up space at protests will mean the difference between success and failure. White people in protests should take direction from the people who are most affected by the issue. The purpose of white people at the protest is to shield the leaders of color and the other protesters against police, counter-protesters, and any other entity that would inhibit the message from going out.

White people should not speak to the media during these protests. The media will immediately go to white people first, as they are most comfortable getting information from white people as presumed authorities. The media will also want the unusual in a protest, and that means white people, especially if there are only a few. The other job of white people during a protest is to check other white people. If a white person is taking the spotlight, move the spotlight to the real leaders.

Money. Accomplices will raise funds and seek ways to support movements led and run by Black and community people. The United Way is great, but your dollars will have a greater impact with smaller, more focused organizations where CEOs do not make millions of dollars annually.

White communities. Create and coordinate the creation of anti-racism trainings and book clubs in white spaces. Disrupt white communities and push them to be inclusive. Hold book clubs on *White Fragility* (DiAngelo, 2018) or in schools and school groups. Read *We Want to Do More Than Survive* (Love, 2019c). Have these book clubs at brunch so others will listen to the conversations. Be open and loud while doing it.

Advocacy on Social Media. Join groups fighting injustice and teaching others about white supremacy's societal influence. Share those items pointedly to teach your social media circle about racism. Also, diversify and extend beyond your current circle. Find people to befriend who will challenge and teach you. Many prominent African American scholars use social media to communicate with anyone who will follow. However, this has become more difficult recently with the right-wing takeover of social media. Feel free to challenge other white people in your posts when necessary. White supremacy thrives in silent agreement or tacit understanding. Disrupt that silence with your voice.

At Work. Beyond the classroom to the structures of the district and school, white people must be disruptors of white supremacy in hiring decisions. Diverse faculty are needed to support students and democratize schools in America. The teaching force is too white. Disrupt by demanding the hiring of diverse teachers and administrators, and support them in their work so they stay in teaching.

Electoral Politics. Be a disruptive force in local politics. Know your representatives well and make sure they see you frequently. When it comes to elected positions in the district, teachers should be the largest voting bloc. These are people who literally decide your day-to-day fate. They make funding, staffing, and curricular decisions, and teachers have very little input unless they demand it.

For too long, teachers have assumed that they would be protected from draconian cuts and meddling by outsiders through their representatives. It should be obvious now that teachers are on their own, and until they vote in LARGE numbers and decide who will be voted on in primaries and caucuses, they will continue to be discounted. Lastly, consider running. No one is better qualified than teachers to run schools, cities, towns, counties, and states. Teachers are trained and ready. Imagine a country run by compassionate teachers in solidarity with communities. What a change that would be.

Confronting Violence. Violence, intimidation, and micro-aggressions are everyday occurrences in schools. This does not mean that they should go unchallenged. Besides demanding that students be kind to one another, teachers must also be ready not to accept jokes or non-jokes that oppress marginalized people. That means correcting adults and children as needed in classrooms, meetings, or emails.

Obviously, it means removing Confederate names from schools and replacing racist mascots. Also, it means teaching people why these are wrong. Teach them that it is not that *standards have changed* or that *political correctness* has run amok, but that these things were always wrong. Teach them that white supremacy and white normality kept white people from seeing them as wrong, but they always knew that they were racist.

Your Children and Your Students. Accomplices are not hiding their work with communities of color. Be bold. Have pictures of your life as an accomplice viewable by students. Have scrapbooks out with your work. Have photos on the desk. Be in the newspaper and on TV as part of movements. Accomplices are public and proud. Also, bring children and students along when accomplice work is going on. See your students and celebrate them at protests, events, and meetings. Bring your own children with you to events and meetings. Let them see how change is made (Osler, 2016).

The Law. Remember, laws are about power. They are made by people seeking to encourage or curb behaviors, not handed down by any infallible source. Laws are impermanent and change at the whim of whoever is in power. Racist laws can carry consequences, but not always. Here in Texas, racist, unconstitutional laws are frequently passed with no penalties beyond loss of funding for failing to enforce or comply with them. Why? Funding is a political decision. Most of the time, funding is not a right. If a project is not funded, there is no standing to sue the government because the legislature sets funding priorities, and there is a very high bar to prove that funding is based on an unconstitutional method. Because many Texas laws are blatantly racist, if they added a penalty of prison for not following or enforcing them and causing demonstrable harm, the courts would get involved sooner. If there is no quantifiable harm, the courts are unlikely to get involved, and it is much more difficult to change the law, as that is up to the legislature.

If there is one thing we have learned since 2016, it is that laws only matter if people enforce them. Sometimes people are willing to enforce them, and sometimes they are not. Politicians have often acted as though they are above the law, and with recent Supreme Court decisions and actions by the Federal administration, we now know they are. So, while it may be stomach-turning to think this way, it is not unreasonable to ask WWTD, What Would *They* Do? *They* are powerful and unscrupulous legislators, corrupt and racist attorneys general, governors, or presidents. Would they follow a law that *they* found unjust, unfair, or inconvenient?

Sometimes, the best answer is to avoid doing what *they* want you to do. Teachers and administrators will have to evaluate which laws will be enforced, which are stalled, and which are ignored. Educators tend to want to be the *best,* which often means being the first to comply. We need to stop that. Be the last to comply. Comply unwillingly. Drag your feet. Sabotage the reports. Corrupt the data. Undermine those who want to jump headfirst into complying with laws that will harm our students. If you are able to do so, join lawsuits and muck up the gears of power.

We are one year into the new Administration as I finish this second edition. They have declared there are only two genders, taken over the entire federal budget to weed out "wokeness and DEI," banned wokeness and DEI in "all schools," using Executive Orders and other performative and unconstitutional memorandums. Roundups of immigrants by masked, heavily armed people, targeting schools and children to pressure parents. Unqualified billionaires are occupying Cabinet positions. While all these ridiculous antics and purposeful chaos will ultimately fail, the damage they are causing is on us. Unfortunately, governments of the United States, from the local school boards to the executive branch in Washington, DC, are capricious, inept, cruel, and corrupt. Therefore, it is morally necessary to evaluate and disrupt the mandates imposed by the powerful that target our students and communities.

For those who want to think that they should be above that kind of unlawfulness or that it is immoral to be non-compliant, remember that sit-ins, marches, the Freedom Rides, the Montgomery Bus Boycott, Rosa Parks sitting in the front of the bus, and Gandhi's March to Sea were all illegal. Pastors criticized Dr. King for breaking the law. They called the Birmingham campaign "unwise and untimely" and asked him to wait until the rest of the community came around. He responded from the jail in Birmingham, Alabama after being arrested for marching.

> We know through painful experience that freedom is never voluntarily given by the oppressor; it must be demanded by the oppressed. Frankly, I have yet to engage in a direct action campaign that was "well timed" in the view of those who have not suffered unduly from the disease of segregation. For years now, I have heard the word "Wait!" It rings in the ear of every Negro with piercing familiarity. This "Wait" has almost always meant "Never." We must come to see, with one of our distinguished jurists, that "justice too long delayed is justice denied." (King, 1963)

In the face of unjust laws, educators must remember that compliance is not a moral absolute—it is a choice that must be weighed against the ethical obligation to protect students. Laws are tools of power, shaped by those who wield them, and their legitimacy depends not on their existence but on their alignment with justice. When laws perpetuate harm, educators have a responsibility to resist, just as those who came before us resisted unjust systems that oppressed the communities we serve. The history of civil rights movements demonstrates that progress requires acts of courage and defiance, not passive acceptance.

To resist does not mean acting recklessly, but rather acting strategically and with purpose. Resistance can take many forms: delaying compliance, exposing harm, sabotaging enforcement systems, or joining collective legal challenges. These actions are not about lawlessness but about prioritizing students' well-being and the integrity of education over blind adherence to policies designed to oppress. As Dr. King reminded us from his Birmingham cell, waiting for a *better time* to resist injustice is a luxury that those who suffer under oppression cannot afford. The urgency of justice demands action, even when it is uncomfortable or difficult.

White educators have the power to disrupt systems of harm through collective resistance, solidarity, and a commitment to moral integrity. When laws threaten equality, inclusion, and truth, compliance becomes complicity. Resistance becomes a duty. The tools of defiance may be small—a delayed report, a reworded policy, a refusal to yield—but they carry the weight of justice. By resisting unjust laws, educators continue the legacy of those who dared to say NO to systems of oppression and YES to hope, joy, and love.

Being an accomplice for students and communities of color will transform teaching, teachers, and their schools and communities (Harden

& Harden-Moore, 2019). However, there are choices. Teachers can keep going as they have, perpetuating white supremacy until the end, but the end will come. Beyond demographic changes, the societal wave ahead will demand that teachers change. Whiteness is a dead end. To teach well is to change the world. Change it to a world your Black students want to live in.

Potatoes and the Art of Resistance

While listening to National Public Radio in my car years ago, I heard a commentator tell a story that has stayed with me long after the details of the broadcast were forgotten. It went something like this.

During the Second World War, in a Nazi prison camp, several captured GIs were tasked daily with growing and processing potatoes that were then shipped off to feed the Nazi soldiers. Potatoes are a staple in war and in feeding armies, as they store well and can be used in many ways to feed soldiers, even under fire. These prisoners, as was typical, were underfed and under-clothed, and I cannot imagine the despair they must have been fighting to stay alive in that situation. They were literally feeding their own captors and oppressors of millions. They even had no tools with which to do their jobs. They dug in the dirt with their bare hands to grow these potatoes. One thing that became available to them was small bits of barbed wire left on the ground from the construction of the camp.

As the potatoes were harvested, the prisoners took a small piece of the barbed wire and surreptitiously pierced the skin of as many potatoes as they could. This compromised the integrity of the potatoes as they were being shipped to the front. Now, each potato was more likely to rot before reaching the soldiers at the front, and one rotten potato could compromise the others. The prisoners were never sure that their small acts of resistance were successful. They hoped that it was, but in the end, the fact that they resisted was the most significant. They did survive, and that survival was an important act of rebellion. The Nazis wanted to work them to death, benefit from their labor, and dispose of them. In the end, it was their captors who were disposed of.

For white teachers working in states where racist laws are passed and books are banned, the story of the GIs in the Nazi prison camp offers a powerful metaphor for resistance. Just as the prisoners used the small pieces of barbed wire to sabotage the potatoes, educators can find ways to resist oppressive systems, even when direct confrontation seems impossible or dangerous. These small acts—introducing critical thinking into lessons, fostering inclusive classroom discussions, or quietly sharing banned books— may seem insignificant in the moment, but collectively, they can undermine the foundations of hate and ignorance.

Resistance is not always about grand gestures; often, it is about the courage to persist and to refuse complicity in systems that harm and oppress. Like the GIs, you may never fully know the impact of your actions, but the act of standing against injustice, even in small ways, holds immense power. These acts are meaningful and necessary, whether it's advocating for a marginalized student, finding creative ways to introduce diverse perspectives, or simply surviving and maintaining your role as an ally in a hostile environment.

The prisoners' survival was their ultimate defiance, and for teachers, remaining in the profession while upholding solidarity and the values of equity, inclusion, and truth is an act of profound rebellion. Each day that teachers act with integrity, they resist. Each lesson that empowers students to think critically, each conversation that validates a marginalized voice, and each quiet refusal to let censorship win, adds up to a collective force for change.

In a speech given in 1922, Mahatma Gandhi explained, "In my humble opinion, non-cooperation with evil is as much a duty as is cooperation with good." Remember, oppressive systems aim to sow fear and silence, but resistance—however small—is never futile. The work of an educator, even under oppressive conditions, is a form of hope and defiance. Like the prisoners who fought back with barbed wire and bare hands, teachers are part of a larger struggle for justice, and their courage inspires others to join the fight.

Practical Examples in Times of Chaos and Crisis: The Pandemic in Minneapolis

In March 2020, I submitted the first edition of this book to the publisher after six years of researching, writing, and editing. As I was making the final edits, a worldwide pandemic hit, challenging all the structures that hold a social system based on White supremacy in place. The stress on the system was considerable, and white people were asked to sacrifice things they once took for granted for the greater good. The responses to the emergency revealed who we are as individuals and as a nation. As expected, a small but vocal contingent of white people revealed they were not equipped for it.

However, the crisis inspired a new appreciation for *essential* workers like nurses and doctors, who were lauded through symbolic messages of care and gratitude, such as clapping for them at the end of their shift, and porch lights illuminated whole cities in the evenings. Parents on social media expressed their thanks to teachers who were called upon to radically change classroom instruction in both sincere and humorous ways. For retail workers, people acknowledged the contributions of the lowest-paid employees at grocery stores, mechanics, gas stations, and fast food restaurants. Through it all, the feelings of appreciation were met with critical voices who asked whether these symbolic gestures would lead to real change in how workers are paid, how benefits are secured, and if healthcare would be acknowledged as a right in the wealthiest country in the world.

The sudden school shutdowns after spring break were traumatic for teachers during the pandemic. Teachers were suddenly expected, with a few days' notice, to retool their curriculum and pedagogy to an online format. Teachers worked furiously, sometimes with little resources, often with little sleep, to connect with all their students. Even teachers with little to no background in virtual learning formats spent days researching new online teaching strategies and tools to provide the most effective instruction they could for their students. This emergency exposed disparities in students' access to technology and the internet, and highlighted the glaring inequality in access to information in America, often called the *digital divide*. It unveiled the privilege of economic classes when telecommuting parents could facilitate lessons at home. America saw the wealth gap as white people complained that they were hunkered down with their children in homes that included every possible comfort. As an observer on several platforms, I witnessed teachers break down as they described their exhaustion, feelings of inadequacy to the task, and the heartbreaking stories they heard from their students. My college students told me of their struggles with children, job losses, and emergency living arrangements due to the crisis.

People across the nation, from all walks of life, worked in solidarity, even though they were physically separated by the need to contain COVID-19.

Time and again, I watched teachers build and enact solidarity in small and large ways. They held car parades in neighborhoods to bolster their students' spirits, and others engaged in more structural acts of solidarity by fundraising online for computers, servers, and cameras so students could participate in classes. Teachers told stories of extraordinary feats to reach students who had no means of communication at their houses and celebrated their return online. Seniors who missed prom, graduation, and a long list of *lasts*—their last game, the last day of classes, the last time cleaning out their locker— had teachers and administrators create online proms and virtual graduations, with teachers recording well-wishes for grads as they crossed virtual stages.

While all this was happening, teachers advocated for more resources for themselves and their students to deliver curriculum and keep students engaged. They demanded them from their schools, districts, and states. The governmental response to the crises was demonstrably ineffective, and teachers took up much of the slack. These acts of solidarity mattered to students and communities, and the relationships that were built and preserved would be needed as the next crises erupted.

Minneapolis

My hometown of Minneapolis is a wonderful place with a diversity that surprises many who visit. That said, it is also a place of segregation and great violence by the police. The state of Minnesota is #2 in the nation for racial inequality, right behind Wisconsin. Black people, those who identify as African American and more recent immigrants, make up 19 percent of the population of Minneapolis. However, they make up two-thirds of those who are subject to force by police. I have witnessed the Minneapolis police brutalize students, protesters, and unarmed adults my entire adult life. As a teacher, I worked to shield my students from their wrath and advocated for the removal of police from our school and the Minneapolis school district.

On May 25, 2020, businesses began reopening even though the threat from COVID-19 was still very real. George Floyd entered Cup Foods on 38th and Chicago Avenue in Minneapolis. It is a neighborhood I know well, as it is only about a mile and a half from South High, where I taught. On that spring day, Mr. Floyd was detained and murdered by strangulation by a police officer who knelt on top of his neck while he was face down and handcuffed. This occurred in broad daylight, in front of multiple witnesses, with cellphone cameras recording. The police officer who strangled Mr. Floyd seemed unfazed by the attention during this horrific event. As Mr. Floyd begged for air and repeated, "I can't breathe," the officer continued to press his knee into his victim. Three other officers, two of them rookies, kept crowds away as Mr. Floyd lay dying.

Mr. Floyd died that day, and the video taken of his death by a seventeen-year-old girl immediately raced across the globe. Demands for justice rose just as swiftly. In Minneapolis, people of all races took to rain-soaked streets the next day to protest the brutality of the death and to demand the arrests of all four officers involved. Minneapolis police met them in riot gear. Police fired teargas and rubber bullets directly at protesters who were marching peacefully in the streets. They fired gas canisters out of moving vehicles. They fired at journalists covering the protests and generally sought to escalate the tension.

Acts of Caring Solidarity in this new stage of crises were displayed everywhere in Minneapolis, from the streets to the schools. A few examples are given here, but many more were done in private and will only be known to those involved. Beginning on the first day of protests, Minneapolis teachers were out in force, marching with community members, getting gassed by police, and demanding justice for Mr. Floyd and their students who face harassment and potential death at the hands of law enforcement daily. As Lake Street businesses and the third Precinct Police Station burned in an uprising that night, teachers checked on students online and by phone to ensure they were secure and out of harm's way. The next day, local artists, including Greta McLain, whose murals grace South High and the cover of this book, created a mural of Mr. Floyd on the side of Cup Foods that has become a memorial. The day after the burnings, teachers and community members flooded the streets to clean up and help businesses board up to prevent further damage. After much of the food distribution infrastructure had broken down due to fires, teachers organized food drives and created bags to distribute to local families. After a week of protests, the Minneapolis school board voted unanimously to sever its ties with the Minneapolis Police Department. The idea was that Minneapolis police would no longer patrol the halls of Minneapolis public schools. The schools planned to take the summer to develop a new plan that, hopefully, would replace School Resource Officers with counselors, social workers, and educators who can help students resolve conflicts without sending them to juvenile detention. Shortly after, the

Minneapolis Parks and Recreation system followed suit. A few days after that, in a stunning development, Minneapolis voted to disband the entire Minneapolis Police Department (MPD). It would be replaced with a new, community-based public service department.

In the days that followed Mr. Floyd's death, national and worldwide protests erupted with people all over the globe. People were making the connection between state violence and the ideology of white supremacy and calling for change. To illustrate, after the uprising in Minneapolis, young people have gone after edifices of white supremacy across the country and the world. The symbols of white supremacy, such as Confederate monuments and statues, began to fall, toppled by crowds of people, young, old, Black, and White, in places like Richmond and Norfolk, Virginia. Over one hundred of these trophies to a failed ideology were removed by the people who had lived among them for too long.

Players, coaches, and many others apologized to Collin Kaepernick, the 49ers player who knelt in protest of police brutality four years prior and was blacklisted. In Europe, people pulled down the statues of a slave trader in Bristol, England, and in Belgium, they are pulling down the former King of Belgium, Leopold II, who enslaved the Congo in the 1800s. In the United States, cities painted BLACK LIVES MATTER on their roads, even the one that led to the White House in DC. The mayor of DC changed the name of the square outside the White House to BLACK LIVES MATTER square. While the gestures were often symbolic, they were also powerful. Standing in solidarity comes in both symbolic and substantive forms. The structural and the personal are equally important. One without the other does not create a more equitable community.

After the 2025 presidential inauguration, most of these public affirmations were systematically removed as part of a broader effort to whitewash American cities and their histories. Under the current administration, murals were painted over, street names were reverted, and public statements of solidarity were reclassified as partisan disruptions rather than democratic expressions of community will. This erasure is not incidental; it is a deliberate attempt to obscure the nation's ongoing racial struggles and to restore a sanitized narrative of American life—one in which state power remains unchallenged by demands for justice. The removal of these symbols demonstrates their potency: if they were merely decorative, they would have been ignored. Instead, their presence so forcefully confronted entrenched systems of racial hierarchy that eliminating them became a political priority, signaling an effort to reclaim public space for a vision of America that resists accountability and rejects the truth these symbols once boldly declared.

In a more substantive change, after Minneapolis removed police officers from schools in 2020, the district replaced them with eleven unarmed public safety support specialists by September of the same year. This change led to fewer students being punished and significantly fewer interactions with law enforcement.

> During the 2020–21 school year, when Minneapolis police officers staffed schools, there were nearly 250 instances where student discipline involved law enforcement in some way, ranging from a conversation with an officer to legal action. In the first half of [the 21–22 school year], it happened just 13 times. (Janzer, 2022, online)

However, racial disparities in disciplinary actions persisted, with Black students disproportionately affected, with one-third of the student body identifying as African American, but "accounted for 70% of disciplinary actions in the first half of last school year" (Janzer, 2022, online). While schools nationwide reported increased disruptive behaviors post-pandemic, educators in Minneapolis generally did not attribute these challenges to the absence of police officers. Educators and administrators found that restorative practices and community-focused approaches effectively addressed safety and discipline (Janzer, 2022).

In June 2020, nine members of the Minneapolis City Council announced their intent to dismantle the MPD (Minneapolis Police Department) and explore alternative public safety models. However, this pledge did not lead to immediate disbandment, as the specific plans and steps were not clearly defined. In November 2021, Minneapolis voters faced Question 2, a ballot measure proposing replacing the MPD with a Department of Public Safety. The measure aimed to adopt a comprehensive public health approach to safety but was ultimately rejected by 56.2 percent of voters. Voters from the western, more white, affluent part of Minneapolis organized an effort to vote no, explicitly telling voters that a "NO" vote did not make them "racist" but were citizens concerned for their safety. They joined with conservative members of the Black community to defeat the measure. After the vote, many embittered activists who had been fighting police brutality in Minneapolis for generations told white voters that it was time to "hand over the Black Lives Matter signs" that were ubiquitous in the yards of west side homes.

As of 2025, the MPD continues to operate, though it has undergone various reforms and remains under scrutiny. Investigations by the US Department of Justice and the Minnesota Department of Human Rights have led to preliminary agreements for further reforms, though binding consent decrees have not been finalized. Unfortunately, those efforts have been discontinued under the new administration (Lynch & Gaudsward, 2024).

Lessons and Impact

The events of 2020 show the profound and interconnected challenges faced during the COVID-19 pandemic and the uprising following George Floyd's murder in Minneapolis. These crises laid bare the systemic inequities entrenched in American society and showed that solidarity allowed people to work together to address them. It was not missionaries dropping from some far-flung place that lifted the people of Minneapolis during the crisis. It was not the Federal Government, as our country's leaders were wholly inept, as the varied crises exposed. Teachers and other community members demonstrated Caring Solidarity in extraordinary ways, from supporting students during unprecedented educational disruption to organizing food drives and demanding systemic changes in public safety. While born of immediate necessity, these acts exemplify how communities can mobilize to create meaningful change.

Witnessing people put themselves in harm's way, facing injury from rubber bullets to demand justice, should inspire us all to meet their sacrifices with our own courage. The tragic losses of Joseph Rosenbaum and Anthony Huber in Wisconsin, both killed by a seventeen-year-old white supremacist who specifically came to Wisconsin to kill protesters, and Renee Nicole Good, murdered by an ICE officer in broad daylight while trying to leave a Minneapolis street, less than a mile from where George Floyd was murdered. These killings underscore the stakes of standing against injustice. Their bravery reminds us of the personal cost that can accompany being an accomplice. It is vital to recognize that symbolic gestures and shaping narratives are potent tools against inequality, yet they can provoke the same level of resistance and violence as direct actions. This reality calls for unwavering resolve—be aware and ready to stand when others run and to push when others ease away in fear. Symbolic actions, while deeply impactful, must be paired with substantive efforts to dismantle oppressive systems and build a society rooted in justice and equity.

The progress in Minneapolis Public Schools, from removing police from schools to implementing restorative practices, demonstrates that change is possible when teachers and administrators work in solidarity with communities. The commitment is long, the journey is complex, and the work is hard. It will cost, but ultimately, it is our most important historical endeavor. We can create a world where all people know they belong and are valued.

Discussion Question from Chapter 9

1   How does the concept of an accomplice differ from that of an ally or advocate? What risks and responsibilities are unique to the role of an accomplice in fostering equity and dismantling systemic oppression in schools?

2   Powell and Kelly argued that risk distinguishes an accomplice from an ally. What specific risks might white teachers take when acting as accomplices in solidarity with Black and Brown students? How can they leverage their privilege effectively in these situations?

3   The chapter describes various ways educators can disrupt white supremacy in their institutions. Which actions described—such as confronting racist policies, supporting protests, or advocating for restorative practices—resonate with you, and why? How might these actions transform schools?

4   The chapter stresses the importance of pairing symbolic actions with substantive changes. How can educators ensure their actions as accomplices have a meaningful impact rather than being performative? Share examples of both symbolic and substantive acts in an educational context.

5   Being an accomplice often involves engaging in activism outside of school, such as attending protests, supporting community initiatives, or challenging unjust laws. How can teachers balance their professional responsibilities with their commitment to broader social justice efforts?

6   The chapter highlights disparities in school funding and systemic inequities, such as the school-to-prison pipeline. How should teachers

in solidarity address these structural issues within their classrooms and advocate for change at the institutional level?

7   Discuss the role of resistant capital, as outlined by Yosso, in empowering students of color to challenge systems of oppression. How can white educators incorporate resistant capital into their curriculum?

Actionable Classroom Practices from Chapter 9

- **Use Your Privilege to Shield Students**

  Act as a buffer for students of color in disciplinary situations. If a situation escalates, step in to mediate or de-escalate before administration or law enforcement is involved, ensuring students remain in the classroom rather than entering the school-to-prison pipeline.

- **Incorporate Restorative Practices**

  Replace punitive discipline methods with restorative practices in your classroom. For example, when conflict arises, facilitate a circle process to allow students to share their perspectives and collaboratively resolve the issue.

- **Interrupt Microaggressions and Racist Behaviors**

  If you witness a colleague or student engaging in microaggressions or making racially insensitive comments, call it out respectfully but firmly. For example, you could say, "That's not an appropriate way to describe this student's behavior. Let's focus on solutions instead."

- **Support Student Activism**

  Actively encourage and support students who are organizing around issues of social justice. For instance, help them plan a school-wide event, create materials, or ensure they have access to resources such as meeting space or technology.

- **Attend and Advocate at School Board Meetings**

  Attend local school board meetings to advocate for changes that benefit marginalized students, such as removing police from schools or increasing funding for mental health resources and counselors.

- **Mentor Students in Navigating Power Structures**

  Teach students how to advocate for themselves in school and beyond. This could include guiding them on how to write effective letters, request meetings with administrators, or speak up about inequities in a professional manner.

- **Publicly Support Equity Initiatives**

  Use your social media platforms, school communications, or community outreach to champion equity initiatives, such as sharing articles about anti-racism or promoting events that address systemic injustices.

- **Leverage Resources for Marginalized Communities**

  Provide resources to marginalized students and their families. For example, share grant or scholarship opportunities, invite community leaders to speak to your class or organize a donation drive to meet immediate needs like school supplies or food security.

10 Teachers as Public Intellectuals in Solidarity with Students

Henry Giroux (2024) highlighted educators' critical role in combating authoritarianism and fostering democratic values. Giroux warned of the dangers posed by far-right ideologies that weaponize education to promote indoctrination, suppress intellectual freedom, and perpetuate systemic oppression. Drawing from Holocaust survivor Primo Levi's insights on fascism, Giroux underscored the urgency for educators to resist efforts to rewrite history, propagate hate, and dismantle public education as a democratic project.

Like Freire and others, Giroux argued that education is inherently political and that educators, as public intellectuals, are responsible for challenging systems of oppression, fostering critical thinking, exposing structural inequalities, and promoting social justice. He critiqued the right-wing push for *patriotic education* as a guise for white supremacist indoctrination and stressed the importance of developing a language of critique and possibility. This includes creating new pedagogical frameworks that empower students to analyze societal injustices and envision transformative change. Giroux argued that the fight for democratic education is inseparable from the broader struggle for economic and social justice. Educators are best suited to lead efforts to create counter-public spheres that resist oppressive ideologies, foster critical consciousness, and advocate for a sustainable and equitable future. Resistance is not optional; it is a moral and civic necessity in the face of rising extremism and the erosion of democratic values.

White teachers occupy a unique position in the educational landscape, where privilege affords them access to spaces, conversations, and audiences that can be leveraged to advocate for justice, uplift the teaching profession, and stand in solidarity with students. While privilege can be a barrier to recognizing inequities, it can also be a powerful tool for disrupting misinformation, challenging structural oppression, and building inclusive communities within and beyond the classroom. To navigate this responsibility, white teachers should embrace their role as advocates and allies, balancing courage, humility, and intentionality in their actions.

One of the most critical roles white teachers can play is correcting misinformation. Public education is under siege by false narratives. For example, claims that Critical Race Theory is indoctrinating students, that teachers are pushing divisive agendas, and that inclusive curricula threaten traditional values not only undermine the profession but also harm students. White teachers can push back against these falsehoods by sharing credible information, amplifying the voices of experts, and reframing discussions to emphasize truth. When misinformation arises—whether in conversations or online spaces—white teachers can step in, not to dominate the dialogue but to provide clarity and encourage reflection. Framing corrections constructively, through questions and evidence, can foster understanding, hopefully without escalating conflict.

Advocating for the teaching profession also requires a deliberate effort to counter negative stereotypes. Teachers are portrayed in right-wing media as overpaid or ineffective, narratives that fuel disrespect for the profession and hinder systemic reform. White teachers can combat these misconceptions by celebrating their colleagues' successes, highlighting transformative classroom work, and mentoring newer educators to build a supportive professional network. Advocacy also involves engaging with unions and professional organizations to amplify educators' collective voices and push for better policies, resources, and protections.

Standing in Caring Solidarity with students demands courage, knowledge, and commitment. It begins with listening to students and creating opportunities for them to share their experiences. By centering student voices, teachers send a powerful message that their perspectives are valued and essential to the learning environment. White teachers who are in solidarity with students and communities use their privilege to advocate for resources and programming that benefit students from marginalized communities, ensuring their needs are met and their identities are celebrated. This advocacy extends beyond the classroom, pushing for systemic changes that address inequities in funding, discipline policies, and access to quality education.

Solidarity also requires confronting uncomfortable truths, particularly the ways white supremacy operates within schools and communities. Charles Mills argued in *The Racial Contract* (1997) that systemic inequities are maintained through deliberate ignorance—an epistemology that shields white people from acknowledging their complicity in oppressive structures. White teachers have a responsibility to disrupt this ignorance, both within themselves and in their communities. Caring Solidarity means addressing instances of bias and exclusion, fostering dialogues on challenging topics, and actively supporting students and colleagues who face discrimination.

At the same time, white teachers must navigate these efforts with care and self-reflection. Solidarity does not mean speaking over marginalized voices or positioning oneself as a savior. Instead, it involves stepping back to amplify those voices and sharing the spotlight with colleagues, students, and families directly impacted by racism. Being in Caring Solidarity also means recognizing when to step forward and use privilege as a shield—whether by speaking out at school board meetings, addressing harmful policies, or pushing back against retaliation—while creating space for others to lead when they feel ready.

To sustain this work, white teachers must also prioritize resilience and hope. Advocacy is demanding and often met with resistance, but small victories—whether in the form of a meaningful conversation, a student's breakthrough, or a classroom project that fosters understanding—can make a significant impact. By sharing stories of resistance and highlighting individuals and movements that have fought for justice, white teachers can inspire students to believe in their own power and the possibilities for change. Encouraging students to take ownership of their learning and participate in initiatives that reflect their identities reinforces this hope.

Finally, building coalitions is essential to creating lasting change. White teachers are not alone in this fight; many colleagues, parents, and community members share their commitment to equity and justice. Strengthening these connections through professional learning communities, advocacy organizations, and family partnerships provides the support needed to counter Conservative challenges. Along with the teacher's union, organizations like the Zinn Education Project, Teaching for Change, and Rethinking Schools offer resources and networks to help educators resist censorship, promote social justice, and create inclusive classrooms.

Ultimately, white teachers have a choice. They can remain passive beneficiaries of privilege or use their position to advance equity and justice.

By embracing the latter, they can disrupt oppressive narratives, uplift the profession, and create classrooms where all students are valued and empowered. In doing so, they not only fulfill their ethical responsibility as educators but also contribute to a larger movement for a more inclusive and equitable society. Furthermore, as frontline agents of change, white teachers have the power—and the obligation—to make a difference.

Navigating the intersection of advocacy and safety is critical for white teachers who wish to leverage their privilege effectively. While standing in solidarity with students and challenging systemic oppression is essential, doing so in the public sphere—especially on social media or in community-facing roles—requires careful consideration. The power of social media as a tool for advocacy is undeniable, yet it also presents risks that can undermine professional standing or personal safety if not approached thoughtfully. By balancing bold advocacy with strategic caution, teachers can create a public presence that promotes justice while safeguarding their role in the profession. The following list of do's and don'ts provides practical guidance for maintaining professionalism, amplifying equity, and staying secure online.

Do's

1 **Know Your District's Policies**:
   - Familiarize yourself with your district's social media guidelines and any relevant state laws regarding online activity for public employees.
   - Make sure you are using your voice as a citizen and not speaking for a district.

2 **Create Professional Boundaries**:
   - Use separate accounts for personal and professional purposes.
   - Ensure professional accounts are focused on education-related content, advocacy, and resources.

3 **Use Privacy Settings Wisely**:
   - Adjust privacy settings to limit who can view your personal posts.
   - Regularly review these settings to stay ahead of platform updates.

4   **Focus on Educational Content**:
    - Share articles, lesson ideas, and resources related to equity, justice, and inclusive education.
    - Highlight student success stories (while respecting FERPA, The Family Educational Rights and Privacy Act of 1974).

5   **Engage Thoughtfully**:
    - Use social media to promote constructive dialogue and share factual information.
    - Amplify the voices of organizations, scholars, and activists aligned with your values.

6   **Use Cautious Language**:
    - Frame your advocacy in terms of professional integrity and educational goals.
    - Emphasize your commitment to supporting all students and creating inclusive learning environments.

7   **Leverage Professional Platforms**:
    - Use platforms like LinkedIn or Bluesky to connect with educators and advocacy organizations. Avoid platforms with many trolls and bots.
    - Share successes in your classroom and ideas for inclusive teaching.

8   **Be Strategic with Hashtags**:
    - Use advocacy hashtags like #EdEquity, #AntiRacistEducation, or #TeachTruth to join broader conversations.

9   **Document Harassment**:
    - If you face harassment online, document the interactions and report abusive behavior to the platform and, if necessary, to your employer or legal support.

10 **Promote Online Civility**:
    - Model respectful and solution-focused communication, even when engaging in challenging topics.

Don'ts

1 Don't Overshare Personal Information:

- Do not post your address, phone number, or other private details.
- Be cautious about sharing photos or content that reveal your location.

2 Don't Engage in Heated Arguments:

- Avoid responding to trolls or engaging in public spats that could escalate or be taken out of context.

3 Don't Post During School Hours:

- Posting during work hours can lead to questions about your focus and professionalism.

4 Don't Share Student Information:

- Do not post photos, names, or identifying details of students without explicit parental consent.
- Even with consent, consider whether sharing is necessary.

5 Don't Use Offensive or Inflammatory Language:

- Avoid posts that could be interpreted as disrespectful, even if they are intended as humor.

6 Don't Assume Your Posts Are Private:

- Even with strong privacy settings, content can be screenshotted or shared.

7 Steer Clear of Partisan Political Posts:

- Focus on educational equity and justice rather than overt endorsements or criticisms of political candidates to avoid potential conflicts with district policies.

8 Don't Share Unverified Information:

- Fact-check before sharing news, articles, or statistics to avoid spreading misinformation.

9 Don't Vent About Work:

- Do not post complaints about colleagues, administrators, or students online, as it could harm relationships and your professional reputation.

- This can also be cause for dismissal, making all your solidarity work suspect. Think about how each post can increase solidarity, not tear it down.

10   Don't Use School Resources for Advocacy Posts:
- Avoid posting from school computers or using district accounts for personal advocacy, as this could violate policies.

Tips for Balancing Advocacy and Safety

- **Use Your Voice Thoughtfully**: Frame advocacy as a professional commitment to equity, solidarity, and quality education for your students. Highlight shared values like fairness, inclusion, and respect.

- **Leverage Collective Advocacy**: Join professional organizations or teacher coalitions that advocate for justice. This helps diffuse individual risks while amplifying impact.

- **Know When to Step Back**: If a post or conversation attracts negative attention, disengage rather than escalate.

- **Rely on Trusted Networks**: Collaborate with educators, unions, and advocacy groups for guidance on navigating public pushback.

- **Create Backup Plans**: Be prepared to deactivate accounts temporarily or refer harassment to legal or union support if necessary.

Discussion Questions for Chapter 10

1   Giroux argued that education is inherently political and that educators have a responsibility to challenge systems of oppression. How can teachers incorporate critical pedagogy into their classrooms to foster democratic values and critical thinking? What are some concrete lesson ideas or classroom strategies that align with this approach?

2   Drawing from Charles Mills' concept of the *Racial Contract*, the chapter discusses how white supremacy is maintained through deliberate ignorance. How can white educators critically reflect on their own positionality and avoid falling into patterns of complicity? What strategies can help them engage in ongoing self-education and accountability in their advocacy for students and colleagues from marginalized communities?

3   The chapter discusses how white teachers can leverage their privilege to combat misinformation and support marginalized students. What are some specific strategies white teachers can use to disrupt oppressive narratives while ensuring they amplify the voices of marginalized groups rather than overshadow them? How can they remain accountable in this work?

4   According to the chapter, misinformation and stereotypes about teachers and inclusive curricula are pervasive. What role do educators have in countering these narratives in their communities and online? Discuss how educators can engage in fact-based advocacy while avoiding the pitfalls of online confrontations and misinformation themselves.

5   The chapter highlights the importance of solidarity and resilience among educators advocating for equity and justice. What are some ways teachers can build coalitions with colleagues, parents, and community organizations to strengthen their efforts?

11 Refusing to Give In to Banning and Bullying

When I began this book project in 2013, there were rumblings about what was to come, but I was honestly stunned when Americans elected Trump. As Dave Chappelle said after the 2016 election, I should not have been, "I know the whites," he mocked our surprise. I know them, too, and yet I still cannot shake the hope that white people can do better. Many do, but not enough of us are willing, able, and ready to live in a multiracial democracy. As the first term dragged on, whipping us from outrageous cruelty to blatantly illegal and treasonous acts without consequences, I had hoped that America had learned her lesson. However, with a second term, things are getting a lot worse for teachers, families, and our students of color. I say "our" because my current students are also under threat.

As a teacher and teacher-leader in the early 2000s, I found myself battling white supremacists over curriculum at the statehouse and in public forums like newspapers and blog sites (Spies et al., 2004). During this period, I faced threats to my job from legislators, received hostile emails in my school inbox, and even had unsigned letters sent to my home and workplace filled with derogatory comments, threats, and accusations. But because I was part of a broad coalition of teachers, parents, education professors, and professional organizations, we were able to come together to resist these awful reactionaries. Through persistence and solidarity, we won. As a result of that work and talking about it afterward in research presentations and a publication, I was offered a fellowship to attend Indiana University to get my PhD. My involvement with the resistance led me to more opportunities than I could have ever imagined, but that is a story for a later book.

In 2009, I left Minneapolis to join a doctoral program in Indiana. Although I had traveled through parts of the South, such as Oklahoma, to visit family and Florida, where my grandparents lived, I had never lived in a region where blatant racism was part of daily discourse. Indiana, I found out after I arrived, has a deeply entrenched history of white supremacy. The Ku Klux Klan was planted there in 1915 and grew to have the largest membership in the country by 1922. This legacy of segregation and racial violence still permeates the state's social fabric. The history of Klan-controlled towns and the segregation of Indianapolis public schools is both horrifying and instructive. For instance, educated Black residents of Indianapolis crafted eloquent letters and treatises published in newspapers, appealing to their neighbors to acknowledge their humanity and to prevent Hoosiers (people in Indiana) from segregating their schools and their lives (Pierce, 2012). This *polite protest* was not successful, and Indiana is still a highly segregated, racially hostile state.

This history was at the forefront of my mind in the summer of 2018 when I was invited to deliver a workshop on Culturally Relevant and Sustaining Pedagogy to a predominantly white group of high school teachers in a Midwestern suburb of a nearby state (Boucher, 2020; Paris, 2012). I approached this Midwestern suburb after Trump's first election with apprehension. I was aware of that region's history and feared my talk would provoke anger and white fragility (DiAngelo, 2018; Leiker, 2002). Their community mirrored so many others in the United States: racially segregated (Gutierrez, 2017; Mid-America Regional Council, 2014) yet experiencing a slow influx of people of color (Adler et al., 2019). The town's geography made these divides starkly visible, with one side deemed the *wrong* side and the other the *right* (white) side. Teachers unhesitatingly labeled schools as *good* or *bad*, with their evaluations tied to the racial and socioeconomic demographics of the student body. But rather than the anger I was worried about, I encountered fear. The teachers I met were polite and attentive but visibly troubled.

During the session, I recommended incorporating the works of Black authors into the curriculum, naming James Baldwin as a possibility. A white, middle-aged female social studies teacher timorously pushed back, recounting her experience receiving angry phone calls from parents after using a James Baldwin quote as a warm-up writing exercise. Her frustration was palpable—not only with what she experienced but also with me, the invited expert. Her challenge was clear. How could I so confidently suggest that she work in solidarity with her students when even a single sentence on the board provoked backlash?

In response, I asked the group: "Who are we afraid of?" An uncomfortable silence filled the room until I answered my own question: "We are afraid of white people."

Her reaction and the group's unease troubled me. Until that moment, I had not fully considered the concept of racial policing among white people, particularly of white, middle-class women. As a white man raised in the liberal, privileged enclave of Minneapolis, I had never experienced fear of other white people, despite my experiences years before. I always thought that these few knuckle-draggers were outliers and that the white people in America, generally, would not be threatened using Black knowledge in a classroom devoted to inquiry and investigation of the past. I assumed that white people were, deep down, as concerned with truth as I was.

I was wrong. Over the last decade, living and working in three Southern states, I have become aware of the racial rules that govern social and professional interactions here. While these rules are subtle in Minneapolis, they are overt and aggressively enforced in states like Indiana, Florida, and Texas.

What struck me was not the existence of these divides—ubiquitous across America—but the teachers' unwillingness to confront them. They listened to my presentation with interest but seemed skeptical about their ability to implement the strategies I suggested. Their hesitation was not rooted in ignorance or apathy but in fear—fear of their white neighbors, pastors, parents, and even students. In follow-up conversations, some teachers expressed a sincere commitment to racial inclusivity and justice but admitted being apprehensive about acting on those commitments. They feared social stigma, job loss, and even violence for supporting students of color or LGBTQ+ students (Brammer, 2017).

This realization was a profound shift for me. Across the country, I had heard teachers voice similar concerns, but I had not fully grasped their implications. What I witnessed was that most white people feel trapped by the implicit threat of losing their standing within white social structures. They remain in solidarity with whiteness—only partially out of sociopolitical allegiance but primarily out of fear. For these teachers, publicly standing with their students of color felt like crossing an unspoken line—a line drawn and enforced by other white people (Berman & Schmidt, 2017).

This dynamic complicates critical whiteness scholarship, which often focuses on the privileges white people hold and assumes that awareness of racialized power will naturally lead to action (DiAngelo, 2018; Sleeter,

2005). My observations challenge this assumption. They highlight an often-overlooked factor: white fear of other white people. This fear is a powerful force that perpetuates conservative and cautious approaches to race in schools. It silences even well-intentioned educators, trapping them in a cycle of passivity, and addressing this dynamic is critical if we are going to disrupt systemic oppression in education.

The Racial Contract and the Politics of Ignorance

As introduced in Chapter 10, Mills's *The Racial Contract* (1997) offers a critical framework for understanding this fear. Mills argued that white supremacy requires an intentional ignorance among white people to shield them from the cognitive dissonance of acknowledging the systemic harm their privilege perpetuates. He described the "racial contract" as a counterpart to the Enlightenment's "social contract." While the latter promised safety and freedom to citizens, the racial contract relegated colonized people to subservience, demanding their loyalty to a system that actively oppressed them (Mills, 1997, p. 11). Mills explained that this system necessitates a willful blindness:

> White misunderstanding, misrepresentation, evasion, and self-deception on matters related to race are among the most pervasive mental phenomena of the past few hundred years, a cognitive and moral economy psychically required for conquest, colonization, and enslavement. And these phenomena ... are prescribed by the terms of the Racial Contract. (Mills, 1997, p. 18)

This deliberate ignorance—what Mills termed an "epistemology of ignorance"—is sustained through narratives that portray systemic injustices as exceptions rather than the norm. He critiqued historians who framed US political culture as fundamentally egalitarian, ignoring the centrality of racism and white supremacy in shaping society (Mills, 2007, p. 17).

Confronting this ignorance requires more than awareness; it demands a willingness to challenge the social policing that enforces it. For educators, this means finding the courage to act in solidarity with their students despite the risks. Only by breaking this cycle of fear can we begin dismantling the racial contract that shapes American society.

Critical Race Theory and Moms for Liberty

Mills's insights provide a powerful lens to understand the historical and ongoing mechanisms of systemic racism, particularly the deliberate construction of ignorance to maintain racial hierarchies. This foundation unites with the panic over Critical Race Theory (CRT), the current administration's efforts to erase Diversity, Equity, and Inclusion (DEI), and the removal of any knowledge created by people of color in schools and the US Government.

CRT interrogates how racism is embedded within legal, political, and social institutions. While Mills was not a Critical Race Theorist, his work dovetails with CRT, as his focus was on the epistemological dimensions of racial injustice. CRT examines how these patterns of exclusion and oppression are perpetuated through structural and institutional practices. Together, these frameworks challenge the dominant narratives of neutrality and fairness, exposing how systemic inequities persist under the guise of progress. These frameworks lay bare the lies of much of the US education system that focuses on white goodness and enlightened progress.

Critical Race Theory (CRT) emerged from the Critical Legal Studies (CLS) movement in the 1970s, offering a sharp critique of how the law, even after landmark decisions like *Brown v. Board of Education* (1954), continued to uphold racial hierarchies. Scholars like Derrick Bell argued that the law is not neutral or objective but a product of social power structures that inherently disadvantage marginalized groups (Bell, 1980). Bell's "interest convergence" posited that racial progress only occurs when it aligns with the interests of white elites (Delgado & Stefancic, 1997). This framework shifted the focus of equality discourse toward the systemic and structural impact of race rather than individual acts of prejudice.

In education, CRT scholars Gloria Ladson-Billings and William Tate extended these critiques, focusing on how schools reproduce white supremacy through curricula, pedagogy, and policy (Ladson-Billings & Tate, 1995). According to Ladson-Billings (2013), CRT scholars subscribe to tenets identified by Delgado and Stefancic (1997):

- Racism is a normal part of American Society and is not an aberration. It is baked into law, society, and politics.

- Racial progress is only made when the interests of whites in power converge with Black and Indigenous people.

- Race is socially constructed and not biological.

- There are intersecting levels of oppression that are felt by different people, and the law seldom addresses that concept. People must have been harmed for a single reason and often cannot claim that there are multiple layers to their experience with discrimination.
- The words and experiences of Black and Indigenous people create a counternarrative that must be considered when producing laws and policies.

CRT's framework became a powerful tool for examining inequities in education, but it also became a lightning rod for Conservative backlash. Beginning in the early 2010s, right-wing commentators in the United States and the UK began targeting CRT, framing it as an ideological threat to white identity. By 2020, these critiques reached a fever pitch, as Conservatives worldwide blamed CRT for multiracial protests following the murder of George Floyd and the removal of Confederate monuments and other symbols of white supremacy worldwide (Birnbaum, 2020; Farrer, 2020; Harlan et al., 2020).

This rhetoric coalesced around the term "wokeness," which Conservatives weaponized to describe any attempt to challenge systemic inequality. Right-wing media amplified fabricated stories of CRT being taught in K-12 schools—despite CRT being a legal framework rarely taught outside graduate-level courses (Wolfe-Rocca & Nold, 2022). These narratives painted CRT as a divisive, anti-white ideology, claiming it indoctrinated children into feelings of guilt and self-loathing (Blackburn, 2021; Wong, 2021). The ensuing panic provided the foundation for legislative bans and organized resistance to any knowledge that did not derive specifically from white supremacy.

Beginning in the spring of 2020, mask mandates implemented to control the spread of COVID-19 became a focal point of disinformation, fueled not only by right-wing media but also by the Whitehouse and supporters of the President. Extremists, misled by lies circulating online and in right-wing media, labeled the virus a *hoax*, amplifying conspiracy theories. Protests against mask mandates initially gained attention, but as public interest waned amid the grim reality of over one million American deaths from the disease, organizers shifted their focus.

In 2021, this resistance gained a national face with the founding of Moms for Liberty in Florida. Ostensibly a parents' rights organization, Moms for Liberty quickly became a central force in the movement to ban books and curricula addressing race, gender, and sexuality (SPLC, 2024). The group's mission aligned seamlessly with the anti-CRT hysteria, framing their activism as a defense of parental control over education. However, their actions revealed a broader white supremacist agenda: suppressing discussions of systemic inequities and marginalizing already vulnerable communities.

Seeking to stoke anger and fear among less-educated white populations, Moms for Liberty spearheaded a coordinated strategy to mobilize white parents' anxieties, creating a moral panic that extended far beyond debates about school safety. By the summer of 2021, school board meetings across the country became battlegrounds for this unrest, where white parents were conflating mask mandates, CRT, and the visibility of trans students into one big ball of anger, fear, and ignorance. While some protesters were local parents, many were outside agitators emboldened by the group's inflammatory rhetoric. These confrontations frequently escalated into threats, harassment, and violence, targeting educators, librarians, and board members (Borter et al., 2022).

By 2023, the group had expanded its focus to include bans on books addressing gender identity and sexuality, characterizing these materials as *pornographic*. Texas became a leader in this crusade, with lawmakers and activists targeting school libraries and classrooms. In one instance, over one hundred books were removed from school libraries in a single Texas district after a Republican state lawmaker flagged 432 titles for review. Among the banned books were Pulitzer Prize-winning works like *Maus*, a graphic novel depicting the Holocaust, and numerous texts addressing slavery, segregation, and LGBTQ+ identities (Alfonseca, 2022).

Moms for Liberty's rhetoric mirrored earlier Conservative attacks on CRT, invoking fears of white replacement to justify sweeping censorship. The group presented itself as a defender of traditional values, claiming that its actions protected children from *inappropriate* material. In reality, their crusading sought to erase the experiences and histories of anyone they found inferior, reinforcing the epistemology of ignorance described by Mills. By framing their efforts as apolitical and focused solely on "protecting children," Moms for Liberty obscured their role in erasing anyone they did not consider white, straight, and Christian (Alfonseca, 2022).

Legislative Backlash: Banning CRT and Multicultural Education

White supremacist lawmakers seized on the momentum generated by Moms for Liberty, introducing bills across the United States to ban CRT and other content deemed controversial. Texas was an early adopter of cut-and-paste legislation from the Heritage Foundation, framed with race-neutral language specifically to ban students from learning about race, which was adopted in all former Confederate states. Texas Senate Bill 3, passed in 2021, directly targeted CRT principles, banning the teaching of ideas that frame systemic racism as central to American history or law. The law also prohibited teaching that slavery and racism were foundational to the nation's founding values (Castillo et al., 2022). Furthermore, the bill explicitly banned the *1619 Project* from K-12 schools, seeking to suppress narratives that challenge the myth of American exceptionalism (Hannah-Jones, 2019; Lopez, 2021a; 2021b; Najarro, 2022).

The results have been chilling. Texas now leads the nation in banning multicultural and gender-related content in schools (Lopez, 2022). Schools have been flooded with challenges to library books, many of which address issues of identity and systemic injustice. The coordinated efforts to suppress these materials reflect a broader resistance to confronting uncomfortable truths about American society.

In June 2023, the Southern Poverty Law Center (SPLC) officially designated Moms for Liberty as an "extremist organization" (Altschuler, 2023; SPLC, 2024). This classification marked a significant escalation in the scrutiny of the group, which has rapidly gained prominence as a driving force behind efforts to censor educational materials and limit discussions of race, gender, and sexuality in schools. The SPLC's decision was grounded in a thorough examination of the organization's activities, noting that while the group's website promotes a relatively innocuous agenda centered on parental rights, its actual practices reveal a more troubling pattern of targeting teachers and school officials. The SPLC also highlighted how Moms for Liberty's social media posts, policies, and practices often advance conspiracy theories and disseminate "hateful imagery and rhetoric against the LGBTQ community" (SPLC, 2024).

The designation underscored the growing concern among advocacy and professional organizations about the impact of Moms for Liberty's campaigns. The American Historical Association (AHA) strongly condemned the group's advocacy of censorship and its support for legislation severely restricting academic freedom. The AHA stated that such measures "render it impossible for historians to teach with professional integrity without risking job loss and other penalties" (AHA, 2023). This critique reflects a broader alarm about how these actions undermine the teaching of history and the principles of open inquiry and intellectual honesty that are foundational to education.

The backlash against CRT and the rise of Moms for Liberty illustrate the enduring power of white fear and the racial contract. As Mills argued, white supremacy relies on an epistemology of ignorance that shields individuals from confronting inequality. The panic over CRT and the censorship of educational materials reinforces this ignorance, ensuring that white narratives remain unchallenged.

Standing in Solidarity: What White Teachers Need To Know and Do

As attacks on Critical Race Theory (CRT), multicultural education, and inclusive curricula intensify, teachers committed to solidarity must be equipped with the knowledge, tools, and strategies to resist these efforts and advocate for their students. Standing against these attacks requires courage, a deep understanding of the systemic forces, and deliberate action to disrupt the status quo. Below are key insights and strategies for teachers to consider as they navigate this landscape.

Understand the Landscape of Oppression

To stand in solidarity, white teachers must first understand the systemic nature of the forces they are confronting. These include:

- **The Racial Contract**: As Charles Mills (1997) described, white supremacy is not an aberration but a foundational aspect of American society. Teachers must recognize how this racial contract manifests in schools— through inequitable funding, biased curricula, and disciplinary practices that disproportionately harm students of color.

- **Intersectionality**: Teachers need to consider how overlapping systems of oppression—based on race, gender, class, sexuality, and ability— affect their students differently (Crenshaw, 1997). Understanding these intersections helps educators identify and address specific barriers their students face.

- **Misinformation Campaigns**: Teachers should educate themselves on the myths surrounding CRT and related concepts. Conservative rhetoric often conflates CRT with any discussion of race or equity, framing it as divisive or harmful. Being well versed in the actual principles of CRT allows teachers to counter these falsehoods effectively.

Build and Strengthen Coalitions

Solidarity is not a solo effort. Know that you are not alone. Teachers across the country are waiting for someone to inspire them and show them how to overcome this culture of ignorance sweeping the nation. Teachers must collaborate to create supportive networks that amplify their voices and protect them from isolation. This includes:

- **Building Alliances with Colleagues**: Forming professional learning communities focused on equity can provide a safe space to share resources, discuss challenges, and strategize responses to attacks on inclusive education.

- **Engaging Parents and Community Members**: Parents of color support honest and inclusive education but feel excluded from conversations, and white parents are fearful of their neighbors. Engaging with intelligent white parents, along with parents of color who are understandably frightened and cautious at the moment, will go a long way toward making sure your students can engage in actual education.

- Teachers can hold community forums, share reading lists, and invite parents to participate in discussions about the importance of culturally relevant curricula.

- **Connecting with Advocacy Organizations**: Groups such as the Zinn Education Project (https://www.zinnedproject.org), Teaching for Change (https://www.teachingforchange.org), and Rethinking Schools (https://www.rethinkingschools.org) provide valuable resources and support for educators working to resist censorship and promote social justice in education.

- **JOIN THE UNION**: Teachers' unions, for all their problems—and there are many—are one of the few lifelines that can make a difference in this age of fear. However, we must also work to make these unions less timid, finger-wagging, and more effective through younger, more energetic leadership and a more confrontational stance to battle the forces destroying our schools and democracy.

Practice Courageous Truth-Telling

Solidarity requires the courage to speak truth to power, even when it is uncomfortable or risky. White teachers can:

- **Incorporate Counternarratives**: Following CRT principles, teachers can integrate the voices and experiences of marginalized communities into their lessons. This might include primary sources, literature, and art that challenge dominant narratives.

- **Teach Critical Media Literacy**: Students must learn to analyze and question the media they consume. By teaching them to identify bias, recognize propaganda, and evaluate sources, teachers can empower students to resist misinformation campaigns.

- **Create Opportunities for Dialogue**: Facilitating classroom discussions on topics like race, gender, and identity helps students develop empathy and critical thinking skills. Ground rules for respectful dialogue can create a safe space for these conversations (Brown, 2023; Singleton & Linton, 2006).

- **The Right-Wing Organizations Are Grifters**: Dialogue is essential, but it is also vital not to begin doubting yourself or your reality in the face of these efforts to demonize you or anti-racist work. These are not serious, intelligent people. The leaders of Moms for Liberty are ideologues, but their main objective is to rake in millions of dollars from frightened, uninformed, and misinformed white people. They have succeeded in that beyond their dreams. They are now being exposed as hypocrites, involved in sordid sex scandals, and more misbehavior. Don't take their arguments seriously. Don't give ground on logic or reality. Don't capitulate.

Know Your Rights and Protections

As backlash grows, white teachers will face administrative pushback, community criticism, and legislative scrutiny. They will be accused of being race traitors and criminal behavior. It is essential to:

- **Understand Local Policies**: Familiarize yourself with district policies, state laws, and national curriculum and teacher speech guidelines. This knowledge can help you navigate potential conflicts and advocate for your rights.

- **Document Incidents**: If you face challenges or censorship, document the events thoroughly. Keeping detailed records can provide evidence if you need to escalate concerns to your union or legal counsel.

- **Leverage Union Support**: Teachers' unions have resources and legal teams dedicated to defending educators against unfair treatment. Engage with your union to access these protections.

- **Join and Leverage Professional Organizations**: Professional organizations play a critical role in supporting teachers committed to equity, inclusion, and excellence in education. Joining these organizations provides access to valuable resources and connects educators with a community of like-minded professionals who can amplify their voices and efforts.

Model Resilience and Hope

Perhaps most importantly, teachers in solidarity must model resilience and hope for their students. In the face of adversity, educators can:

- **Highlight Stories of Resistance**: Share examples of individuals and movements that have fought for justice and won. These stories inspire students to believe in the possibility of change.

- **Empower Students' Voices**: Encourage students to take ownership of their education by creating projects, campaigns, or presentations that reflect their identities and perspectives.

- **Celebrate Small Victories**: Resistance is a marathon, not a sprint. Recognizing incremental progress—whether it's a meaningful conversation, a student's breakthrough, or a classroom project—can sustain motivation.

Advocate for Systemic Change

Standing in solidarity also means working toward systemic reform. White teachers can:

- **Support Policies That Promote Equity**: Advocate for funding equity, restorative justice practices, and inclusive curricula at the district and state levels.
- **Collaborate with Activists and Researchers**. Partnering with scholars, activists, and community organizations can provide new perspectives and resources for your work.
- **Challenge Harmful Legislation**: Join advocacy efforts to oppose laws that restrict honest education. Writing op-eds, testifying at hearings, and organizing petitions are ways to push back against censorship and discrimination.

Teachers standing in solidarity against attacks on inclusive education face significant difficulties, but their role is vital. By understanding systemic oppression, building coalitions, speaking truth, and modeling resilience, educators can resist these efforts and create classrooms that empower all students. As Mills (1997) argued, dismantling the racial contract requires not only acknowledging its existence but also actively dismantling the structures that sustain it. As frontline agents of change, white teachers have the power to disrupt these systems. The fact is that while white people have been able to enjoy enough privilege that their inactions have had few consequences for them, those days are quickly coming to an end. We all have to choose the type of community and the type of country we want. If democracy is to survive, if we are to survive, we must stand in opposition to this culture of ignorance.

Discussion Questions for Chapter 11

1   The author describes white teachers' fear of backlash as a significant barrier to implementing inclusive practices in schools. How does this fear reflect the broader dynamics of racial policing described in Charles Mills's *The Racial Contract*? What strategies might educators use to overcome these fears and advocate for systemic change?

2   The chapter critiques the backlash against Critical Race Theory (CRT) and the rise of organizations like Moms for Liberty. How does the misinformation about CRT contribute to the "epistemology of ignorance" Mills outlines? In what ways can educators combat this misinformation effectively?

3   The chapter emphasizes the importance of solidarity and coalition-building among educators, parents, and community organizations. What specific actions can teachers take to form these coalitions and advocate for inclusive education while navigating hostile political climates?

4   The chapter highlights the importance of modeling resilience and hope for students. What practical ways can educators empower students to engage critically with issues of race, gender, and equity, even in the face of censorship and backlash? How can storytelling and counternarratives foster resilience?

12 Conclusion

Some will say that the school system is doing precisely what it was intended to do. They will rightly point to the history of schooling in America and show forthrightly, with numerous well-cited examples, that American schools were never meant to be egalitarian or to lift the disenfranchised. They will show that it was always designed to sift out the chaff and deliver the white to an abundant future. They contend that the purpose of schools is to create workers and weed out nonconformists. While I am not blind to the evidence, I believe that we have the power to disrupt and dismantle this system and rebuild it to reflect a new set of principles. I believe that public schools can be the incubators of democratic thinking and action. All human systems are changeable, problems are solvable, and benefits are abundant when we decide to act together for the betterment of our communities.

There are many issues in education, and there are many groups that need solidarity, including gay and lesbian students, transgender students, Latinx students, and a host of racial and ethnic groups that have been marginalized and oppressed within our schools. The school-to-prison pipeline is a moral imperative of the first order; however, the pipeline does not only affect African American students. Latinx people, people with disabilities, and people of all races and gender identities are also caught up in a system with one goal: to maintain white, male, straight, Christian supremacy in law, economics, and politics. We have jailed our citizens at an alarming rate, and the costs in economic terms, human terms, and democratic terms are astronomical.

Teachers live at the intersection of these identities and oppressive forces (Crenshaw, 1997). So, while I have worked to shine a light on one, I hope others will shine the light of solidarity in a thousand different directions. We cannot forget that our acts of solidarity are sometimes the difference between life and death, especially for kids who do not identify as part of the gender binary (Wozolek et al., 2016).

Teaching is arduous work, and teaching well is even more challenging. However, teaching well is the most rewarding way to spend a working life I can imagine. The rewards are innumerable, and the frustrations are equally so. Still, those frustrations are far outweighed by the satisfaction of students growing into adults who set the world ablaze with their intellect, drive, energy, and idealism. That is the kind of teaching that Caring Solidarity brings—a world-changing, life-altering conglomeration of experiences. That is what I hope for you.

Looking back, someone should have stopped the first enslavers who arrived in 1619. Four hundred years ago, one hundred years ago, even a month ago, people should have stood against oppression and violence directed at people of color. In the idealized version of America, white people would have acted in solidarity with all who have inhabited this land. A few did, but the vast majority remained complicit, allowing white supremacy to take root from the moment the first Europeans set foot on these shores. If now is the moment when people are finally ready to reject the sickness of white superiority and embrace genuine solidarity, then let us begin.

One of my former tenth graders, Greta McLain, studied art in Minneapolis and murals in California and Mexico. Now, as an adult, she, along with other collaborators, is turning the city of Minneapolis into a wonderland of color and vibrant walls that reflect the beauty and diversity of the city that lives under a blanket of snow and cold for almost half the year. Some pictures of her art grace the cover of this book. Her work with communities, kids, adults, and other artists is an example for all of us to follow.

She gathers students to talk about their lives and, in solidarity with them, helps them tell their stories on paper, then on parachute cloth, and finally on the walls of schools and community centers. On one project, Greta replaced a faded, vandalized mural at South High School, where I taught her and her brother. The mural's tagline explains who South students are and inspires everyone who sees it. Amongst the colors, people, and symbols that represent the students who designed it are the words,

"I am not in this world to adapt to it, rather to transform it."

May that be said of all of us.

References

Adler, E., Williams, M. R., & Smith, S. (2019). KC area has been one of the most racially segregated in America. But not anymore. *Kansas City Star*. https://www.kansasc ity.com/news/local/article223888475.html

Alfonseca, K. (2022). Students protest book bans by distributing "Maus," "Beloved." *ABC News*. https://abcnews.go.com/US/students-protest-book-bans-distribut ing-maus-beloved/story?id=82622456

Alfonseca, K. (2024). The forces behind Harvard President Claudine Gay's resignation. *ABC News*. https://abcnews.go.com/US/forces-harvard-president-claudine-gays-resignation/story?id=106071191

Allen, R. L. (2009). What about poor white people? In W. Ayers, T. M. Quinn, & D. Stovall (Eds.), *Handbook of social justice in education* (pp. 209–225). Routledge.

Allen, R. L., & Liou, D. D. (2018). Managing whiteness: The call for educational leadership to breach the contractual expectations of white supremacy. *Urban Education*, *54*(5), 677–705.

Alonso, G., Anderson, N. S., Su, C., & Theoharis, J. (2009). *Our schools suck: Students talk back to a segregated nation on the failures of urban education*. New York University Press.

Altschuler, G. C. (2023, July 9). Six reasons why Moms for Liberty is an extremist organization. *The Hill*. https://thehill.com/opinion/education/4086179-six-reas ons-why-moms-for-liberty-is-an-extremist-organization/

American Historical Association (AHA). (2023, June 26). AHA letter opposing Museum of the American Revolution's hosting of Moms for Liberty event. *AHA*. https://www.historians.org/news/aha-letter-opposing-museum-of-the-ameri can-revolutions-hosting-of-moms-for-liberty-event/

Anderson, C. (2017). *White rage: The unspoken truth of our racial divide*. Bloomsbury.

Annamma, S. A., Anyon, Y., Joseph, N. M., Farrar, J., Greer, E., Downing, B., & Simmons, J. (2016). Black girls and school discipline: The complexities of being overrepresented and understudied. *Urban Education*, *54*(2), 211–242. https://doi. org/10.1177/0042085916646610

Appiah, K. A. (2007). *Cosmopolitanism: Ethics in a world of strangers*. Penguin Books.

Applebaum, B. (2011). *Being white, being good: White complicity, white moral responsibility, and social justice pedagogy.* Lexington Books.

Azoulay, K. G. (1997). Experience, empathy and strategic essentialism. *Cultural Studies, 11*(1), 94–116.

Banks, J. A. (1995). Multicultural education: Historical development, dimensions, and practice. In J. A. Banks & C. A. Mcgee Banks (Eds.), *Handbook of research on multicultural education* (pp. 3–24). Macmillan.

Banks, J. A. (1997). *Educating citizens in a multicultural society.* Teachers College Press.

Banks, J. A., & Banks, C. A. (2016). *Multicultural education: Issues and perspectives.* John Wiley & Sons.

Baron-Cohen, S. (2022). *The science of evil: On empathy and the origins of cruelty.* Basic Books.

Bartolomé, L. (1994). Beyond the methods fetish: Toward a humanizing pedagogy. *Harvard Educational Review, 64*(2), 173–195.

Bayertz, K. (2013). Four uses of solidarity. In K. Bayertz (Ed.), *Solidarity* (pp. 3–28). Springer Netherlands.

Bell, D. A. (1980). Brown v. Board of Education and the interest-convergence dilemma. *Harvard Law Review, 93*(3), 518. https://doi.org/10.2307/1340546

Bello, C. (2023). The EU's population is set to shrink by 6% by 2100. *Euronews.* https://www.euronews.com/next/2023/04/04/china-sees-first-population-decline-in-six-decades-where-does-the-eu-stand

Berman, M., & Schmidt, S. (2017). He yelled "Get out of my country," witnesses say, and then shot 2 men from India, killing one. *Washington Post.* https://www.washingtonpost.com/news/morning-mix/wp/201 7 /02/24/get-out-of-my-country-kansan-reportedly-yelled-beforeshooting-2-men-from-india-killing-one/?utm term=.5fd 168753aca

Berry, T. R. (2018). *States of grace: Counterstories of a Black woman in the academy.* Peter Lang.

Bidwell, C. (2010). *Successful white mathematics teachers of African American students* [Unpublished doctoral dissertation]. Georgia State University.

Birnbaum, M. (2020). Europe said U.S. influence had waned under Trump. Then, Black Lives Matter protests rocked the continent. *Washington Post.* https://www.washingtonpost.com/world/europe/europe-said-us-influence-hadwaned-under-trump-then-black-livesmatter-protests-rocked-thecontinent/2020/06/17/23f88ff2-ab4c-11ea-a43b-be9f6494a87d_story.html

Blackburn, M. (2021). Why is critical race theory dangerous for our kids? *U.S. Senator Marsha Blackburn of Tennessee.* https://www.blackburn.senate.gov/2021/7/why-is-critical-race-theory-dangerousfor-our-kids

Blunden, A. (2003). Honneth's "Struggle for recognition." *Ethical Politics.* https://ethicalpolitics.org/ablunden/works/honneth.htm

Bonilla-Silva, E. (2010). *Racism without racists: Color-blind racism and the persistence of racial inequality in America* (3rd ed.). Rowman & Littlefield.

Borter, G., Ax, J., & Tanfani, J. (2022). School Boards get death threats over race, gender, mask policies. *Reuters*. https://www.reuters.com/investigates/special-report/usa-education-threats/

Bosch, T. (2017). Twitter activism and youth in South Africa: The case of #RhodesMustFall. *Information, Communication & Society, 20*(2), 221–232.

Boucher, M. L. (2020). The white conundrum: White social studies teachers, fear, and the racial contract. In A. Hawkman & S. B. Shear (Eds.), *Marking the "invisible": Articulating whiteness in social studies education* (pp. 239–268). Essay, Information Age Publishing.

Boucher, M. L., & Helfenbein, R. J. (2015). The push and the pull: Deficit models, Ruby Payne, and becoming a "warm demander." *The Urban Review, 47*(4), 742–758.

Bowditch, C. (1993). Getting rid of troublemakers: High school disciplinary procedures and the production of dropouts. *Social Problems, 40*(4), 493–509.

Bradbury, B., Corak, M., Waldfogel, J., & Washbrook, E. (2015). *Too many children left behind: The U.S. achievement gap in comparative perspective*. Russell Sage Foundation.

Brammer, J. P. (2017). "Make America straight again": Students harassed at homecoming parade. *NBC News*. www.nbcnews.com/feature/nbc-out/make-america-straight-again-studentsharassed-homecoming-parade-n804626

Britzman, D. P. (2003). *Practice makes practice: A critical study of learning to teach*. State University of New York Press.

Brown, A. L. (2012). On human kinds and role models: A critical discussion about the African American male teacher. *Educational Studies, 48*(3), 296–315.

Brown, B. (2023). *Dare to lead: Brave work, tough conversations, whole hearts*. Random House.

Brown-Jeffy, S., & Cooper, J. E. (2011). Toward a conceptual framework of culturally relevant pedagogy: An overview of the conceptual and theoretical literature. *Teacher Education Quarterly, 38*(1), 65–84.

Browne, J. (2007). Rooted in slavery: Prison labor exploitation. *Race, Poverty & the Environment, 14*(1), 42–44.

Bryan, N. (2017). White teachers' role in sustaining the school-to-prison pipeline: Recommendations for teacher education. *The Urban Review, 49*(2), 326–345.

Cammarota, J. (2011). Blindsided by the avatar: White saviors and allies out of Hollywood and in education. *Review of Education, Pedagogy, and Cultural Studies, 33*(3), 242–259.

Carlson, T. (2024). Full speech: Tucker Carlson delivers remarks at Turning Point Rally in Duluth, GA - 10/23/24. *Rumble*. https://rumble.com/v5jvaz1-full-speech-tucker-carlson-delivers-remarks-at-turning-point-rally-in-dulut.html

Case, K. (2018). How NOT to be an ally – Part 2 "He-peat, re-white, and amplification." http://www.drkimcase.com/how-not-to-be-an-ally-part-2-he-peat-re-white-and-amplification/

Casey, Z. A. (2016). *A pedagogy of anticapitalist racism: Whiteness, neoliberalism, and resistance in education*. SUNY Press.

Castillo, M., Craven, M., Gómez, I., & Latham Sikes, C. (2022). What Texas' classroom censorship law means for students & schools. *Texas SB 3 guide – IDRA* https://www.idra.org/wpcontent/uploads/2022/02/What-Texas-Classroom-Censorship-Law-Means-for-Students-and-Schools-IDRA-2022.pdf

Cazden, C. B., & Leggett, E. L. (1976). Culturally responsive education: A discussion of Lau Remedies II (Rep.). *U.S. Department of Health, Education, and Welfare*. pp. 1–52. (ERIC Document Reproduction Service No. ED135 241). https://files.eric.ed.gov/fulltext/ED135241.pdf

Chappelle, D. (2016). Dave Chappelle: SNL monologue [November 12, 2016] - Transcript. *Scraps from the loft*. https://scrapsfromtheloft.com/comedy/david-chappelles-snl-monologue-2016-transcript/?utm_source=chatgpt.com

Chu, J. M. (Director). (2024). *Wicked* [Film]. Universal Pictures.

Coates, T. (2008, May). "This is how we lost to the white man": The audacity of Bill Cosby's Black conservatism. *The Atlantic*. https://www.theatlantic.com/magazine/archive/2008/05/-this-is-how-we-lost-to-the-white-man/306774/

Coates, T.-N. (2015). *Between the world and me*. Spiegel & Grau.

Coates, T. (2017, September 14). The first white president. *The Atlantic*. www.theatlantic.com/magazine/archive/2017/10/the-first-white-president-ta-nehisi-coates/537909/

Cochran-Smith, M. (2000). Blind vision: Unlearning racism in teacher education. *Harvard Educational Review*, *70*(2), 157–190.

Cochran-Smith, M. (2003). Learning and unlearning: The education of teacher educators. *Teaching and Teacher Education*, *19*(1), 5–28.

Coleman, B. (2007). *Successful white teachers of Black students: Teaching across racial lines in urban middle school science classrooms* [Unpublished doctoral dissertation]. University of Massachusetts-Amherst.

Coleman, J. S. (1966). Equality of educational opportunity (Rep. No. FS 5.238:38001). *US Dept of Health, Education, and Welfare*. pp. 1–749. (ERIC Document Reproduction Service No. ED012275).

Cooper, P. M. (2003). Teaching within a community. *Journal of Teacher Education*, *54*(5), 413–427.

Couvson, M. (2016). *Pushout: The criminalization of Black girls in schools*. The New Press.

Clayton, A. (2023). From military weapon to cultural symbol: How the AR-15 has defined the US gun debate. *The Guardian*. https://www.theguardian.com/us-news/2023/nov/01/ar-15-republican-american-gun-book

Crenshaw, K. (1997). Demarginalizing the intersection of race and sex: A Black feminist critique of antidiscrimination doctrine, feminist theory, and antiracist politics. In K. Maschke (Ed.), *Feminist legal theories* (pp. 23–54). Routledge.

Crenshaw, K. (1991). Mapping the margins: Intersectionality, identity, and violence against women of color. *Stanford Law Review, 43*(6), 1241–1300.

Crocco, M. S., & Costigan, A. T. (2007). The narrowing of curriculum and pedagogy in the age of accountability Urban Educators Speak Out. *Urban Education, 42*(6), 512–535.

Cuellar, A. E., & Markowitz, S. (2015). School suspension and the school-to-prison pipeline. *International Review of Law and Economics, 43*, 98–106.

Danielewicz, J. (2001). *Teaching selves: Identity, pedagogy, and teacher education.* State University of New York Press.

Darling-Hammond, L., Friedlaender, D., & Snyder, J. (2014, June). *Student-centered schools: Policy supports for closing the opportunity gap* (Rep.). doi:10.1007/s11256-007-0066-6

De Lissovoy, N. D. (2010). Rethinking education and emancipation: Being, teaching, and power. *Harvard Educational Review, 80*(2), 203–221. doi:10.17763/haer.80.2.h6r65285tu252448

De Lissovoy, N., & Brown, A. L. (2013). Antiracist solidarity in critical education: Contemporary problems and possibilities. *The Urban Review, 45*(5), 1–22.

DeLage, J. (2016). Police unions blast teachers' Minneapolis Philando Castile protest. *Pioneer Press Online.* https://www.twincities.com/2016/07/19/teachers-arres ted-in-minneapolis-philando-castile-protest/

Delgado, R. (1996). Rodrigo's eleventh chronicle: Empathy and false empathy. *California Law Review, 84*(1), 61–100. doi:10.2307/3480903

Delgado, R., & Stefancic, J. (1997). *Critical white studies: Looking behind the mirror.* Temple University Press.

Delpit, L. (2006). *Other people's children: Cultural conflict in the classroom.* New Press.

DiAngelo, R. (2011). White fragility. *The International Journal of Critical Pedagogy, 3*(3), 54–70.

DiAngelo, R. J. (2018). *White fragility: Why it's so hard to talk to white people about racism.* Beacon Press.

Dixson, A. D. (2018). "What's going on?": A critical race theory perspective on Black Lives Matter and activism in education. *Urban Education, 53*(2), 231–247.

Du Bois, W. E. (1903/1994). *The souls of Black folk.* Dover Publications.

Duckworth, A. L., & Quinn, P. D. (2009). Development and validation of the short grit scale (Grit–S). *Journal of Personality Assessment, 91*(2), 166–174.

Duckworth, A. L., Peterson, C., Matthews, M. D., & Kelly, D. R. (2007). Grit: Perseverance and passion for long-term goals. *Journal of Personality and Social Psychology, 92*(6), 1087–1101. doi:10.1037/0022-3514.92.6.1087

Dunbar-Ortiz, R. (2019). *An indigenous peoples' history of the United States for young people.* Beacon Press. (Original work published in 2014).

Duncan, K. E. (2018). "They hate on me!" Black teachers interrupting their white colleagues' racism. *Educational Studies, 55*(2), 197–213. doi:10.1080/00131946.2018.1500463

Duncan-Andrade, J. (2007). Gangstas, wankstas, and ridas: Defining, developing, and supporting effective teachers in urban schools. *International Journal of Qualitative Studies in Education, 20*(6), 617–638.

Duncan-Andrade, J. M., & Morrell, E. (2008). *The art of critical pedagogy: Possibilities for moving from theory to practice in urban schools.* Peter Lang.

EdBuild. (2016, August 23). *Fault Lines: America's most segregating school district borders* (Rep.). https://s3.amazonaws.com/edbuild-public-data/data/fault+lines/EdBuild-Fault-Lines-2016.pdf

Edbuild. (2019, February). Nonwhite school districts get $23 billion less than white districts. https://edbuild.org/content/23-billion#CA

The Education Opportunity Project at Stanford University. (2024). The segregation explorer. *The Educational Opportunity Project at Stanford University.* https://edopportunity.org/segregation/explorer/

Eslinger, J. C. (2013). Caring and understanding "as nearly as possible": Towards culturally responsive caring across differences. *Critical Intersections in Education: An OISE/UT Students' Journal, 1*(1), 1–11.

Fallis, R. K., & Opotow, S. (2003). Are students failing school or are schools failing students? *Journal of Social Issues, 58*(1), 103–119.

Fanon, F. (1961/2004). *The wretched of the earth.* Grove Press.

Farrer, M. (2020). Who was Edward Colston and why was his Bristol statue toppled? *The Guardian.* https://www.theguardian.com/uk-news/2020/jun/08/who-was-edwardcolston-and-why-was-his-bristol-statuetoppled-slave-trader-black-lives-matterprotests

Feistritzer, C. E., Griffin, S., & Linnajarvi, A. (2011). Profile of teachers in the U.S., 2011. *National Center for Education Information.* https://www.teachertoolkit.co.uk/wp-content/uploads/2016/06/pot2011final-blog.pdf

Flaherty, J. (2019). Arizona teachers went on strike. Now lawmakers aim to ban politics in classrooms. *Phoenix New Times.* https://www.phoenixnewtimes.com/news/arizona-legislators-politics-speech-class-teachers-strike-townsend-11212255

Figley, C. R. (2015). *Compassion fatigue: Coping with secondary traumatic stress disorder in those who treat the traumatized.* Routledge.

Frankenberg, R. (1993). Growing up white: Feminism, racism and the social geography of childhood. *Feminist Review, 45*, 51. doi:10.2307/1395347

Freire, P. (2014). *Pedagogy of the oppressed: 30th anniversary edition.* M. B. Ramos (Trans.). Bloomsbury.

Frey, W. H. (2022). *The US will become "minority White" in 2045, Census Projects.* *Brookings*. https://www.brookings.edu/articles/the-us-will-become-minority-white-in-2045-census-projects/

Friedersdorf, C. (2019, August 9). Dismantling Tucker Carlson's white-supremacy argument. *The Atlantic*. https://www.theatlantic.com/ideas/archive/2019/08/tucker-carlson-white-supremacy/595789/

Fromm, E. (1956). *The art of loving*. Continuum Publications.

Fry, R. (2009). The rapid growth and changing complexion of suburban public schools (Rep.). *Pew Trusts*. https://www.pewtrusts.org/en/research-and-analysis/reports/2009/03/31/the-rapid-growth-and-changing-complexion-of-suburban-public-schools

Fuentes, A. (2012). Arresting development: Zero tolerance and the criminalization of children. *Rethinking Schools*, *26*(2), 18–23.

Gay, G. (2010). *Culturally responsive teaching: Theory, research, and practice*. Teachers College. (Original work published in 2000).

Gaztambide-Fernández, R. A. (2012). Decolonization and the pedagogy of solidarity. *Decolonization: Indigeneity, Education & Society*, *1*(1), 41–67.

Gershenson, S., Hart, C. M., Lindsay, C. A., & Papageorge, N. W. (2017). *The long-run impacts of same-race teachers* (Rep. No. IZA DP No. 10630). IZA – Institute of IZA – Institute of Labor Economics (pp. 1–61). http://ftp.iza.org/dp10630.pdf

Giroux, H. A. (2024). Educators as public intellectuals and the challenge of Fascism. *Policy Futures in Education*, *22*(8), 1533–1539. https://doi.org/10.1177/14782103241226844

Godley, A. J., Sweetland, J., Wheeler, R. S., Minnici, A., & Carpenter, B. D. (2006). Preparing teachers for dialectally diverse classrooms. *Educational Researcher*, *35*(8), 30–37. doi:10.3102/0013189x035008030

Goff, P. A., Jackson, M. C., Leone, B. A., Culotta, C. M., & Ditomasso, N. A. (2014). The essence of innocence: Consequences of dehumanizing Black children. *Journal of Personality and Social Psychology*, *106*(4), 526–545. doi:10.1037/a0035663

Goldberg, D. T. (1995). *Multiculturalism: A critical reader*. Blackwell Publications.

Gonyea, D. (2017, October 24). Majority of white Americans say they believe whites face discrimination. www.npr.org/2017/10/24/559604836/majority-of-white-americans-think-theyre-discriminated-against

Gorski, P. (1999). A brief history of multicultural education. *EdChange*. www.edchange.org/multicultural/papers/edchange_history.html

Gorski, P. (2006). The classist underpinnings of Ruby Payne's framework. *Teachers College Record*, 12322. 1–5. https://www.researchgate.net/profile/Paul-Gorski/publication/283017178_The_Classist_Underpinnings_of_Ruby_Payne%27s_Framework/links/5bb9f1bf4585159e8d880ab9/The-Classist-Underpinnings-of-Ruby-Paynes-Framework.pdf

Gutierrez, L. (2017). Kansas City is among the most economically segregated cities in the U.S. *Kansas City Star*. https://www.kansascity.com/news/local/articlel 4 7826924.html

Gray, A. (2019). The bias of "professionalism" standards. *Stanford Social Innovation Review*. https://ssir.org/articles/entry/the_bias_of_professionalism_standards?

Gregory, A., & Weinstein, R. (2008). The discipline gap and African Americans: Defiance or cooperation in the high school classroom. *Journal of School Psychology*, *46*(4), 455–475.

Hannah-Jones, N. (2019). The 1619 project. *New York Times*. https://www.nytimes.com/interactive/2019/08/14/magazine/1619-americaslavery.html

Hackman, R. (2015). "We need co-conspirators, not allies": How white Americans can fight racism. *The Guardian*. www.theguardian.com/world/2015/jun/26/how-white-americans-can-fight-racism

Harden, K., & Harden-Moore, T. (2019). Moving from ally to accomplice: How far are you willing to go to disrupt racism in the workplace? *Diverse*. https://diverseeducation.com/article/138623/

Harlan, S., Morris, L., & Birnbaum, M. (2020). Protesters in Europe push for a new reckoning of their own countries' racism. *Washington Post*. https://www.washingtonpost.com/world/europe/george-floyd-protests-londonberlin-brussels-rome-madrid-policeracism-europe/2020/06/07/06c340c4-a829-11ea-b619-3f9133bbb482_story.html

Harris, A. (2019, May 28). The new secession. *The Atlantic*. www.theatlantic.com/education/archive/2019/05/resegregation-baton-rouge-public-schools/589381/

Harris, C. I. (1993). Whiteness as property. *Harvard Law Review*, *106*(8), 1707.

Harvey, D. L., & Reed, M. H. (1996). The culture of poverty: An ideological analysis. *Sociological Perspectives*, *39*(4), 465–495. doi:10.2307/1389418

Harvey, J. (2007). Moral solidarity and empathetic understanding: The moral value and scope of the relationship. *Journal of Social Philosophy*, *38*(1), 22–37. doi:10.1111/j.1467-9833.2007.00364.x

Haskins, R., & Rouse, C. (2005). *Closing achievement gaps – Policy brief* (Rep.). https://www.brookings.edu/wp-content/uploads/2016/06/20050301foc.pdf

Hayes, C., & Juarez, B. (2012). There is no culturally responsive teaching spoken here: A critical race perspective. *Democracy and Education*, *20*(1), 1–14.

Helfenbein, R. J. (2003). Troubling multiculturalism: The new work order, anti anti-essentialism, and a cultural studies approach to education. *Multicultural Perspectives*, *5*(4), 10–16. doi:10.1207/s15327892mcp0504_3

Helms, J. E. (1990). *Black and white racial identity: Theory, research, and practice*. Praeger.

Herman, K. C., Hickmon-Rosa, J., & Reinke, W. M. (2017). Empirically derived profiles of teacher stress, burnout, self-efficacy, and coping and associated student outcomes. *Journal of Positive Behavior Interventions, 20*(2), 90–100. doi:10.1177/1098300717732066

Hermes, M. (2005). White teachers, Native students: Rethinking culture-based education. In J. Phillion, M. F. He, & F. M. Connelly (Eds.), *Narrative and experience in multicultural education* (pp. 95–115). Sage Publications.

Hirschfield, P. J. (2008). Preparing for prison?: The criminalization of school discipline in the USA. *Theoretical Criminology, 12*(1), 79–101. doi:10.1177/1362480607085795

Hoffman, D. M. (1996). Culture and self in multicultural education: Reflections on discourse, text, and practice. *American Educational Research Journal, 33*(3), 545–569. doi:10.2307/1163276

Honneth, A. (1995). *The struggle for recognition: The moral grammar of social conflicts.* MIT Press.

hooks, B. (1994). *Teaching to transgress: Education as the practice of freedom.* Routledge.

hooks, B. (2000). *All about love: New visions.* William Morrow.

hooks, B. (2013). *Writing beyond race: Living theory and practice.* Routledge.

Howard, T. C. (2002). Hearing footsteps in the dark: African American students' descriptions of effective teachers. *Journal of Education for Students Placed at Risk (JESPAR), 7*(4), 425–444. doi:10.1207/s15327671espr0704_4

Howard, T. C. (2010). *Why race and culture matter in schools: Closing the achievement gap in America's classrooms.* Teachers College Press.

Hughey, M. W. (2010). The white savior film and reviewers' reception. *Symbolic Interaction, 33*(3), 475–496. doi:10.1525/si.2010.33.3.475

Huntington, S. P. (1996). *The clash of civilizations and the remaking of world order.* Simon & Schuster.

Ignatiev, N., & Garvey, J. (1996). *Race traitor.* Routledge.

Indigenous Action Media. (2014, May 4). Accomplices not allies: Abolishing the ally industrial complex. http://www.indigenousaction.org/accomplices-not-allies-abolishing-the-ally-industrial-complex/

Ingersoll, R. M., & May, H. (2011, September). *Recruitment, retention and the minority teacher shortage.* (No. pre ResearchReport # Rr-69). http://www.cpre.org/what-national-data-tell-us-about-minority-teacher-turnover (ERIC Document Reproduction Service No. ED526355).

Irving, D. (2014). *Waking up white: And finding myself in the story of race.* Elephant Room Press.

Isensee, L. (2015). Why calling slaves "workers" is more than an editing error. www.npr.org/sections/ed/2015/10/23/450826208/why-calling-slaves-workers-is-more-than-an-editing-error

Janzer, C. (2022). What happened after Minneapolis removed police officers from schools. *Juvenile Justice Information Exchange*. https://jjie.org/2022/08/03/what-happened-after-minneapolis-removed-police-officers-from-schools/?

Johnson, W. (2019). "Extermination and enslavement": The twin horrors of the American dawn. *Washington Post*. www.washingtonpost.com/educat ion/2019/08/28/historians-slavery-myths/

Jupp, J. C., Berry, T. R., & Lensmire, T. J. (2016). Second-wave white teacher identity studies. *Review of Educational Research*, *86*(4), 1151–1191. doi:10.3102/0034654316629798

Kanpol, B., & McLaren, P. (1995). *Critical multiculturalism: Uncommon voices in a common struggle*. Bergin & Garvey.

Katsarou, E., Picower, B., & Stovall, D. (2010). Acts of solidarity: Developing urban social justice educators in the struggle for quality public education. *Teacher Education Quarterly*, *37*(3), 137–153.

Keating, A. (1995). Interrogating "whiteness," (De)constructing "race." *College English*, *57*(8), 901. doi:10.2307/378620

Kendi, I. X. (2016). *Stamped from the beginning: The definitive history of racist ideas in America*. Nation Books.

Kilander, G. (2022, April 6). "Do you hate Mexicans?" JD Vance accused of racism over new campaign ad. *The Independent*. https://www.the-independent.com/news/world/americas/us-politics/jd-vance-racism-campaign-ad-b2052191.html

Kim, C. Y., & Geronimo, I. (2009). Policing in schools: Developing a governance document for school resource officers in K-12 schools (ACLU White Paper) (Rep.). *American Civil Liberties Union (ACLU)*. http://www.aclu.org/files/pdfs/racialjustice/whitepaper_policinginschools.pdf

King, J. E. (1991). Dysconscious racism: Ideology, identity, and the miseducation of teachers. *The Journal of Negro Education*, *60*(2), 133–146. doi:10.2307/2295605

King, M. L., Jr. (1963). Letter from a Birmingham jail. *University of Pennsylvania*. https://www.africa.upenn.edu/Articles_Gen/Letter_Birmingham.html

King, M. L., Jr. (2017). Man's sin and God's grace. *The Martin Luther King, Jr. Research and Education Institute*. https://kinginstitute.stanford.edu/king-papers/docume nts/mans-sin-and-gods-grace

Kleinfeld, J. (1975). Effective teachers of Eskimo and Indian students. *The School Review*, *83*(2), 301–344. doi:10.1086/443191

Kobayashi, A., & Peake, L. (2000). Racism out of place: Thoughts on whiteness and an antiracist geography in the new millennium. *Annals of the Association of American Geographers*, *90*(2), 392–403. doi:10.1111/0004-5608.00202

Kohl, H. R. (1992). *From archetype to zeitgeist: Powerful ideas for powerful thinking*. Little, Brown and Company.

Kolbert, E., & Hammond, R. (2018). Skin deep: What is race, exactly? *National Geographic*, *233*(4), 29–41.

Krogstad, J. M., & Fry, R. (2014). Department of Education projects public schools will be "majority-minority" this fall. www.pewresearch.org/fact-tank/2014/08/18/u-s-public-schools-expected-to-be-majority-minority-starting-this-fall/

Kucsera, J. (2014, March 26). New York State's extreme school segregation: inequality, inaction and a damaged future (Rep.). *The Civil Rights Project at UCLA*. www.civilrightsproject.ucla.edu/research/k-12-education/integration-and-diversity/ny-norflet-report-placeholder

Kuhfeld, M., Gershoff, E., & Paschall, K. (2018). The development of racial/ethnic and socioeconomic achievement gaps during the school years. *Journal of Applied Developmental Psychology*, *57*, 62–73. https://doi.org/10.1016/j.appdev.2018.07.001

Ladson-Billings, G. (1994). *The dreamkeepers: Successful teachers of African American children*. Jossey-Bass.

Ladson-Billings, G. (1995). Toward a theory of culturally relevant pedagogy. *American Educational Research Journal*, *32*(3), 465. doi:10.2307/1163320

Ladson-Billings, G. (2006). From the achievement gap to the education debt: Understanding achievement in U.S. schools. *Educational Researcher*, *35*(7), 3–12. doi:10.3102/0013189x035007003

Ladson-Billings, G. (2007). Pushing past the achievement gap: An essay on the language of deficit. *The Journal of Negro Education*, *7*(6), 316–323.

Ladson-Billings, G. (2008). A letter to our next president. *Journal of Teacher Education*, *59*(3), 235–239. doi:10.1177/0022487108317466

Ladson-Billings, G. (2013). Critical race theory—what it is not. In M. Lynn & A. D. Dixson (Eds.), *Handbook of critical race theory in education* (pp. 34–47). Routledge.

Ladson-Billings, G., & Tate, W. F. (1995). Toward a critical race theory of education. *Critical Race Theory in Education*, *97*(1), 47–68.

Lam, K. (2019). New Hampshire lawmaker Werner horn: "Owning slaves doesn't make You racist." *USA Today*. https://www.usatoday.com/story/news/nation/2019/07/18/new-hampshire-lawmaker-werner-horn-owning-slaves-racism-economics/1773670001/

Levine-Rasky, C. (2000). Framing whiteness: Working through the tensions in introducing whiteness to educators. *Race Ethnicity and Education*, *3*(3), 271–292. doi:10.1080/713693039

Lewis, T. (2022). Guns now kill more children and young adults than car crashes. *Scientific American*. https://www.scientificamerican.com/article/guns-now-kill-more-children-and-young-adults-than-car-crashes/

Leiker, J. N. (2002). Race relations in the sunflower state. *Kansas History*, *25*(3), 214–236.

Lieberman, M., & Kim, H. Y. (2024). School shootings in 2024: More than last year, but fewer deaths. *Education Week*. https://www.edweek.org/leadership/school-shootings-in-2024-more-than-last-year-but-fewer-deaths/2024/12

Lipman, P. (2013). *The new political economy of urban education neoliberalism, Race, and the right to the city*. Taylor and Francis.

Lipsitz, G. (2006). *The possessive investment in whiteness: How white people profit from identity politics*. Temple University Press.

Loewus, L. (2018). The nation's teaching force is still mostly white and female. *Edweek*. www.edweek.org/ew/articles/2017/08/15/the-nations-teach ing-force-is-still-mostly.html

Lopez, B. (2021a). Republican bill that limits how race, slavery, and history are taught in Texas schools becomes law. *The Texas Tribune*. https://www.texastribune. org/2021/12/02/texas-critical-race-theory-law/

Lopez, B. (2021b). Death threats and doxxing: The outcomes of mask mandate and critical race theory fights at a Texas School Board. *The Texas Tribune*. https://www. texastribune.org/2021/12/15/texas-school-boards-political-fights/

Lopez, B. (2022). Texas has banned more books than any other state, new report shows. *The Texas Tribune*. https://www.texastribune.org/2022/09/19/ texas-book-bans/

Losen, D., & Skiba, R. L. (2010). Suspended education: Urban middle schools in crisis (Rep.). *Escholarship*. https://escholarship.org/content/qt8fh0s5dv/qt8fh0s5dv.pdf

Love, B. L. (2014). "I see Trayvon Martin": What teachers can learn from the tragic death of a young Black male. *The Urban Review, 46*(2), 292–306. doi:10.1007/ s11256-013-0260-7

Love, B. L. (2016). Anti-black state violence, classroom edition: The spirit murdering of black children. *Journal of Curriculum and Pedagogy, 13*(1), 22–25. https://doi. org/10.1080/15505170.2016.1138258

Love, B. L. (2019a, February 12). "Grit is in our DNA": Why teaching grit is inherently anti-Black. *Edweek*. www.edweek.org/ew/articles/2019/02/13/ grit-is-in-our-dna-why-teaching.html

Love, B. L. (2019b, March 18). Dear white teachers: You can't love your Black students if you don't know them. *Edweek*. www.edweek.org/ew/articles/2019/03/20/ dear-white-teachers-you-cant-love-your.html?r=1885209627

Love, B. L. (2019c). *We want to do more than survive: Abolitionist teaching and the pursuit of educational freedom*. Beacon Press.

Lynch, S. N., & Gaudsward, A. (2024, October 29). Biden's justice dept has yet to reach accords in police misconduct cases. *Reuters*. https://www.reuters.com/legal/bid ens-justice-dept-has-yet-reach-accords-police-misconduct-cases-2024-10-29/

Ma, A. (2024). 70 years ago, school integration was a dream many believed could actually happen. It hasn't. *AP News*. https://apnews.com/article/school-integrat ion-brown-board-supreme-court-9d84858db3717620a77bfae0b478cab8

Maguire, G. (1995). *Wicked: The life and times of the Wicked Witch of the West*. HarperCollins.

Malik, R. (2017). New data reveal 250 preschoolers are suspended or expelled every day. *American Progress*. www.americanprogress.org/issues/early childhood /news/2017/11/06/442280/new-data-reveal-250-preschoolers-suspended-expelled-every-day/

Masoom, S. (2017). 2016 should mark the end of the "ally." *Huffington Post*. www. huffpost.com/entry/2016-should-mark-the-end_b_9044904

Matias, C. E. (2016a). *Feeling white: Whiteness, emotionality, and education*. Sense.

Matias, C. E. (2016b). "Why do you make me hate myself?": Re-teaching whiteness, abuse, and love in urban teacher education. *Teaching Education, 27*(2), 194–211. doi:10.1080/10476210.2015.1068749

Matias, C. E., & Allen, R. L. (2013). Loving whiteness to death: Sadomasochism, emotionality, and the possibility of humanizing love. *Berkeley Review of Education, 4*(2), 285–309. doi:10.5070/b84110066

Matias, C. E., & Zembylas, M. (2014). "When saying you care is not really caring": Emotions of disgust, whiteness ideology, and teacher education. *Critical Studies in Education, 55*(3), 319–337. doi:10.1080/17508487.2014.922489

Matos, A. (2015). Despite Minneapolis moratorium, K-1 kids still getting suspended. *Star Tribune*. www.startribune.com/despite-minneapolis-moratorium-k-1-schoolk ids-still-getting-suspended/330535511/

Mapping police violence. (2024). https://mappingpoliceviolence.us/

May, S. (1999). *Critical multiculturalism: Rethinking multicultural and antiracist education*. Routledge Falmer.

McCarty, T. L., & Lee, T. S. (2014). Critical culturally sustaining/revitalizing pedagogy and indigenous education sovereignty. *Harvard Educational Review, 84*(1), 101–124. doi:10.17763/haer.84.1.q83746nl5pj34216

Mcintosh, P. (2001). White privilege: Unpacking the invisible the knapsack. In P. S. Rothenberg (Ed.). *Race, class, and gender in the United States: An integrated study* (pp. 188–192). Worth Publishers. (Original work published in 1988).

McLaren, K. (2013). *The art of empathy: A complete guide to life's most essential skill*. Sounds True, Inc.

Melville, H. (1850/1985). Hawthorne and his Mosses: By a Virginian spending July in Vermont. In H. Hayford (Ed.), *Melville: Pierre, Israel Potter, the Piazza tales, the confidence-man, uncollected prose*, Billy Budd Erica series/novels and tales (Vol. 3, pp. 1154–1471). Library of America.

Mervosh, S. (2019). How much wealthier are white school districts than nonwhite ones? $23 billion, report says. *New York Times*. https://www.nytimes. com/2019/02/27/education/school-districts-funding-white-minorities.html?mod ule=inline

Mettler, K. (2016). "Good trouble": How John Lewis fuses new and old tactics to teach about civil disobedience. *Washington Post*. www.washingtonpost.com/news/

morning-mix/wp/2016/06/23/good-trouble-how-john-lewis-fuses-new-and-old-tactics-to-teach-about-civil-disobedience/

Michael, A. (2015). *Raising race questions: Whiteness and inquiry in education.* Teachers College Press.

Michael, A., Coleman-King, C., Lee, S., Ramirez, C., & Bentley-Edwards, K. (2017). Naming the unnamed: White culture in relief. In C. A. Warren & S. D. Hancock (Eds.), *White women's work: Examining the intersectionality of teaching identity, and race* (pp. 19–43). Information Age Publishing.

Michie, G. (2007). Seeing, hearing, and talking race: Lessons for white teachers from four teachers of color. *Multicultural Perspectives, 9*(1), 3–9. doi:10.1080/15210960701333633

Mid-America Regional Council. (2014). Fair Housing Assessment (Rep.). Mid-America Regional Council on behalf of the Cities of Blue Springs, Independence and Kansas City, Missouri; the city of Leavenworth, Kansas; and the Unified Government of Wyandotte County/ Kansas City, Kansas website: http: //www. marc.org/Regional-Planning/Housing/pdf/ 4B-Segregation-Integration. aspx

Mills, C. W. (1997). *The racial contract.* Cornel University Press.

Mills, C. W. (2007). White ignorance. In S. Sullivan & N. Tuana (Eds.), *Race and epistemologies of ignorance* (pp. 11–38). State University of New York Press.

Milner, H. R. (2006). The promise of Black teacher's success with Black students. *Education Foundations, 20*(3–4), 89–104.

Milner, H. R. (2010). *Start where you are, but don't stay there: Understanding diversity, opportunity gaps, and teaching in today's classrooms.* Harvard Education Press.

Milstein, C. (2015). *Taking sides: Revolutionary solidarity and the poverty of liberalism.* AK Press.

Moll, L. C., Amanti, C., Neff, D., & Gonzalez, N. (1992). Funds of knowledge for teaching: Using a qualitative approach to connect homes and classrooms. *Theory into Practice, 31*(2), 132–141. https://doi.org/10.1080/00405849209543534

Monroe, C. R. (2005). Why are "bad boys" always Black?: Causes of disproportionality in school discipline and recommendations for change. *The Clearing House: A Journal of Educational Strategies, Issues and Ideas, 79*(1), 45–50. doi:10.3200/tchs.79.1.45-50

Morris, E. W., & Perry, B. L. (2016). The punishment gap: School suspension and racial disparities in achievement. *Social Problems, 63*(1), 68–86. doi:10.1093/socpro/spv026

Movement for Black Lives. (2016, August). Platform. https://policy.m4bl.org/platform/

Musu-Gillette, L., De Brey, C., McFarland, J., Hussar, W., & Sonnenberg, W. (2017, July). Status and trends in the education of racial and ethnic groups 2017. *National Center for Education Statistics.* https://nces.ed.gov/programs/raceindicators/indicator_rbb.asp

Najarro, I. (2022). Whatever happened with Texas' anti-CRT law? *Education Week*. https://www.edweek.org/teachinglearning/whatever-happened-with-texasa nti-crt-law/2022/12

Nasaw, D. (2016). Americans' view of race relations at two-decade low—WSJ/ NBC News Poll [Web log post]. *The Wall Street Journal*. https://blogs.wsj.com/ washwire/2015/12/16/americans-view-of-race-relations-at-two-decade-low-wsj nbc-news-poll/

Nazaryan, A. (2017). Whites only: School segregation is back, from Birmingham to San Francisco. *Newsweek*. https://www.newsweek.com/2017/05/19/race-scho ols-592637.html

Newkirk, V. R., II. (2016). This is why Black Lives Matter is not going away. *The Atlantic*. www.theatlantic.com/politics/archive/2016/08/movement-black-lives-platf orm/494309/

Nieto, S. (1999). Multiculturalism, social justice, and critical teaching. In I. Shor & C. Pari (Eds.), *Education is politics: Critical teaching across differences, K-12* (pp. 1–20). Boynton/Cook Heinemann.

Nieto, S. (2006). Solidarity, courage and heart: What teacher educators can learn from a new generation of teachers. *Intercultural Education, 17*(5), 457–473. doi:10.1080/14675980601060443

Noddings, N. (1984). *Caring: A feminine approach to ethics and moral education*. University of California Press.

Noddings, N. (1995). Teaching themes of care. In L. W. Anderson (Ed.), Handbook of research on teaching (4th ed., pp. 363–380). Macmillan.

Okonofua, J. A., & Eberhardt, J. L. (2015). Two strikes: Race and the disciplining of young students. *Psychological Science, 26*(5), 617–624. doi:10.1177/0956797615570365

Orfield, G., Frankenberg, E., Ee, J., & Kuscera, J. (2014, May 15). Brown at 60: Great progress, a long retreat and an uncertain future (Rep.). *The Civil Rights Project at UCLA*. https://www.civilrightsproject.ucla.edu/research/k-12-education/integrat ion-and-diversity/brown-at-60-great-progress-a-long-retreat-and-an-uncertain-future/Brown-at-60-051814.pdf

Osei-Kofi, N. (2005). Pathologizing the poor: A framework for understanding Ruby Payne's work. *Equity & Excellence in Education, 38*, 367–375.

Osler, J. (Ed.). (2016). Opportunities for white people in the fight for racial justice. *White Accomplices*. https://www.whiteaccomplices.org/

Paley, V. G. (1979). White teacher. Harvard University Press.

Painter, N. I. (2010). *The history of white people*. W.W. Norton.

Palos, A. L., & McGinnis, E. I. (Directors). (2012). *Precious Knowledge* [Motion picture on DVD]. Public Broadcasting Service PBS.

Pane, D. M., & Rocco, T. S. (2014). *Transforming the school-to-prison pipeline: Lessons from the classroom*. Sense.

Paris, D. (2012). Culturally sustaining pedagogy: A needed change in stance, terminology, and practice. *Educational Researcher, 41*(3), 93–97. doi:10.3102/0013189x12441244

Paris, D., & Alim, H. S. (2017). *Culturally sustaining pedagogies: Teaching and learning for justice in a changing world*. Teachers College Press.

Park, M., Levenson, E., & Jorgensen, S. (2018, March 2). West Virginia governor defends role in teachers strike: "I'm not king." *CNN*. www.cnn.com/2018/03/01/us/west-virginia-teachers-strike/index.html

Parsons, E. C. (2005). From caring as a relation to culturally relevant caring: A white teacher's bridge to black students. *Equity & Excellence in Education, 38*(1), 25–34. doi:10.1080/10665680390907884

Patel, V. S. (2011). Moving toward an inclusive model of allyship for racial justice. *The Vermont Connection, 32*, 78–88.

Payne, C. R., & Welsh, B. H. (2000). The progressive development of multicultural education before and after the 1960s: A theoretical framework. *The Teacher Educator, 36*(1), 29–48. doi:10.1080/08878730009555249

Payne, R. K. (2013). *A framework for understanding poverty*. Aha! Process.

Perna, M. C. (2024). *No more teachers: The epic crisis facing education in 2024*. Forbes. https://www.forbes.com/sites/markcperna/2024/01/03/no-more-teachers-the-epic-crisis-facing-education-in-2024/

Peters, M. A. (2015). Why is my curriculum white? *Educational Philosophy and Theory, 47*(7), 641–646. doi:10.1080/00131857.2015.1037227

Pew Research Center. (2015, May 12). America's changing religious landscape (Rep.). *Pew Forum*. https://www.pewforum.org/2015/05/12/americas-changing-religious-landscape/

Phillippo, K. (2012). "You're trying to know me": Students from nondominant groups respond to teacher personalism. *The Urban Review, 44*(4), 441–467. doi:10.1007/s11256-011-0195-9

Pierce, R. B. (2012). *Polite protest: The political economy of race in Indianapolis, 1920–1970*. Indiana University Press.

Powell, J., & Kelly, A. (2017). Accomplices in the academy in the age of Black Lives Matter. *Journal of Critical Thought and Praxis, 6*(2), 42–65.

Renkl, M. (2018, July 30). Opinion | How to talk to a racist. White liberals, you're doing it all wrong. *New York Times*. https://www.nytimes.com/2018/07/30/opinion/how-to-talk-to-a-racist.html

Reason, R. D., Millar, E. A., & Scales, T. C. (2005). Toward a model of racial justice ally development. *Journal of College Student Development, 46*(5), 530–546. doi:10.1353/csd.2005.0054

Ris, E. W. (2015). Grit: A short history of a useful concept. *Journal of Educational Controversy, 10*(1), 1–18. https://cedar.wwu.edu/jec/vol10/iss1/3

Rothstein, R. (2013). For public schools, segregation then, segregation since: Education and the unfinished march (Rep.). *Economic Policy Institute.* https://www.epi.org/files/2013/Unfinished-March-School-Segregation.pdf

Rothstein, R. (2017). *The color of law: A forgotten history of how our government segregated America.* Liveright Publishing.

Sawyer, L. (2016). Arrests follow in Minneapolis as teachers, activists protest Philando Castile's death. *Star Tribune.* www.startribune.com/teachers-join-activists-to-prot est-castile-shooting/387511391/?refresh=true

Scholz, S. J. (2012). *Political solidarity.* Penn State University Press.

Scott, E. (2019). "This is us": Eddie Glaude's comments on America and white supremacy, annotated. *Washington Post.* https://www.washingtonpost.com/polit ics/2019/08/06/this-is-us-eddie-glaudes-comments-america-white-supremacy- annotated/

Seltzer, K. (2019). Reconceptualizing "home" and "school" language: Taking a critical translingual approach in the English classroom. *TESOL Quarterly.* https://doi. org/10.1002/tesq.530

Shevalier, R., & Mckenzie, B. A. (2012). Culturally responsive teaching as an ethics-and care-based approach to urban education. *Urban Education, 47*(6), 1086–1105. doi:10.1177/0042085912441483

Singer, T., & Klimecki, O. M. (2014). Empathy and compassion. *Current Biology, 24*(18). https://doi.org/10.1016/j.cub.2014.06.054

Singleton, G. E., & Linton, C. (2006). *Courageous conversations about race: A field guide for achieving equity in schools.* Corwin Press.

Skiba, R. J., Horner, R. H., Chung, C., Rausch, M. K., May, S. L., & Tobin, T. (2011). Race is not neutral: A national investigation of African American and Latino disproportionality in school discipline. *School Psychology Review, 40*(1), 85–107.

Skiba, R. J., Michael, R. S., Nardo, A. C., & Peterson, R. L. (2002). The color of discipline: Sources of racial and gender disproportionality in school punishment. *The Urban Review, 34*(4), 317–342.

Skiba, R. J., Peterson, R. L., & Williams, T. (1997). Office referrals and suspension: Disciplinary intervention in middle schools. *Education and Treatment of Children, 20*(3), 295–315.

Sleeter, C. E. (2001). An analysis of the critiques of multicultural education. In J. A. Banks & C. A. Banks (Eds.), *Handbook of research on multicultural education* (pp. 81–94). Jossey-Bass.

Sleeter, C. E. (2005). How teachers construct race. In C. McCarthy, Crichlow, G. Dimitriadis, & N. Dolby (Eds.), *Race, Identity, and Representation in Education* (2nd ed., pp. 243–256). Routledge.

Sleeter, C. E., & Soriano, E. (Eds.). (2012). *Creating solidarity across diverse communities: International perspectives in education* (pp. 1–19). Teachers College Press.

Smiley, A. D., & Helfenbein, R. J. (2011). Becoming teachers: The Payne effect. *Multicultural Perspectives, 13*(1), 5–15. doi:10.1080/15210960.2011.548177

Solomona, R. P., Portelli, J. P., Daniel, B., & Campbell, A. (2005). The discourse of denial: How white teacher candidates construct race, racism and "white privilege." *Race Ethnicity and Education, 8*(2), 147–169. doi:10.1080/13613320500110519

Solorzano, D. (1997). Images and words that wound: Critical race theory, racial stereotyping, and teacher education. *Teacher Education Quarterly, 24*(3), 5–19.

Solorzano, D. G., & Yosso, T. J. (2002). Critical race methodology: Counter-storytelling as an analytical framework for education research. *Qualitative Inquiry, 8*(1), 23–44. doi:10.1177/1077800402008001003

Sondel, B., Baggett, H. C., & Dunn, A. H. (2018). "For millions of people, this is real trauma": A pedagogy of political trauma in the wake of the 2016 U.S. Presidential election. *Teaching and Teacher Education, 70*, 175–185. doi:10.1016/j. tate.2017.11.017

Souto-Manning, M. (2013). Competence as linguistic alignment: Linguistic diversities, affinity groups, and the politics of educational success. *Linguistics and Education, 24*(3), 305–315. doi:10.1016/j.linged.2012.12.009

Southern Poverty Law Center (SPLC). (2017). Hate groups increase for second consecutive year as Trump electrifies radical right. https://www.splcenter.org/ news/2017/02/15/hate-groups-increase-second-consecutive-year-trump-electrif ies-radical-right

Southern Poverty Law Center (SPLC). (2024). Moms for liberty. https://www.splcen ter.org/resources/extremist-files/moms-liberty/

Spector, C. (2024). 70 years after Brown v. Board of Education, new research shows rise in school segregation. *Stanford Graduate School of Education.* https:// ed.stanford.edu/news/70-years-after-brown-v-board-education-new-resea rch-shows-rise-school-segregation

Spies, P., Bloom, J., Boucher, M. L., Norling, L., & Theisen, R. (2004). From crisis to civic engagement: The struggle over social studies standards in Minnesota. *Social Education, 68*(7), 457–463.

Stokas, A. G. (2015). A genealogy of grit: Education in the new gilded age. *Educational Theory, 65*(5), 513–528. doi:10.1111/edth.12130

Stotko, E. M., Ingram, R., & Beaty-O'Ferrall, M. E. (2007). Promising strategies for attracting and retaining successful urban teachers. *Urban Education, 42*(1), 30–51. doi:10.1177/0042085906293927

Stovall, D. (2006). WE CAN RELATE: Hip-hop culture, critical pedagogy, and the secondary classroom. *Urban Education, 41*(6), 585–602. doi:10.1177/0042085906292513

Straubhaar, R. (2014). The stark reality of the "White saviour" complex and the need for critical consciousness: A document analysis of the early journals of a Freirean educator. *Compare: A Journal of Comparative and International Education*, *45*(3), 381–400. doi:10.1080/03057925.2013.876306

Suissa, J., & Chetty, D. (2018). Editorial. *Ethics and Education*, *13*(1), 1–3. doi:https://doi.org/10.1080/17449642.2018.1430932

Sullivan, S. (2014). *Good white people: The problem with middle-class white anti-racism*. State University of New York Press.

Taie, S., & Goldring, R. (2017). Characteristics of public elementary and secondary school principals in the United States: Results from the 2015-16 national teacher and principal survey. National Center for Education Statistics, Institute of Education Sciences. https://nces.ed.gov/pubs2017/2017070.pdf

Taie, S., & Lewis, L. (2022). *Characteristics of 2020–21 Public and Private K–12 School Teachers in the United States: Results From the National Teacher and Principal Survey*. National Institute For Education statistics.

Tatum, B. D. (1992). Talking about race, learning about racism: The application of racial identity development theory in the classroom. *Harvard Educational Review*, *62*(1), 1–24. doi:10.17763/haer.62.1.146k5v980r703023

Ullucci, K. (2012). Knowing we are White: Narrative as critical praxis. *Teaching Education*, *23*(1), 89–107. doi:10.1080/10476210.2011.622747

US Government Accountability Office. (2024, September 10). K-12 Education: Nationally, Black girls receive more frequent and more severe discipline in school than other girls (GAO Report No. GAO-24-106787). Retrieved from https://www.gao.gov/assets/gao-24-106787.pdf

Utt, J. (2013, July 01). So, you call yourself an ally: 10 things all "allies" need to know. *Everyday Feminism*. https://everydayfeminism.com/2013/11/things-allies-need-to-know/

Utt, J., & Tochluk, S. (2016). White teacher, know thyself: Improving anti-racist praxis through racial identity development. *Urban Education*, *55*(1), 125–152 doi:10.1177/0042085916648741.

Valencia, R. R. (2010). *Dismantling contemporary deficit thinking: Educational thought and practice*. Routledge.

Valenzuela, J. (2021). How a simple visual tool can help teachers connect with students. *Edutopia*. https://www.edutopia.org/article/how-simple-visual-tool-can-help-teachers-connect-students/

Valenzuela, J. (2023). A blueprint for restorative conversations. *Edutopia*. https://www.edutopia.org/article/using-restorative-conversations-mend-relationships-schools/

Villegas, A. M., Strom, K., & Lucas, T. (2012). Closing the racial/ethnic gap between students of color and their teachers: An elusive goal. *Equity & Excellence in Education*, *45*(2), 283–301. doi:10.1080/10665684.2012.656541

Wacquant, L. (2001). Deadly symbiosis. *Punishment & Society*, *3*(1), 95–133. doi:10.1177/14624740122228276

Waters, R. (2010). Understanding allyhood as a developmental process. *About Campus, 15*(5), 2–8. doi:10.1002/abc.20035

Wald, J., & Losen, D. J. (2003). Defining and redirecting a school-to-prison pipeline. *New Directions for Youth Development, 2003*(99), 9–15. doi:10.1002/yd.51

Ware, F. (2006). Warm demander pedagogy: Culturally responsive teaching that supports a culture of achievements for African American students. *Urban Education, 41*(4), 427–456.

Warren, C. A. (2013). Towards a pedagogy for the application of empathy in culturally diverse classrooms. *The Urban Review, 46*(3), 395–419. doi:10.1007/s11256-013-0262-5

Warren, C. A. (2018). Empathy, teacher dispositions, and preparation for culturally responsive pedagogy. *Journal of Teacher Education, 69*(2), 169–183. doi:10.1177/0022487117712487

Warren, C. A., & Hotchkins, B. K. (2014). Teacher education and the enduring significance of "false empathy." *The Urban Review, 47*(2), 266–292. doi:10.1007/s11256-014-0292-7

Warren, C. A., & Talley, L. M. (2017). "Nice white ladies": Race, whiteness, and the preparation of a more culturally responsive teacher workforce. In C. A. Warren & S. A. Hancock (Eds.), *White women's work: Examining the intersectionality of teaching identity, and race* (pp. 147–175). Information Age Publishing.

West, L. (2013). A complete guide to "hipster racism." *Jezebel.* https://jezebel.com/a-complete-guide-to-hipster-racism-5905291

Whitaker, A., Torres-Guillén, S., Morton, M., Jordan, H., Coyle, S., Mann, A., & Sun, W. (2017). Cops and no counselors: How the lack of school mental health staff is harming students (Rep.). *American Civil Liberties Union (ACLU).* www.aclu.org/report/cops-and-no-counselors

White, K., & Ruelas, R. (2016). Desert Vista high school girl apologizes for n-word incident. *AZ Central.* www.azcentral.com/story/news/local/ahwatukee/2016/01/25/desert-vista-high-school-protest-petition-shirts/79309158/

Wilde, L. (2007). The concept of solidarity: Emerging from the theoretical shadows? *The British Journal of Politics and International Relations, 9*(1), 171–181. doi:10.1111/j.1467-856x.2007.00275.x

Williamson, L. A. (2011). Getting more Black men into the classroom. *Learning for Justice.* www.tolerance.org/blog/getting-more-black-men-classroom

Woodson, C. G. (1933). The mis-education of the Negro. *History Is a Weapon.* https://historyisaweapon.com/defcon1/misedne.html

Wolfe-Rocca, U., & Nold, C. (2022). Opinion: Why the narrative that critical race theory "makes white kids feel guilty" is a lie. *The Hechinger Report.* https://hechingerreport.org/opinionwhy-the-narrative-that-critical-racetheory-makes-white-kids-feel-guilty-is-alie/

Wong, J. C. (2021). From viral videos to Fox News: How rightwing media fueled the critical race theory panic. *The Guardian*. https://www.theguardian.com/educat ion/2021/jun/30/critical-race-theoryrightwing-social-media-viral-video

Wozolek, B., Wootton, L., & Demlow, A. (2016). The school-to-coffin pipeline: Queer youth, suicide, and living the in-between. *Cultural Studies ↔ Critical Methodologies, 17*(5), 392–398. doi:10.1177/1532708616673659

Wu, N. (2019, August 22). Newt Gingrich says slavery needs to be put "in context," calls 1619 project a "lie." *USA Today*. www.usatoday.com/story/news/polit ics/2019/08/19/newt-gingrich-calls-new-york-times-1619-project-a-lie/204 9622001/

Wyly, E. K., & Hammel, D. J. (2004). Gentrification, segregation, and discrimination in the American urban system. *Environment and Planning A: Economy and Space, 36*(7), 1215–1241. doi:10.1068/a3610

Xiong, C., & Stahl, B. (2017, June 22). Video: "I don't want you to get shooted," daughter pleads to mother moments after Castile shooting. *Star Tribune*. www. startribune.com/video-i-don-t-want-you-to-get-shooted-daughter-pleads-to-mother-moments-after-castile-shooting/429948923/

Yosso, T. J. (2005). Whose culture has capital? A critical race theory discussion of community cultural wealth. *Race Ethnicity and Education, 8*(1), 69–91. doi:10.1080/1361332052000341006

Yull, D. G., & Wilson, M. A. (2018). Allies, accomplices, or troublemakers Black families and scholar activists working for social justice in a race-conscious parent engagement program. *Critical Education, 9*(8), 1–18. http://ojs.library.ubc.ca/ index.php/criticaled/article/view/186343

Zinn, H. (2015). *A people's history of the United States*. HarperPerennial. (Original work published 1980).